## FINES & FEES

Fines will be assessed for all overdue
materials. Fees for lost materials will be
the cost of the item + a processing fee.

## WASHTENAW COMMUNITY COLLEGE
## LIBRARY

# THE CULTURE OF EXCESS

# THE CULTURE OF EXCESS

*How America Lost Self-Control
and Why We Need to Redefine Success*

J. R. Slosar

**PRAEGER**

*An Imprint of ABC-CLIO, LLC*

A B C · C L I O

Santa Barbara, California • Denver, Colorado • Oxford, England

**Library of Congress Cataloging-in-Publication Data**

Slosar, J. R. (Jay R.)
   The culture of excess : how America lost self-control and why we need to redefine success /
J.R. Slosar.
     p. cm.
   Includes bibliographical references and index.
   ISBN 978–0–313–37768–6 (hard copy : alk. paper) — ISBN 978–0–313–37769–3 (ebook)
1. Narcissism—United States. 2. Social values—United States. I. Title.
BF575.N35S55   2009
306.0973—dc22            2009020509


13  12  11  10  9     1  2  3  4  5

This book is also available on the World Wide Web as an eBook.
Visit www.abc-clio.com for details.

ABC-CLIO, LLC
130 Cremona Drive, P.O. Box 1911
Santa Barbara, California 93116-1911

This book is printed on acid-free paper (∞)

Manufactured in the United States of America

For my sister

Joan Wulf

(1942–1986)

# CONTENTS

# ACKNOWLEDGMENTS

*The Culture of Excess* developed gradually from writings that began in 2002. The content areas went through many reworkings and continuous updates and integration into the premise and theme of the book.

The book benefited from support, encouragement, feedback, and analysis from many colleagues and friends who gave input from reading parts of this work. I want to thank my close friend and colleague, forensic psychologist and psychoanalyst, Dr. Richard Lettieri, for his input on the content, review of material, and sharing of his psychoanalytic library. Myron Orleans, Professor Emeritus in Sociology, provided valuable critique and suggestions on almost the entire manuscript. Other colleagues who read parts of the book and offered feedback include Elizabeth Loftus, Dave Smith, and Steve Berger. I would also like to thank Dr. Don McCanne for numerous lectures to my classes on health care and his contribution to Chapter 5.

I benefited from participation for two years in the New Directions Writing Program of the Washington Psychoanalytic Institute. My writing group offered precise critique in organizing material, fully developing themes, and providing much needed integration for early parts of the manuscript. The members of this group included the leaders, Sara Taber and Marc Levine. The members included Sandie Friedman, Kerry Malawista, Hemda Arad, and Elizabeth Wallace. Another director, Sharon Alperovitz, offered encouragement on the content of what I was writing, as did group leader Elisabeth Waugaman.

Jay Wurts provided developmental editing in early stages of reformulating the material in the manuscript. His dissecting and analysis of the material was very helpful. Laura Long provided excellent editorial serv-ices throughout the entire manuscript. Chapman University graduate stu-dent Lee Ann Orme read the entire manuscript and offered suggestions and feedback.

Family members and friends offered encouragement and support, including my brother, Joel Slosar, Tom Wulf, Patty Ginsburg, and Janine Komers. Finally, acquisitions editor, Debra Carvalko, provided the oppor-tunity and guidance for moving the book forward.

Jay Slosar<br>April 27, 2009

# INTRODUCTION

Jonathan, age 12, has an amazing verbal capacity as he describes the fantasy characters in a new video game he is playing. It has more "levels" than I can grasp. The creation of characters and situations he describes seems confusing and scattered to me. But not to him. He is pleased that I let him talk about it, as his parents and other adults do not seem interested. The game is clearly an emotional release for him. I fidget and am aware I must patiently listen as he goes on and on and on. In advanced classes at school, Jonathan has trouble connecting with peers. He angrily describes perceived mistreatment from classmates. He describes a teacher as "humorless," and this is a major factor in how Jonathan responds to him. Jonathan often does not keep up with assignments. In several classes, he is late turning them in, especially if he does not like the teacher or views the teacher as humorless.

It would be wrong to say Jonathan is hyperactive or has attention deficit disorder. He can read an entire book, steadily sitting for several hours—as long as the book has fantasy or a very high level of imagination. "I try to give him other material," his mother reports, but he usually wins on this one. A big reward for him was to be allowed to take a 3D computer class. His parents seek help in setting limits but are also concerned he gets frustrated and despondent at times. They are protective, too, asserting their pride at how he "thinks out of the box." And in the classic battle, his parents limit or stop computer privileges. When this happens, Jonathan gets sullen and depressed. He does not seem to be faking; he seems genuinely sad and lethargic—adopting a "what's the use" attitude. His parents are affected by his despondent and depressed mood. They feel guilty.

Finally, after what seems like a long time from an adult perspective, he finishes his fantasy game description or stops for air. I get my chance to comment on his intense interest in fantasy and probe with a comment about how he thinks. I respond: "It seems you must always have fantasy and new ideas going on in your head." It works—he takes in what I have said. Jonathan responds: "I have to have novelty—all the time." He craves it. Almost anything else is a let down. I am encouraged—he recognizes that he slips away into a deep fantasy world. Despite his awareness, his intense need to do so seems almost addictive. What is he seeking? He has great parents, a wonderful home and is very intelligent.

Jonathan has trouble with our relationship—sometimes he wants to come and talk, especially when he gets depressed. Then the next week he is cranky and angry, blaming me for interfering with his time. He is conflicted. He wants help from me when he is despondent but also wants to manage his mood by himself. Jonathan often reports he is going to be all right. He progresses in therapy, but after some improvement, he asserts his independence and indicates he wants to stop coming. As he emerges into puberty and then high school, it is hard to predict how he will integrate his interests, intellect, and passion within our societal structure and connect with others and the world. Will he still have bouts of depression? Will he get along with peers? As demands increase, can he respond positively to authority figures? Will he be able to integrate his strong intellect with his feelings?

Jonathan's issues are representative of many preteen boys today. He is smart, fast thinking, obsessed with video technology and has a dramatic flare for fantasy. His psychological development derives from a different sense of reality, one developed by growing up on screen media. This different sense of reality and what is possible then conflicts with the reality of the structure of school and actual responsibilities, noticeably affecting his connectedness with others. He withdraws from peers, has much internal brooding and anger, and readily escapes into fantasy. His internal world seems more comfortable when based on digital fantasy than on actual real-life attachment. This has an effect upon his childhood development. Jonathan can appear out of touch with the environment and the world, or even grandiose and out of touch with reality. That is, until he communicates with you about current events and describes the difference between the Shiites and the Sunnis in Iraq. At this point, you are shocked with his fund of information. Somehow, you had concluded he was so deep in his fantasy digital world that he was lost in space. But, like others his age, he can emerge quickly and stun you with accuracy. But when confronted from adults about his fantasy world, he can become depressed. Jonathan's drive for novelty, stimulation, and uniqueness is observed in many others—children, teens, and young adults. Abrupt shifts from digital withdrawal to engagement are evident in others too, if you yourself do not turn away and give up on them. It is a model of human development and our daily lives within a culture of excess that depletes self-control.

We live in a true age of excess. Our thoughts race ahead, especially since we spend about two-thirds of our time doing things we would rather not be doing.[1] The racing thoughts increase anticipation. Our expectations of immediacy are staggering. We lose patience quickly. We become anxious far more easily. Symptoms emerge that make matters far worse. We are overweight, spend and amass huge financial debt, and take excessive amounts of medications. And when we overdo it, we expect someone else to bail us out.

The American culture of excess and wealth yields a paradoxical finding. And the data from research on happiness is clear. All of our materialistic and economic gains do not make us feel better. We lose ourselves for fun in activities like video games, extreme sports, spectator sports, and reality shows. But often these activities are pursued with obsessions that border on addiction. These trends of excess define our culture, altering the definitions of success, love, and happiness. But the new definitions are elusive.

Author Gregg Easterbrook has described this dilemma as "The Progress Paradox."[2] The tremendous economic development and prosperity of the United States should make us all feel wonderful. But it does not. I believe this conflict arises from social and cultural factors that have altered our physical and psychological development. Psychology professor Jean Twenge has referred to today's new workers and young adults as "Generation Me"[3] for whom the boundaries for self-control have been lost. For a generation that puts me first, what it takes to attain "success," a unique identity, or a stable self-concept and mood is constant manipulation that is often deceptive. This is especially evident in what has been described today as "The Cheating Culture."[4] As such, the bar for the definition of cheating has been lowered. In fact, we are not even sure what cheating is anymore.

Over 25 years, the changes I have observed in clinical practice, teaching, and consulting have led to the material in this book. The prospective that comes from my career in applied psychology adds an invaluable dimension to academic research and viewpoints. It is the difference between designing a house and building a house. This work attempts to integrate social, economic, and cultural forces with research data and clinical experience, and then to apply this integration to our culture and society.

Today's profound changes in economic development, technological advancements, and media have received much attention. Many writers have eloquently described the social and cultural factors that predominate today, such as "extreme capitalism," "out-of-control capitalism," "market populism," "supercapitalism," and the "new consumerism." The cumulative and broader psychological impact of a rapid and intense marketplace is extremely powerful and until recently with the financial collapse of 2008 has not been fully realized. The ongoing adaptation is gradual and destructive. If you place a frog in hot water, it jumps out. But if you put the frog in the water and gradually increase the temperature, the frog stays in the water and dies. Today's increase in temperature is the incredible pace, intensity, and competition of the "free market." All of these writers help provide the structure and interactive environment in which the culture of excess has developed; however, few have attempted to integrate these technological, cultural, and economic advancements and their impact on our personality development. In particular, these powerful changes have led to the growth of narcissism within our culture.

Historically, a culture of narcissism was beginning to emerge in the 1970s, a passive decade following the protests and riots of the 1960s. Author Tom Wolfe described the 1970s as the "Me Decade." The popular television program *Dallas* (1978) depicted J. R. Ewing as a manipulative narcissistic figure that we somehow envied. An upcoming episode in which J. R. was shot drew national attention and was put on the cover of *Time* magazine. The movie *Network* (1976) presented newscaster Howard Beall, famous still today for encouraging everyone to open their windows and shout out they are "mad as hell" and not going to take it anymore. Beall would give his monologue, working himself into a frenzy until he passed out on the floor. Later, the network was elated because Beall announced he would commit suicide on the air and their ratings soared. *Network* became a precursor for today's emergence and dominance of "reality" TV shows. The movie *Rollerball* (1975), set in the year 2018, provides a chilling portrayal and prediction of a society in which corporations have replaced countries. "Game! Who said this was just a game?" screams Jonathan E., played by actor James Caan, when playing Rollerball, a futuristic version of gladiator games.

It is most unfortunate that social critic Christopher Lasch is not able to elaborate and update his prescient groundbreaking 1979 work, *The Culture of Narcissism*.[5] Lasch's book can be seen as predicting the election of Ronald Reagan, who would advance free market principles of capitalism that have become today's zeitgeist. Lasch presents the concept of emerging narcissism in our society, a societal trend that illustrates immediacy, consumption, and self-love at the expense of self-reflection and the ability to sustain focus and attention. Lasch's exploration of narcissism expands its emphasis from what psychologists describe as an internal condition developed from childhood to a broader occurrence reflected through all aspects of our society. Rather than arising from trauma in childhood development or some aspect of dysfunctional child/parent attachment, cultural narcissism is rooted in social and cultural factors that create narcissism as a group phenomenon. But consider how Lasch's work was published before the Internet revolution and media development we have today, and you quickly realize what an amazing social critic he was.

Lasch's subtitle, *American Life in an Age of Diminishing Expectations*, was appropriate for the decade of the 1970s, but not today. Today, expectations are unlimited and the observations reported of overpraising and overindulging of children (which has been referred to as "Hothouse Parenting") are accurate and reflect the spirit of twenty-first-century cultural narcissism. Lasch also was addressing a powerful underlying factor that changes our behavior—the factor of expectations. In the Pygmalion effect, teachers were informed that a group of students were gifted, even though they were not. The results were dramatic; the teachers responded differently and the students had dramatic gains. The placebo effect is also based on expectation. If someone takes a pill, they feel better even if the pill has an inactive substance or placebo. The placebo effect is so well documented that it is the gold standard for drug trials. In other words, a new medication must show stronger results than a placebo effect. Decades later, technology has altered expectations from diminishing to expansive. In fact, technology's effect is so dramatic that it has led to an exponential expansiveness of expectations, such that the individual's expectations are grandiose and accompany and create a distorted view of reality. This altered reality includes unlimited expectations, and is what is being passed on to our children.

Lasch was on to this too. In the 1990 afterword to his book, he discusses the "Faustian View of Technology." Referring to technology as "a collective revolt against the limitations of the human condition," Lasch then describes the relationship between technology and narcissism. He writes:

> Careful study of the consequences of our attempts to master nature leads only to a renewed appreciation of our dependence on nature. In the face of this evidence, the persistence of fantasies that envision technological self-sufficiency for the human race indicates that our culture is a culture of narcissism in a much deeper sense than is conveyed by journalistic slogans like "me-ism." No doubt there is too much selfish individualism in American life; but such diagnoses barely scratch the surface.[6]

Today, I believe Lasch would be writing about the unlimited and unrealistic expectations of Americans, and the continued profound and habitual development of cultural narcissism.

## SELF-CONTROL AND IMPULSIVITY

The age of excess creates powerful forces that are gradually changing human development. The psychological damage caused by these forces is most evident in an impulsive society that has had a breakdown in self-control. This means that we take in more than we need, or engage in behavior without thinking it through, behavior that has undesirable consequences. Our boundaries for regulation and self-control get stretched and even collapse, leading to rampant impulsivity.

The outward symptoms of declining self-control appear within the context of cultural narcissism. The combination of narcissistic entitlement with cyber-capitalism results in a developing generation of young adults who struggle with physical and mental health and with moral and character development. Many cultural examples of the lack of self-control are documented, obesity being one of the more dramatic. Today, about two-thirds of adults are either overweight or obese. Thirty percent of adults older than 20, or about 60 million people, are obese. Since the mid-1970s being overweight has tripled in children and adolescents. In the range of 6–19 years, about 16 percent or 9 million persons are overweight.[7] The increase in future health-related problems, from coronary disease to type 2 diabetes, poses a staggering economic burden on a health care system that is already failing. Health care experts have put forth the prediction that young adults today may not live as long as their parents.

Self-control is maintained by keeping one's boundaries and setting limits. Many times we overrespond and compensate not with a lack of self-control but with overcontrol and rigidity. Thus, an important factor in eating includes not just the lack of self-control, but its opposite or over-control. In an interesting paradox, not only is obesity a problem in the United States, but the cultural obsession to be thin results in bulimia and eating disorders for teenage girls and young adult women. Eating disorders have doubled since the 1960s, currently affecting about eight million Americans, 90 percent of whom are young women. The worst eating disorder, anorexia nervosa, can result in death. Recent data shows eating disorders occurring in children as young as seven. Fifteen percent of those with eating disorders attempt suicide.[8] This does not include "binge-eating" disorder, which is binge eating without the purging of bulimia. Thus, binge eating is not a full-fledged psychological diagnosis, but an in-between "provisional" diagnosis. Binge eating is estimated to affect 2 percent of the general population and 8 percent of those who are obese.[9]

Psychologist Mary Pipher has documented the issues and symptoms of eating disorders, the intense pressure to be sexual, and bouts of depression in what she describes as a poisonous culture for young girls.[10] She clearly points out how the poisonous media culture obsesses on the tall and super slim model as the absolute ideal and way to be. The shallowness of this mega-obsession of "beauty" permeates our senses and being, contributing to eating disorders. Pipher clearly illustrates how hard it is for young girls to adjust to teenage years and early adulthood. Her book, *Reviving Ophelia: Saving the Selves of Adolescent Girls*, has been on the *New York Times* best seller list. It is not as if we are unaware of the problem. Although some researchers are reporting the prevalence and incidence of eating disorders in other cultures, it can be strongly argued that anorexia and bulimia are what the *Diagnostic and Statistical Manual of Mental Disorders* calls a "culture-bound syndrome."[11]

Other examples of self-control are harder to measure and explain. Today, 1 out of 75 persons will experience a panic disorder. In addition, 10 percent of healthy people will experience a panic attack in a given year. It is not uncommon to see these symptoms in an emergency room on a regular basis. While the criteria for a psychological diagnosis are more stringent (repeated attacks over a longer period of time), still about 1.6 percent of the adult population, or about 2.4 million Americans, have a panic disorder in a given year. Like most psychological diagnoses, other problems or diagnoses are attached. For example, about 30 percent of those with panic disorder abuse alcohol, and about 17 percent abuse other drugs.[12]

A nationwide survey of more than 9,000 adults reported in the *Archives of General Psychiatry* has indicated that the diagnostic category labeled "intermittent explosive disorder" may be far more prevalent than believed. IED is defined as an outburst way beyond anger that results in serious harm to individuals or property. Researchers estimate that in a given year about 4 percent or 8.5 million Americans experience the disorder.[13] This is not just giving someone the finger on the freeway, as employees, spouses, and children on the wrong end of such an outburst will tell you.

In 2004, researchers reported that gambling has rapidly become our society's favorite leisure endeavor and pastime. One only has to look at all the increased number of casinos—on land and on cruise ships and boats—and betting on sports to observe this dramatic growth. In 2004, gross gambling revenues were estimated at $47.6 billion, an amount deemed larger than receipts from movies, recorded music, spectator sports, and live entertainment combined.[14] Like panic disorders, gambling coexists with other diagnoses, including major depression, substance abuse, and attempted or completed suicides. The dramatic accessibility and increase in gambling, like other impulsive behaviors, takes us in the direction of addiction and crime.

Criminologists have long recognized the link between impulsivity and juvenile delinquency and crime. Impulsivity is the focal point of many major theories of crime and it is still widely researched as a prominent psychological factor. In a 2004 study, researchers Donald Lyman and Joshua Miller reported that criminologists believe impulsivity deserves the most attention in research. They reported two "personality pathways," the lack of premeditation and sensation seeking.[15]

These factors are certainly evident in the recent melodrama of Internet connections and sex. The Internet has become the vehicle for pedophiles to prey on children. The incredibly popular MySpace, the Web page for teens, has become a stalking ground for adult pedophiles.[16] *Dateline* has literally brought the ugly problem into our living room. In the past year, NBC has set up numerous "stings" via Internet chat rooms with actors feigning to be a 13-year-old girl or boy and luring adult men to a house where they delightfully film the event and provide reality TV for us after dinner. So far, they have arrested more than one hundred men and these men are not the dregs of society. Instead, many are professional men— even teachers and doctors—who are married with children. Of course, they all insist the offense is their first. Are they true pedophiles or have they succumbed simply to a self-indulgent impulsive society that lacks self-control and hinders character and moral development? Are we suddenly producing more pedophiles? Law enforcement agencies are thrilled to sign on with the networks to videotape and show the public how they are catching the bad guys—your tax dollars at work. This is despite the fact that actual convictions of those caught in the sting may prove more difficult than the media presentation implies. In addition, sometimes they catch one of their own profession.

## COPING IN CYBER-CAPITALISM

Where is the intense pace of technology and capitalism taking us? The decline in self-control is occurring so rapidly we do not yet notice the cumulative impact. As this gradual process continues, the culture of excess has hindered our own natural healthy defense mechanisms. In an economic era that prized deregulation, our powerful marketplace society has deregulated our internal mechanisms of self-control. We are fatter, have more debt, and our prisons house more people than ever before.

Of most importance is that we learn and believe that we can have anything we want, at any time, and that nothing should hold us back. And, all we need to do is make sure we and our children feel good about ourselves. Fortunately, the do-it-now and feel-good-about-yourself movement has been challenged. In the early 1990s, psychology had an active debate about the self-esteem movement that had resulted in approximately 30 U.S. states enacting more than 170 statutes promoting self-esteem in schools. Many notable psychological researchers pointed out research showing that gang leaders, terrorists, and extremely ethnocentric people all had higher than average self-esteem.[27] In addition, young males with higher than average self-esteem were more likely to engage in sexual activity at an earlier age than would be considered appropriate or desired. On the flip side, psychological research showed that those with low self-esteem were not prone to violence. Noted researcher Roy Baumeister, who acknowledges "probably publishing more studies on self-esteem than anybody else," reports in 1996: "The enthusiastic claims of the self-esteem movement mostly range from fantasy to hogwash." Most notable is his summation: "My conclusion is that self-control is worth ten times as much as self-esteem."[18]

The payoff comes from changing our emphasis from self-esteem to self-control. With emphasis more on the boundaries that maintain self-control, one becomes healthier. The old adage of moderation in all things is a wise one.

## LOVE AND PLAY

What exactly changes in children who are overpraised, have pumped up self-esteem and higher expectations? While Freud emphasized love and work, the equivalent for children is love and play, or as Piaget put it: "Play is the work of the Child." Today's technology has changed the basic activity of play, leading readily to the conclusion that childhood development has been altered.

Susan Linn, an instructor in psychiatry at Harvard Medical School, documents in her book, *Consuming Kids, The Hostile Takeover of Childhood*, how children are potential consumers from birth. In discussing deregulation, Linn notes the significance of the 1984 Federal Trade Commission deregulation of children's TV, which invited corporations to license products, referred to as "branding." Branding now dominates our entire cultural consumption. Linn notes that branding and licensing results in corporate predetermined images and toys that move and talk and "interact" with the child. The child will then "play" with the toy and then discard it for another interactive toy. Linn observes the effect in her own clinical practice, that young children have less creative play and creative development. Instead of using their own blossoming and natural imagination, they play with programmed toys. Linn describes this trend:

> Play comes naturally to children. They play—often without knowing they are doing so—to express themselves and to gain a sense of control over their world. But play is continually devalued and stunted by the loud voice of commerce. Play thrives in environments that provide children with safe boundaries but do not impinge on their ability to think and act spontaneously. It is nurtured with opportunities for silence. For children who are flooded continually with stimuli and commands to react, the cost is high. They have fewer opportunities to learn to initiate action or to influence the world they inhabit, and less chance to exercise the essential human trait of creativity.[19]

Having these toys is "cool" and advertisers know the parental pressure induced, as they market to the "alpha kids," the teens or preteens who are the cool kids, the leaders and trendsetters. When these children buy a product and take it to school, the trend is started and sales take off. What is important is that all this advertising works. Research shows even just a 30-second commercial can influence brand choice in children as young as age two. And the effect is greater with repetition until popular commercials have children completely brainwashed. The repetition is automatic, and Linn estimates the average child takes in about 40,000 commercials a year. Television, of course, is a major conduit. The average American child has three TV sets in their home, and two-thirds of children between age eight and eighteen have TVs in their bedrooms. This figure declines for children aged two to seven, as only 32 percent have sets in their bedrooms, but the infants are not far behind as 26 percent of children under age two have a set in their bedrooms.[20] But forget TV; the pervasiveness of advertising now influences far more readily through screen media.

## REGAINING SELF-CONTROL AND REDEFINING SUCCESS

The changes in development of today's youth are profound as the interaction of economic and social trends have dramatically affected self-control and how we define success. This book focuses on how to stop and change these trends; how to cope as individuals, parents, and decision makers; and how to transition from Generation Me to a Generation We.

Among the issues and examples of the culture of excess this book will explore include:

- How the extraordinary growth of capitalism and market forces blends together and leads to a culture of excess and narcissism.
- How the growth of narcissism in our culture leads to an increase in immediacy and expectations, resulting in impulsivity and lack of self-control. Breakdown in self-control, in turn, leads to other factors such as exaggerated risk-taking and increased deception.
- How the growth of cultural narcissism leads to a noticeable decline in critical thinking and analysis and avoidance of data, numbers, and math. This results in the inability to make meaningful comparisons and effective decisions.

- The cumulative effects of many of these factors lead to changes in psychological development that alters one's sense of self and identity. The compromises made in adapting to intense economic competition lead to a false sense of self and of reality.
- How today's culture has changed in one's search and struggle for a unique identity that is able to represent oneself in a healthy and realistic way. This struggle includes avoiding overcontrol and rigidity, along with coping with constant presentation and anticipation of trauma.

In addition, the book will offer discussion, suggestions, and recommendations for coping and integrating the social and cultural forces that are changing the way we think and behave so that we may move from Generation Me to Generation We. In particular, this process includes:

- How to cope with extreme capitalism by supporting a return to regulation in our institutions and business and government agencies.
- Recognizing how to develop and collect sound information to make meaningful comparisons and effective decisions.
- Redefining success and setting different standards for success in others.
- Reevaluating the philosophy and impact that extreme capitalism has upon today's youth.
- How to go about fostering a new sense of personal identity for today's generation to create Generation We.

The first chapter provides a background of definitions and symptoms of narcissism and its application to our culture and society. The complexity of the concept is presented from history, research, and application. Chapter 2 separates out the factors in the economic marketplace that contribute to cultural narcissism. Chapter 3 focuses on coping with the impact of the factors of cultural narcissism, and explores reality and loss, rigidity and self-destruction, and perfectionism and deception. The fourth chapter looks at our avoidance and anxiety of numbers, math or quantitative analysis, a cultural weakness that opens the door to faulty comparisons and poor decisions. A different perspective is offered in Chapter 5, as our health care system is offered as a primary example of how our society sanctions cultural narcissism and self-defeating behavior. Chapter 6 focuses upon changes in reality and hero images as representative of today's cultural narcissism. An analysis of sports as a dramatic seeking of reality is discussed. Chapter 7 discusses identity theory and development with the focus on today's youth and how they see and present themselves. Finally, the last chapter summarizes, integrates, and offers structural recommendations to help change directions and return to a more balanced and realistic appraisal of our economic system and our day-to-day lives and decisions.

## NOTES

1. Mihalyi Csikszentmihalyi has written extensively about happiness and creative flow. This includes how we spend our time and when we are happy. See Csikszentmihalyi, M. (1997). *Finding flow*. New York: Perseus Books. Csikszentmihalyi, M. (1990). *Flow: The psychology of optimal experience*. New York: HarperCollins. Csikszentmihalyi, M. (1996). *Creativity: Flow and psychology of discovery and invention*. New York: Harper & Row. Csikszentmihalyi, M. (1998). If we are so rich, why aren't we happy? *American Psychologist*, 54 (10): 821–827.

2. For extensive documentation of economic progress in the United States illustrating the contradiction between tremendous progress and lack of fulfillment and happiness, see Easterbrook, G. (2004). *The progress paradox: How life gets better while people feel worse*. New York: Random House.

3. Researcher Jean Twenge has numerous peer-reviewed articles on the study of narcissism. See her book Twenge, J. (2006). *Generation me: Why today's young Americans are more confident, assertive, entitled— and more miserable than ever before*. New York: Free Press. Twenge has documented changes in scores on the Narcissistic Personality Inventory with scores increasing in college students over the years. See Twenge, J., Konrath, S., Foster, J., Campbell, W. K., & Bushman, B. (2008). Egos inflating over time: A cross temporal analysis of the Narcissistic Personality Inventory. *Journal of Personality*, 76 (4): 875–901. Twenge has recently released another book. See Twenge, J., & Campbell, W. Keith. (2009). *The narcissism epidemic: Living in the age of entitlement*. New York: Free Press.

4. Callahan, D. (2004). *The cheating culture: Why more Americans are doing wrong to get ahead*. Orlando, FL: Harcourt. Outlines reasons and

data of a culture constantly cheating, manipulating, and gaming situations to get ahead.

5. Lasch, C. (1979). *The culture of narcissism: American life in an age of diminishing expectations.* New York: Norton.

6. Ibid., p. 245. This quote is in an afterword written in 1990.

7. Voluminous data exists on the worsening problem of obesity. This data was taken from U.S. Department of Agriculture, Economic Research Service. (2004). *The economics of obesity: Report on the workshop held at USDA's Economic Research Service* (Report E-FAN No. 04004, May 2004). See also U.S. Department of Health and Human Services, Centers for Disease Control and Prevention. (n.d.). *Overweight and obesity.* Retrieved December 1, 2008, from http://www.cdc.gov/nccdphp/dnpa/obesity/.

8. Franko, D. L., et al. (2004). What predicts suicide attempts in women with eating disorders? *Psychological Medicine,* 34:843–853. See also Millar, H. R., et al. (2005). Anorexia Nervosa mortality in Northeast Scotland. *American Journal of Psychiatry,* 162:753–757. Numerous textbooks cite current rates of occurrence. See Halgin, R., & Whitbourne, S. K. (2007). Chapter 14: Eating disorders and impulse control disorders. In *Abnormal psychology: Clinical perspective on psychological disorders* (7th ed., pp. 428–462). New York: McGraw-Hill Publishing.

9. McLean Hospital. (2007, February 4). Binge eating more common than other eating disorders, survey finds. *ScienceDaily.* Retrieved August 2, 2008, from http://www.sciencedaily.com/releases/2007/02/070203103249.htm.

10. Pipher, M. (1994). *Reviving Ophelia: Saving the selves of adolescent girls.* New York: Ballantine Books.

11. American Psychiatric Association. (2004). *Diagnostic and statistical manual of mental disorders* (4th ed.). Washington, D.C.: American Psychiatric Association. Culture-bound syndromes are listed at the end as an appendix section.

12. U.S. Department of Health and Human Services, National Institute of Mental Health. (2006). Facts about panic disorder. Washington, D.C.: U.S. Department of Health and Human Services. See also Halgin, R., & Whitbourne, S. K. (2007). Chapter 5: Anxiety disorders. In *Abnormal psychology: Clinical perspective on psychological disorders* (7th ed., pp. 146–177). American Psychological Association (2009), retrieved July

31, 2009 from http://www.apahelpcenter.org/search/?search_string=panic
+attacks.html.

13. Kessler, R. C., & Coccaro, E. F. (2006). The prevalence of DSM-IV
Intermittent Explosive Disorder in the National Comorbidity Survey replication. *Archives of General Psychiatry*, 63:669–678. See also Kaplan,
A. (January 2007). Intermittent Explosive Disorder: Common but underappreciated. *Psychiatric Times*, 24:1.

14. Khantzian, E. (2005). Pathological gambling: A clinical guide to
treatment. *The American Journal of Psychiatry*, 162:1992; Grant, J. E.,
& Potenza, M. N. (Eds.). (2004). *Pathological Gambling: A clinical guide
to treatment*. Washington, D.C.: American Psychiatric Publishing.

15. Lyman, D. R., & Miller, J. D. (December 2004). Personality pathways to impulsive behavior and their relations to deviance: Results from
three samples. *Journal of Quantitative Criminology*, 20 (4): 319–341.
See also Tice, D. T., Bratslavsky, E., & Baumeister, R. (2001). Emotional distress regulation takes precedence over impulse control: If you
feel bad, do it! *Journal of Personality and Social Psychology*, 80 (1):
53–67.

16. Manuel, B., & Churnin, N. (2006, March 5). Parents fear MySpace
is playground for pedophiles. *Dallas Morning News*. http://www
.dallasnews.com/sharedcontent/dws/dn/latestnews/stories/030506dnliv-
myspace.2976283.html; Salkin, A. (2006, December 13). Web site hunts
pedophiles and TV goes along. *The New York Times*, Technology Section.

17. Baumeister, R. F., Calanese K. R., & Vohs, K. D. (2003). Does high
self-esteem cause better performance, interpersonal success, happiness, or
healthier lifestyles? *Psychological Science in the Public Interest*, 4 (1):
1–44.

18. Baumeister, R. F., Smart, L., & Boden, J. (1996). The dark side of
high self-esteem. *Psychological Review*, 65. See also Myers, D. G.
(2005). Chapter 2. The self in a social world. In *Social Psychology* (8th
ed., pp. 62–66). New York: McGraw-Hill Publishing.

19. Linn, S. (2004). Chapter 3: Branded babies: From cradle to consumer. In *Consuming Kids: The hostile takeover of childhood* (p. 62).
New York: The New Press.

20. Ibid., p. 5.

# Chapter 1

# CULTURAL NARCISSISM 2.0

Integration is the first essential.

—Frank Lloyd Wright

Today's college students are called Millenials or Generation Next. The Millenials are incredibly smart and their behavior is not oppositional or defiant. They care about others and do not want to hurt anyone. They do not like conflict or confrontation. It is easy to notice behavior of young college students that is rude. I am reviewing a test in a class lecture so that students can see what items they have missed and be better prepared for the final exam. A young student who sits near the front is going over her answers. I notice she looks up at the clock. A few minutes later, she gets up and walks out of the class. Perhaps, I think, she must make an important call or something. But 10 minutes later she returns with food and drink. The following semester, I announce no food is allowed for the 50-minute class. (I allow the obligatory water bottles.) Invariably, halfway through the semester, students begin to cart in bagels, burritos, and Red Bull, so I need to give a reminder.

In another class, a student arrives about five minutes late, after I am actively lecturing. She immediately sits in her usual spot and begins to talk and show something to her friend. I look over hoping she will get the cue and stop, but she persists for several minutes. I finally politely ask the two to stop. They seem surprised but apologetic. The next class, I again must ask them to stop.

Students frequently get up and walk out of class when I am lecturing, even in just a 50-minute class. If I later ask them, they seem surprised it might bother me, and indicate it is to go to the bathroom. Several students have told me they have a "bladder problem." I always thought this was a condition for older persons. Some students are clearly doing something else on their laptops rather than taking notes, although adults certainly do this too. Others read different material, even another book, while sitting in the front where I can directly notice. I have learned not to confront anyone in the class about most of this unless absolutely necessary. Maybe I am too nice, but the vibes and atmosphere in the class change when you do so. If I can talk to students on the side, they are apologetic and surprised their behavior had been noticed.

Are these students so self-absorbed they are narcissistic? Or are they simply a product of a different culture? My conclusion is that they are a product of today's culture—one that has become a culture of narcissism.

Culture trumps personality. Powerful cultural forces have altered individual personality development. Culture dominates the consumer. Consumer choices are not fully influenced by free will, but by cultural demands. The impact and result of these powerful forces has produced an outcome that can be called a culture of excess. The dramatic expansion of technology, technology coupled with media, and extreme market forces *are the cultural forces* that have led to a culture of excess. All three of these forces are interrelated and feed off each other.

The growth of cultural narcissism is an outcome of these profound cultural forces and an underlying psychological explanation for the decline in self-control, depletion of human resources, and excessive consumption. The basis for the argument that culture is paramount is because the magnitude of these cultural forces has not been fully recognized. We now use the word billion and trillion for dollar amounts as if they were something ordinary and commonplace. Screen media dominates every aspect our lives. In some ways, experts believe that brain development is changing. That is, we demand fast, strong, and immediate information, and when we leave the screen to return to daily life, we have lost sustaining focus and the ability to analyze and think. This contributes further to impulsive behavior and less self-control.

Yet, it is easy to misrepresent the complex concept of narcissism. Older generations have always complained about today's youth, just as I have done. Christopher Lasch, in his 1979 best seller, *The Culture of Narcissism*, noted that narcissism is "readily susceptible to moralistic inflation."[1] He notes humans have always been self-centered and egocentric, and the term is compromised if all selfish behavior is considered narcissistic or if narcissism is used as a metaphor for the human condition. Any discussion of culture and narcissism can easily become moralistic and indicting.

But still, our own individual and societal narcissism rages and technology expand Lasch's "cult of consumption" into hyperspace. The powerful technological and economic forces of our time have created a cycle of expectations, competition, and a drive for unlimited success and perfection that becomes so self-consuming, and so ingrained in our way of being, that previous checks and balances are considered outdated and unnecessary. In the end, the boundaries of constraint necessary for self-control erode.

The historical concept of narcissism emerged from Greek mythology. Briefly, Narcissus was known for his beauty. Through different versions of the story, Narcissus became so self-absorbed with his own reflection in the water, one way or another he died.[2] Thus, Narcissus became associated with the term "self-love." Freud's 1914 seminal paper *On Narcissism: An Introduction* began the definition and study of narcissism by psychoanalysis and psychology. Many substantive books and professional literature compare and contrast the approaches for treatment of the full-fledged Narcissistic Personality Disorder. This literature continues to thrive.

The focus here, however, is upon lower levels of narcissism that have been gradually increasing in all aspects of our society and culture. Lasch expands the exploration of narcissism from an individual internal condition developed from childhood to a group phenomenon—a culture of narcissism—created through social and cultural factors. Cultural narcissism, then, may minimize the idea that narcissism develops because of a trauma in childhood development or some aspect of parent-child development or attachment. Traditional psychoanalytic theory posited that narcissism was caused by a lack of gratification of normal narcissistic needs in infancy and childhood. Adults then make up for this deficiency with an inflated sense of self or a "false self."[3] However, another theory may be that narcissism is the result of an overgratification of narcissistic needs in childhood, often described as overparenting or "helicopter parents."[4] A fixation on the overgratification leads to a lack of integration in the superego and poor regulation of self-esteem. Overgratification develops into the social and cultural correlates already discussed, including impulsivity, poor self-control, and excessive risk-taking.

Cultural narcissism, a concept continued from Christopher Lasch's introduction of the term, is defined as features and symptoms of narcissism in our day-to-day behavior. The characteristics used in the formal diagnostic category of Narcissistic Personality Disorder describe the condition: a sense of entitlement; a preoccupation of fantasies of success, power, brilliance, beauty, or ideal love; a grandiose sense of self-importance; a belief that one is "special" and must associate only with others who are special who can understand them; a need for excessive admiration; an exploitive interpersonal style; a lack of empathy; an envy of others or believe others are envious; and arrogant behaviors and attitudes.[5] Does this sound like anyone you know?

## CONTEXT AND CONTINUUM

Of course, all of us have some of these narcissistic characteristics. Personality inventories have helped to identify different levels of narcissism; that is, a high level or tendency that does not warrant a psychological diagnosis, but might have an effect on one's behavior. Researcher Jean Twenge from San Diego State University has documented the trend of increased narcissism in college students. She has led a research team that surveyed more than 16,000 college students who took the Narcissistic Personality Inventory (NPI) between 1982 and 2006. The results showed a dramatic increase over the years in self-absorption. In her report, *Egos Inflating Over Time*, Twenge found a 30 percent elevation in narcissism during 1982–2006, as measured by scores on the NPI.[6] Twenge referred to today's new workers and young adults as Generation Me and concludes that Generation Me while more "confident, assertive, and entitled" is also "more miserable than ever before." This is the subtitle of her book, *Generation Me*. In discussing today's narcissistic person she writes: "They tend to have problems with impulse control, so that means they are more likely to, for example, be pathological liars or commit white collar crimes."[7] Twenge continues her research that narcissism is rampant. Her 2009 book is titled, *The Narcissism Epidemic*.[8]

Twenge's research has not been without challenge. A separate analysis reported that college students' NPI scores did not increase from 1980 to 2007, but that some small changes were noted in specific "facets of narcissism."[9] These researchers reported that Twenge used samples that were small and possibly subject to selection bias. In utilizing a larger "nationally representative sample," they concluded that the accused self-esteem movement has not contributed to today's generation having an increased impression of themselves.

The NPI assessment has been established in totality as valid and reliable and also shown to predict psychologists' ratings of narcissism.[10] However, the NPI does not have a cutoff score for narcissism and is based upon the specific clinical criteria for Narcissistic Personality Disorder, which have long been criticized as overlapping and not clearly distinct. Mental health clinicians encounter patients with symptoms in multiple dimensions that rarely fit into one diagnostic category. For example, when someone is depressed, they invariably have anxiety and other personality criteria and symptoms.[11] Nine descriptive criteria are offered to fully diagnose Narcissistic Personality Disorder, and diagnosis depends on evidence that five of the nine are present. Thus, a precise definition or agreement on the concept of narcissism is open to debate.

Another personality expert has put forth four different subtypes of narcissism, including elitist, amorous, unprincipled, and compensatory.[12] From a more technical viewpoint, there are issues with precise definition and measurement of narcissism. Despite these limitations, Twenge's conclusion is accepted that narcissism has increased, if not necessarily in individuals, but *within our culture*. The research presented is made to demonstrate the magnitude of the evidence in our current day-to-day living.

Laboratory research on narcissism usually compares the performance of persons who score high on the NPI with that of others. Despite their claims, no clear evidence has been found that narcissists are better performers or producers.[13] However, when narcissists receive "self-enhancement" with promised rewards and public identification and recognition, their performance has been shown to improve.[14] This finding seems to explain the constant complaint from supervisors that today's generation of Millennials must be treated with excessive workplace rewards—a trend that might be described as everyone is a winner. The constant need to provide self-enhancement is draining for those supervising today's young workers.

Other laboratory research reported that narcissists are less forgiving,[15] an interpersonal situation that must increase tension, and contribute to strained personal relationships. Those with narcissistic tendencies also displayed more anger and aggression following an experience of social rejection.[16] In addition, a series of experiments showed that narcissists had less empathy for rape victims, had more enjoyment watching a rape scene in a movie, and were more punitive toward women who would not read a sexual passage out loud to them.[17] This research leads to the most concern about the possible increase in "narcissistic rage" or "shame-based rage." When events or the response of others do not endorse their sense of entitlement, a narcissistic person can erupt in anger. Incidents of domestic and workplace violence are often attributed to narcissistic rage. Reference has been made to narcissistic comments made by the youth who carried out the Columbine school homicides, and much also has been written and discussed about the social conditions at the school.[18]

The increase in cultural narcissism parallels the decline in self-control. Yet a counterbalance exists where narcissism is viewed as leading to drive productivity and success. Is the research by Twenge unduly pessimistic? Laboratory research is one thing, but what about narcissism and its impact in the workplace?

## PRODUCTIVE NARCISSISM

Michael Maccoby is an anthropologist and psychoanalyst who works as a consultant with prominent business executives and sees narcissism from a different and valuable perspective. Writing in the *Harvard Business Review* and his book, *Productive Narcissism*, Maccoby's point of view is that narcissism has been misunderstood.[19] He believes that narcissism is a necessary requirement for a CEO in today's rapidly evolving industries such as media, digital and electronic domains. He posits that most of the very successful leaders in business share narcissistic features. Although Maccoby does not minimize the self-destructive, risk-taking, or "dark side" of narcissism, he believes one can be a "productive narcissist" and cites Jack Welch and Bill Gates as examples. A narcissistic person, he writes, is "the type of person who impresses us as a personality, who disrupts the status quo and brings about change."[20] He further adds:

> Narcissists have little or no psychic demands that they have to do the right thing. Freed from these internal constraints, they are forced to answer, for themselves, what is right, to decide what they value, what, in effect, gives them a sense of meaning. They create their own vision, a sense of purpose that not only engages them but also inspires others to follow them.
>
> Narcissists train themselves from an early age to block out other voices, other opinions, so one of the few voices they trust is their own. They are accustomed to listening to themselves talk, debating different sides of the same issue, finally reaching a decision about what to do and the best way to do it. Lacking the support of others, narcissists have a highly developed "me against the world" way of looking at things. This often comes out as paranoia, a heightened awareness of danger that may be realistic, given narcissistic ambition, competitiveness and unbridled aggressive energy. There's not a

lot of gray area in the narcissistic view of the world—you are either a friend or a foe, for or against the vision.[21]

Examples are found everywhere among our media. Talk radio, news stations, and newspapers are dominated by the biased opinions of those who take the stance you are either with us or against us (friend or foe). Overall, the growth of cultural narcissism may be the underlying reason for the infamous red/blue political dichotomy.

Maccoby's point that the same risk-taking and audacity that can be self-destructive also leads to tremendous innovative change explains an increase in narcissism in the business world where it may be necessary for success. Yet Maccoby's point of view inadvertently supports the premise that narcissism has become normative in American business and society. He argues that a CEO in a rapidly diverse field must have narcissistic features to succeed, or to be successful as a business leader, narcissism is a minimum requirement. In fact, a person with narcissistic features reaches the higher levels of leadership positions.

I have assigned Maccoby's *Harvard Business Review* article to students in a research class who are working for a wide variety of companies. They often are excited about the article and agree with Maccoby's views. Many cite that they have had a narcissistic boss and express how difficult it was to work for him. However, some seem empowered by the article, and I get the sense they intend to go work the next day with the idea they can be more narcissistic because that's the way you attain success and get the job done. In effect, I feel they are relieved and now have authoritative permission to be more narcissistic. I hope I am wrong, and sometimes express my caution that they should be careful in using the term.

Narcissism may have its advantages in the business world, but in the dramatic crash of Wall Street and our financial system in 2009 must give us pause. Is the collapse due to business leaders who have developed narcissistic styles that "have little or no psychic demands that they have to do the right thing"?[22]

Considering the recent economic crisis, awareness of this narcissistic trend would be important to develop a stable society. Neville Symington, an Australian psychoanalyst, has written extensively about narcissism and proposed his own theory about narcissism in today's culture.[23] Writing as far back as 1993, he explains the importance of recognizing narcissistic features.

Narcissism is not only present in individuals but it also contaminates organizations. One of the ways of differentiating a good-enough organization from one that is pathological is through its ability to exclude narcissistic characters from key posts. I have worked in organizations so riven with narcissistic currents that they seemed to have been present since the organization's foundation, and under such circumstances little creative work was done. I have also worked in organizations where, despite there being much narcissism and envy, creative development was fostered. In these places highly narcissistic people were usually prevented from obtaining senior positions. It is important to be able to make some sort of diagnosis of organizations with regard to narcissistic currents.[24]

Symington's overall opinion of narcissism, at least at the clinical level, is described even as a warning. He writes: "It is extremely important to recognize people dominated by a narcissistic character structure. For one thing, such people, however gifted, cause considerable damage to the social structures to which they belong—to their families, their work organizations, clubs, societies."[25]

Symington and Maccoby provide fresh insight into narcissism in context and its possible outcomes in the day-to-day work world. This context and perspective has led others to emphasize viewing narcissism on more of a continuum. Psychoanalyst and personality expert Otto Kernberg presents a continuum from a narcissistic personality to an antisocial personality, someone who continuously violates the norms and rules of society and gets into legal trouble. Kernberg notes that the antisocial person is an extreme example of narcissism that is pathological, and in its worst form, lacks an integration of a superego and a conscience.[26] This could be described as the worst of the worst. One smaller subset of an antisocial personality disorder is referred to as a psychopath who can even kill without remorse or conscience. When considering this continuum, has our society moved over toward greater pathological narcissism, approaching the antisocial side? Or, as Maccoby maintains, is narcissism necessary and desirable for a decision maker to succeed? If the answer is yes, has narcissism led to dramatic innovation or increased criminal behavior? Figure 1.1 provides a visual and a continuum for degrees of narcissism. While this provides a visual, one can jump from subclinical narcissism to an antisocial *act*. Movement to the right increases the probability of antisocial behavior.

Psychologist Robert Hare, probably the world's foremost expert on psychopathy, reports that about 20 percent of the prison population are psychopaths, and that this 20 percent account for more than half of all

## NARCISSISM SCALE/CONTINUUM

**Figure 1.1**   Continuum scale for narcissism shows agreement on far right of antisocial behavior and the negative consequences. Diagnosis for Narcissistic Personality Disorder is less precise with five of nine criteria to be met for individual. Subclinical narcissism is posited as increasing in culture as also is the general societal movement to the right of the scale. Movement toward the right of the scale indicates increased probability of an antisocial act, as opposed to consistent antisocial behavior.

violent crimes.[27] After 40 years of scientific research and development of a widely used assessment instrument to detect psychopathy,[28] Hare has spoken out about CEOs. In 2002, speaking to a law enforcement audience, Hare described top executives of well-known bankrupt companies as just as callous and cold-blooded as psychopaths. He contrasted an immense societal response to physical violence with the ignoring of the economic violence caused by failing companies. Hare believes it is time to transition from assessing psychopathy in jails to assessing it on Wall Street. Or, as he told *Fast Company* magazine: "I always said that if I wasn't studying psychopaths in prison, I'd do so at the stock exchange."[29] Hare calls for screening of top executives to eliminate those with psychopathic tendencies and prevent them from occupying the top positions. And, appearing in the Canadian documentary, *The Corporation*,[30] he goes much further, checking off the criteria for psychopathy demonstrated in corporate behavior as a whole, and making the official diagnosis—corporations are psychopaths.

His strong statement can only meet with extreme defensiveness and umbrage from the insulted business sector. If you want to start an instant fight, just tell some brokers or business leaders that corporations are psychopaths. Hare also links corporations and CEOs together. A decent CEO will prevent the corporation from doing harm. He is responding from the perspective of a clinical psychologist and diagnostician and is probably overdiagnosing or overgeneralizing. Hare has continued his position, his recent book is titled: *Snakes in Suits: When Psychopaths Go to Work*.[31] Are corporations in and of themselves destined to be harmful? Hare takes the issue to another level. Can a clear distinction be made between productive narcissism that is acceptable and, according to Maccoby, even necessary for innovative change, and that which is antisocial behavior and narcissism run wild? It may be that there used to be a clear line, but today's society has changed, and the growing power of cultural narcissism makes everything a blur. Without a clear boundary, we flounder, not knowing or fully realizing what is right and wrong, not knowing or fully realizing sometimes what is real.

## EXCESSIVE RISK-TAKING

Maccoby, who does not minimize the cons of narcissism, asks why we go along with narcissistic leaders. His answer is: "When narcissists win, they win big."[32] Everyone wants to win big. And quickly. We see this everywhere, from the search for our 15 minutes of fame (remember Joe the Plumber in the 2008 election)[33] to who wants to be a millionaire, to the rampant volatility on Wall Street. Gambling, speculation, and excessive risk-taking are an operational mode of cultural narcissism.

While gambling has always been a destructive force, its growth and popularity are dramatic, even without the expansive access to Internet gambling, which is theoretically illegal in the United States. And capitalism, free markets, and government encourage the rage. In the recent economic downturn of 2007, casinos in the United States declined in revenue, but not as badly as other industries. In Las Vegas, gambling site for the wealthy foreign spender, revenues actually increased in 2007.[34] State governments are now beginning to offer scratch-off lotto tickets for $20 and $50. In 2008, California voters, encouraged by government leaders to help raise revenue and close the ever occurring budget gap, passed three ballot propositions to dramatically increase slot machines at Indian casinos, considered the largest expansion of gambling in history.[35] Families and friends now routinely get together to play the latest rage, Texas Hold 'em poker, which when packaged as a game became one of the hottest-selling Christmas gifts. ESPN constantly broadcasts a "sports" show of poker tournaments. Pushing carts loaded with cash, the colorful winners of huge amounts outmanipulate the losers. Special programs emphasize how women can become professional gamblers, too.[36]

What is simply a more sophisticated form of gambling runs rampant on Wall Street. Shrewd managers speculate, accumulate huge amounts of money, and influence economic trends. The latest vehicle that government now must try to reign in is the "hedge fund." These are simply funds that accumulate a huge amount of money from "investors" and dramatically trade securities at a turnover rate reported to be 300–400 percent, far greater than any typical investment fund. Currently, hedge funds operate without public disclosure of their activity, with extremely high fees that yielded in 2005 an average compensation for a hedge fund manager of $363 million.[37] Hedge funds are estimated to account for about 40 percent of all Wall Street trades. Yet despite their reported lucrative success or image, more than 1,800 hedge funds failed between 1995 and 2003.[38]

In the recent economic chaos of October 2008, the most significant new trend was volatility. The volatility index (VIX), a method measuring the swings in the stock market, has gone way up. The VIX, also called the "fear index," is a warning not to invest in a shaky stock market. Rampant speculation occurs because, of course, you can "invest" in the VIX. It is not uncommon to see wild swings in the stock market from several hundred points down to several hundred points up in one day, a volatility that used to be unheard of.[39] Experts now know that how the Dow Jones Index is doing during the trading day is irrelevant. All that matters is the last 10 minutes when the money pours in or is taken out, and what the final close is.

Despite the excessive speculation on Wall Street, those in charge of regulating promote the activity. Even since 2007, authorities have eliminated an "uptick rule," which allows for greater speculation to drive a stock down.[40] Authorities also have lowered the asset requirements that a financial entity must have, allowing for more financial risk-taking. More about these deregulations in the next chapter, but the main point is that government fosters and develops excessive risk-taking. Our financial system welcomes entrepreneurial narcissism, risk-taking, and the end result—a crash when self-control breaks down.

What is the correct term for this activity? Is it "investment," "risk-taking" or are these just synonyms for gambling? Buying a low-cost lotto ticket or playing the increased number of slot machines is one form of the growth in gambling. The other form is a sophisticated marketplace that uses much larger amounts of money to speculate and take risks. Recently, frequent reports and claims have been made that speculation has contributed to drastic increases in oil prices. In July 2008 the price of oil was about $150 per barrel. In November 2008 the price dropped below $50 per barrel. Few think this extreme volatility is due to supply and demand.[41]

The gambling on Wall Street is matched by the American consumer. Savings rates in the United States have declined since 1970, dropping in

2005 to below zero. Americans were spending more than they made. Apparently, good times in real estate and the stock market led to this risk-taking. Recently, the savings rate hovered around 1–2 percent, finally showing an increase to 3 percent in 2008 and 6 percent in 2009. In comparison, the savings rate in Japan has declined below 5 percent since 2002, and in Germany the savings rate has held steady at about 10 percent since 2000.

While spending more than you make is risk-taking that cannot be sustained, nothing reflects the culture of excess more than our spending. U.S. consumer spending as a percentage of gross domestic product (GDP) has risen above 70 percent. By comparison, Germany and Japan spend at a level of 55 percent. In the end, rising consumer spending occurs with declining savings and exemplifies the excessive risk-taking of a culture of excess.[42] Today the culture of excess is the definition of success.

The overall increase in risk-taking in our social, economic, and cultural environment is truly staggering. The dramatic financial risk-taking, or gambling, has become so excessive that when the risks fail, deception and fraud also increase. The constant frenetic pace and risk-taking deplete our human resources. Simply the lengthy and complicated investigations alone of fraudulent financial schemes drain precious time and resources. Eventually, we need relief or some sort of self-preservation to avoid a complete breakdown in self-control and a collapse. In desperation, we must use manipulating and cheating as defensive maneuvers of compensation.

## THE CULTURAL FACTOR IN NARCISSISM

A confounding factor that relates to narcissism is the historic American tradition of "rugged individualism." The term is prominent in describing our ethic in the birth and development of our democracy. The term implies strongly that one has the right to a full development of one's potential— no matter what. The self-made or self-educated man (and today proudly including women) is the icon of what our country is about.[43] Individualism remains important even as technology has dramatically changed our lives, redefining individualism in modern times. Historic individualism is certainly related to narcissism, and this is highlighted when we look at different cultures.

Social psychology has fully documented our individualism as defining one's identity not by group identity or factors but by personal attributes.

One of the core concepts of social behavior in Western culture is the fundamental attribution error. This is defined as repeatedly making judgments that blame the individual, overemphasizing the person's traits and underestimating the situation. Other cultures are different. Their perspective has more appreciation for the situation in which a person's behavior occurs. For example, when psychologist Kaiping Peng analyzed newspaper accounts of recent murders, he found a distinct difference between American and Chinese reporting. American reporters emphasized the personal traits of the murderers, while Chinese reporters emphasized the situational factors.[44]

The Iraq occupation and Abu Ghraib prison scandal provides another example—are the young soldiers who committed atrocious acts lacking in character and moral development? Or, are they in an ongoing, despicable, and inhumane condition that would cause anyone eventually to break down and display abhorrent behavior? Our Western culture's first inclination is to blame the individual.

The fundamental attribution error is a profound concept. Malcolm Gladwell, popular writer of *Blink* and *Tipping Point*, was asked to respond in two seconds to different terms. When presented with the fundamental attribution error, he said: "If there was anything close to a theory of everything, it's that. That's the most profound observation about the way human beings operate than almost anything."[45]

But in Asian and African cultures, collectivism—giving an emphasis to a group's goals—and defining identity in relation to others is the dominant perspective. Other experiments dramatically illustrate cultural differences and how simple events are perceived differently. For example, psychologists Heejun Kim and Hazel Markus presented a picture of five pencils, with four of them the color green and the other the color orange. When Americans were asked to choose one of these pencils, 77 percent chose the pencil of a different color. Given the same choice, only 31 percent of Asian subjects picked the pencil of a different color.[46] Imagine how this simple perceptual difference and choice has a profound effect on workplace relations, working on a team or negotiating a conflict among persons with different cultural backgrounds.

Now dramatically heighten one side of the equation—the individualistic perspective that bigger and different are better. This display of fierce individualism increases the level of conflict with others who have a different cultural sense of self and belonging. It is not hard to see and feel this tension and conflict in our daily lives. In another experiment, when shown an underwater scene, Asian subjects usually described the relationships among the fish and the environment. But American subjects were more focused upon a single big fish![47]

Collectivism and group identity also seem to allow Asian culture to readily acknowledge shame and respond. When 32 people were killed at Virginia Tech in April 2007, the Korean community was appalled that the disturbed young man was from South Korea. Cho Seung-Hui was only eight when he left South Korea with his parents and was basically raised in the United States. But President Roh Moo-Hyun of South Korea issued two statements of condolences immediately after the shootings, and then made a public statement of apology. Foreign Minister Song Min-Soon sent a letter to Secretary of State Condoleezza Rice offering condolences. Koreans in all parts of the United States gathered at churches in response to the shooting.[48] It is hard to imagine Americans responding in a similar manner.

On the lighter side, what happens when our highly developed culture of narcissism goes up against the perspectives of other more collectivistic cultures? Our entrepreneurial narcissism may trump collectivistic culture and convert different cultural groups through the strong hypnotic trance of materialism. Consider the Yakima Indian tribe who in 2001 performed ceremonial rain dances in response to a severe drought in the Pacific Northwest. The tribe then sent a bill to the local federal government facility, the Bonneville Power Administration. The bill, for $32,000, was unfortunately rejected. "We're not paying," said Bonneville spokesman Mike Hansen, "the Yakima tribe basically went off and did something on their own and sent us the bill."[49] One can certainly interpret the Yakimas' bill as an appropriate cultural response of entrepreneurial narcissism. Sort of like—bill it, and they will pay.

In Southern California the Indian tribes have attained immense success and profits from their gambling casinos. They want to build more casinos, competitors oppose them, and there is a huge battle over taxes. Many Californians believe that with such large profits the tribes should pay taxes. But adapting to the dominant culture, the tribes respond that they do not want to pay any taxes and believe their sovereignty protects them from having to. Sound familiar?

The Indian tribes are trying hard to learn the political rules of manipulation. They have given large amounts of their new revenue to lobbyists, expecting the "return" of power and influence. Unfortunately, powerful and well-connected lobbyist Jack Abramoff took them to the cleaners. He collected money from all sides and basically stole their new profits until he was indicted and pled guilty to tax evasion, fraud, and conspiracy to bribe public officials.[50]

While there is considerable research about Western-Asian differences, are other cultures narcissistic? There is no clear evidence, though the recent economic growth of China offers amusing anecdotal reports. Beijing's six million square feet shopping mall Golden Resources has been dubbed the "Great Mall of China." With more than a thousand shops, it is described as "the perfect shopping experience." According to one report, the merchandise included a pedigree silver tabby cat (with American parents) for sale at the equivalent of US$3,600.[51] Take that, you American consumers.

And as for the Great Wall, U.S. skateboarding champ Danny Way jumped the wall in 2005, clearing a 61-foot gap at 50 miles per hour. This special event followed 10 years of events jumping the wall, including a bicyclist who died trying.[52] Young persons in China are quoted in newspapers as seeking and worrying about how they will attain their fortune. A serious competition may be brewing for our top position as a culture of excess and a culture of narcissism.

Cultural narcissism 2.0 is the second generation of cultural narcissism. As the modern day version, cultural narcissism 2.0 includes the assimilation of technology, screen media, and extreme capitalism. The second version of cultural narcissism has far greater impact on our society than when it was first observed. Cultural narcissism is played out daily in the marketplace. The definition of success and making it is determined by the new culture. Entrepreneurial activity is a coveted goal. Deregulation is a core pathway to success. Economic policy represents cultural narcissism 2.0 and defines what success is. Cultural narcissism 2.0 operates in an intensely fast and dynamic environment. It is in this incredible fast-paced culture that we define ourselves and define "success." Yet success is attained by playing within a structure of marketplace mania.

NOTES

1. Lasch, C. (1979). *The culture of narcissism* (pp. 32–33). New York: W. W. Norton.

2. This is a very brief description of the myth of Narcissus. For more elaborate discussions, see Alcorn, M. (1994). *Narcissism and the literary libido* (p. 1–28). New York: New York University Press. Also, Strate, L. (2000). Something from nothing: Seeking a sense of self. *Speech Communication Annual*, 14:14–62.

3. Kohut, H. (1966). Forms and transformations of narcissism. *Journal of the American Psychoanalytic Association*, 14:243–272. Kohut, H. (1971). *The analysis of the self*. New York: International Universities Press.

4. Fernando, J. (1998). The etiology of narcissistic personality disorder. *Psychoanalytic Study of the Child*, 53:141. Fernando, J. (2000). Superego analysis in narcissistic patients with superego pathology. *Canadian Journal of Psychoanalysis*, 8:99–117. See also Symington, N. (1993). *Narcissism: A new theory* (p. 4). London: Karnac Books. Symington notes the cause or origin of narcissism is not the trauma but the "individual's response to it."

5. American Psychiatric Association. (2004). *Diagnostic and statistical manual of mental disorders*. Washington, D.C.: American Psychiatric Association.

6. Twenge, J., Konrath, S., Foster, J., Campbell, W. K., & Bushman, B. (2008). Egos inflating over time: A cross temporal analysis of the narcissistic personality inventory. *Journal of Personality*, 76 (4): 875–901.

7. Twenge, J. (2006). *Generation me: Why today's young Americans are more confident, assertive, entitled—and more miserable than ever before*. New York: The Free Press.

8. Twenge, J., & Campbell, W. Keith. (2009). *The narcissism epidemic: Living in an age of entitlement*. New York: Free Press.

9. Trzesniewski, K., Donnellan, M. B., & Robins, R. (2008). Is "generation me" really more narcissistic than previous generations? *Journal of Personality*, 76 (4): 903–918.

10. Raskin, R. N., & Hall, C. S. (1981). The Narcissistic Personality Inventory: Alternate form reliability and further evidence of construct validity. *Journal of Personality Assessment*, 45:159–162.

11. Raskin, R., & Hall, C. (1979). A Narcissistic Personality Inventory. *Psychological Reports*, 45:590.

12. Trull, T., & Durrett, C. (2005). Categorical and dimensional models of personality disorder. *Annual Review of Clinical Psychology*, 1:335–380. Potter, N. N. (2004). Perplexing issues in personality disorders. *Current Opinion in Psychiatry*, 17:487–492. Westen, D., & Arkowitz-Westen, L. (1998). Limitations of Axis II in diagnosing personality pathology in clinical practice. *American Journal of Psychiatry*, 155:1767–1771.

13. Millon, T., Davis, R., Millon, C., Escovar, L., & Meagher, S. (2000). *Personality disorders in modern life*. New York: Wiley.

14. Wallace, H., & Baumeister, R. (2002). The performance of narcissists rises and falls with perceived opportunity for glory. *Journal of Personality and Social Psychology*, 82:819–834.

15. Exline, J., Baumeister, R., Bushman, B., Campbell, W. K., & Finkel, E. (2004). Too proud to let go: Narcissistic entitlement as a barrier to forgiveness. *Journal of Personality and Social Psychology*, 87: 894–912.

16. Twenge, J. M., & Campbell, W. K. (2003). "Isn't it fun to get the respect that we're going to deserve?" Narcissism, social rejection, and aggression. *Personality and Social Psychology Bulletin*, 29: 261–272.

17. Bushman, B., Bonacci, A., van Dijk, M., & Baumeister, R. (2003). Narcissism, sexual refusal, and aggression: Testing a narcissistic reactance model of sexual coercion. *Journal of Personality and Social Psychology*, 84:1027–1040.

18. Twenge. *Generation me*.

19. Maccoby, M. (2003). *The productive narcissist*. New York: Broadway Books. See also Maccoby, M. (January–February 2000). Narcissistic leaders: The Incredible pros, the inevitable cons. *Harvard Business Review*.

20. Maccoby, M. (2003). *The productive narcissist*. Appendix, p. 262.

21. Ibid., pp. 262–263.

22. Ibid., p. 262.

23. Symington. *Narcissism: A new theory*.

24. Ibid., p. 10.

25. Ibid.

26. Kernberg's position cited in Person, Ethel Spector. (1986). Manipulativeness in entrepreneurs and psychopaths. In Reid, W., Dorr, D., Walker, J., & Bonner, J. (Eds.) *Unmasking the psychopath* (p. 258). New York: W. W. Norton.

27. Hare, R. (1999). *Without conscience: The disturbing world of the psychopaths among us*. New York: Guilford Publications.

28. The instrument is the Hare Psychopathy Checklist (HPCL). Toronto: Multi-Health Systems.

29. *Fast Company*, July 2005 article. See also Carlson, P. (2005, July 8). The CEO as Psychopath. *The Los Angeles Times*, p. E18.

30. Achbar, M., Abbott, J., & Bakan, J. (2005). *The corporation*. Retrieved December 12, 2008 from http://www.thecorporation.com. Documentary based on Bakan, J. (2004). *The corporation: The pathological pursuit of profit and power.* The film interviews 40 experts, including Hare, on how corporations operate.

31. Babiak, P., & Hare, R. (2006). *Snakes in suits: When psychopaths go to work.* New York: Harper-Collins.

32. Maccoby, M. (2003). Preface. In *The productive narcissist* (p. xiv). New York: Broadway Books.

33. Joe the Plumber was cited as a working-class example by John McCain in the 2008 election. He became a media star, had an agent, and wrote a book. After the election, he disavowed John McCain and called Sarah Palin "the real deal."

34. Hittelman. (2008, February 2). We need a better deal with tribes. *The Los Angeles Times*, p. A21.

35. Steele, M. (2008, May 23). Fantasy 5 fantasy fix: Enticing the poor to gamble more is a crazy solution to California's budget mess. *The Los Angeles Times*, p. A29.

36. Mihoces, G. (2008, May 30). Brain trumps hand: Mental acuity under pressure is needed to be successful on poker's big stage. *USA Today: World Series of Poker* [Special Section].

37. Reich, R. (2008). *Supercapitalism* (pp. 112–113). New York: Alfred A. Knopf.

38. Bogle, J. (2005). *The battle for the soul of capitalism* (pp. 120–121). New Haven, CT: Yale University Press.

39. Templeton, D. (2008, October 19). The importance of the VIX index. Retrieved December 12, 2008 from www.seekingalpha.com/article/101949/. Lauricella, T., & Lucchetti, A. (2008, October 23). What's behind the surge in the VIX? *The Wall Street Journal*. Retrieved December 12, 2008 from http://online.wsj.com/article/SB122477812298862775.html.

40. Definition of Uptick rule from *Investopedia* a Forbes Digest Company. http://www.investopedia.com/terms/u/uptickrule.asp.

41. Cho, D. (2008, August 21). A few speculators dominate vast market for oil trading. *The Washington Post*.

42. Brockman, J. (2008, October 17). As economy falters, should we spend or save? National Public Radio. Retrieved December 12, 2008 from http://www.npr.org/templates/story/story.php?storyId=95836911&sc=emaf. Barr, C. (2008, October 16). The bright spot in a dark economy. Retrieved December 12, 2008 from http://money.cnn.com/2008/10/15/news/rainy.day.fortune/index.htm. For documented trends of consumerism and spending, see Schor, J. (2004). *Born to buy.* New York: Scribner; and Schor, J. (2002). *The overspent American.* New York: Scribner.

43. Jacoby, S. (2008). *The age of American unreason* (pp. 58, 71, 74). New York: Pantheon Books.

44. 1994 Study by Kaiping Peng cited in *APA Monitor*, February 2006. Asian-American Psychology: The Culture-Cognition Connection. p. 65.

45. Jaffe, E. (2006). Malcolm in the middle: Gladwell responded in 2 seconds to terms presented by interviewer. *Observer, Association for Psychological Science*, 19 (3): 34.

46. Kim and Marcus's study reported in Myers, D. (2005). *Social psychology* (8th ed., p. 49). New York: McGraw-Hill.

47. Nisbett's study reported in ibid., 47.

48. Sohn, Jie-Ae. (2007, April 18). South Korea shocked by U.S. shooting link. CNN. Retrieved December 12, 2008 from http://www.cnn.com/2007/WORLD/asiapcf/04/17/vatech.seoul/index.html.

49. May, J. (2001, September 6). Bonneville refuses payment for Yakima rain ceremonies. *Indian Country Today.* Retrieved December 12, 2008 from http://www.indiancountrytoday.com/archive/28221764.html.

50. Schmidt, S., & Grimaldi, J. (2006, January 4). Abramoff pleads guilty to three counts. *The Washington Post*, p. A01.

51. Things Asian. (2005, June 27). The great mall of China. Retrieved December 12, 2008 from http://www.thingsasian.com/stories-photos/3446.

52. Cave, C. (2008, August 20). Danny Way jumps Great Wall of China. Retrieved December 12, 2008 from http://skateboard.about.com/od/events/a/DannyWayChina1.htm.

# Chapter 2

# MARKETPLACE MANIA

The good news is, you'll be a millionaire soon. The bad news is, so will everybody else.

The market will fluctuate daily, but by 2010, the Dow will soar past the 50,000 mark.

—Kevin Kelly, Editor, *Wired* magazine
September 1999

There's always a bull market somewhere.

—Jim Cramer, *Mad Money*, CNBC

The last six months have made it abundantly clear that voluntary regulation does not work.

—Christopher Cox, SEC Chair
September 26, 2008

The volume of shares traded on the New York and NASDAQ stock exchanges was 15 million shares a day in 1970. By 1980, it was 80 million a day, and by 1990, 300 million shares a day. But the increase in the next decade was staggering. By 2000, it had increased to almost three billion shares a day. Even after the Internet bubble burst and the market crashed in 2000–2002, daily volume was at 3.3 billion shares in 2004. This amounts to an average turnover rate of 150 percent.[1] The hyperactivity results in tremendous profits for brokers and fund managers. Whether the market goes up or down, the activity is what matters.

Unfortunately, the mania also involves betting on the downside and the ruin of a company. In July 2007, the U.S. Securities and Exchange Commission (SEC) eliminated the uptick rule.[2] In place since 1934, this rule curbed short sellers—those who gamble a stock will go down. Traders can profit by betting on a stock's decline, placing a bet without even holding the stock. This is referred to as naked short selling. The uptick rule prevented short sellers from adding to downward momentum when a stock is already in decline. The rule did not allow an additional trade unless there was an "uptick" or an increase in the stock price. Otherwise, everyone piles on and suddenly a stock is at zero and worthless—while vultures profit.

If eliminating the uptick rule were not enough, the SEC also allowed the major investment banks to increase the amount of debt they could take on. In a 55-minute meeting in April 2004, a meeting that at the time was not covered by any news outlet, five SEC members buckled to a request to grant an exemption to debt/asset requirements. The result allowed the investment firms to pump money into mortgage-backed securities and credit derivatives. At that meeting, one of the lobbying principals representing Goldman Sachs was Henry Paulson, whom President George W. Bush named Treasury Secretary in 2006. Subsequently, when the economy spun out of control in October 2008, Paulson was placed in charge of the huge rescue/bailout plan.[3] Systematically, decision makers routinely promote the mania of the marketplace until it finally collapses. This continued grandiosity—a trend analogous to "irrational exuberance"—is characteristic of cultural narcissism.

The smoke from this hot activity wafts and settles downward to the individual. Marketplace mania defines the conditions of success. As a powerful cultural force, it impacts each of us to develop our own manic drive to succeed, do it all, and make our own fortune. In the end, we have a strong desire to be active and risk-taking—to have unlimited potential. On an individual basis, cultural forces press us to take charge, to seize the entrepreneurial spirit, and to take our own risks. Even more so, it is a persona, a way of being, and the means toward a socially sanctioned and approved road to success.

## ENTREPRENEURIAL NARCISSISM

"For certain executives, there is no ceiling." So reads a large newspaper ad in the *Los Angeles Times* for an "Executive M.B.A." program which is "where you go when you're reaching for the top." The ad boasts that the program is ranked in the top 25 in the nation, citing *U.S. News & World Report* and *Business Week* as the references. The program is designed for those "seasoned mid-to-senior-level business managers," who can attend small classes only on every third weekend for 24 months.[4] The ad accurately reflects the cultural zeitgeist, as today's business executive must adopt an entrepreneurial vision of unlimited success. The road there is often getting an MBA degree. It seems this is where you are taught business principles in the service of becoming a high-level employee who thinks like an entrepreneur.

The growth in MBAs is worldwide, to match the entrepreneur with globalization. Since 1994, there has been more than a 25 percent year-by-year increase in graduating MBAs. Career surveys report that MBAs have a salary increase of about 20 percent when graduating, and around 53 percent three to five years after graduation. In 2006, an 18 percent increase in MBA hiring by major companies was reported. This followed a reported 18 percent increase in 2005. Many of these programs, as illustrated by the ad above, have been condensed to less than two years in length.[5] Fast and profitable, the MBA degree is the royal road to financial success.

The cultural drive to be an entrepreneurial risk-taker with no upper limits is a major contributor to the growth of manipulation and narcissism. In a 1986 essay, "Manipulativeness in Entrepreneurs and Psychopaths," psychoanalyst Ethel Spector Person describes similarities between the way both entrepreneurs and antisocial psychopaths manipulate others.[6] Person writes that entrepreneurs use manipulation to focus directly on success (profit) and a productive life, while the antisocial/psychopath harms others and gradually deteriorates. For the entrepreneur, the manipulation is elective, for the psychopath, it is obligatory. The use of manipulation can be positive and creative, or exploitive and destructive. But today, within the structure of marketplace mania, manipulation is no longer elective but demanded beyond human decency by the intense pace and competition within a culture of excess. Manipulation now feels normal within an environment that demands it. And as higher levels of normative manipulation are required, our society moves increasingly toward antisocial and destructive tendencies.

Sometimes, this manipulation occurs, interestingly, within a company whose executives are supposed to command an organizational, management structure and a bureaucracy, rather than their own personal, risk-taking entrepreneurial needs. Today's CEOs and CFOs seem to act more like entrepreneurs than company executives, spinning lucrative side deals outside the structure of the company they are supposed to represent. The Enron story is replete with examples.

The cultural trend of entrepreneurship does not mean you must go out and start your own company. Rather, entrepreneurial narcissism fuses together with the development of cultural narcissism and represents a person who maintains independence, flexibility and becomes rich. (However, creating their own wealth does not mean they add wealth to society. Many who become wealthy through entrepreneurial activity do not always create or build something, but rather devise some sort of paper financial transactions that make themselves or their company wealthy.) Flexibility is certainly key, as today's "worker" demands flexibility, the opportunity to moonlight, and no upward limit on their potential or financial success.[7] Entrepreneurial narcissism is desired not just in business or with business leaders but is a preferred way of life. The unbridled spirit of entrepreneurial narcissism is so popular we admire and want leaders who display these features. In 2002, California voters had elected Gray Davis as governor, but nine months later threw him out in a special recall election. Davis's speedy demise did not bother angry voters, as a movie star was on the sidelines waiting in the wings. Enter actor Arnold Schwarzenegger, who announced he was running for governor on the *Tonight Show* with Jay Leno.[8] (Later, Leno introduced Schwarzenegger on his victorious election night.) Commanding the power of his bodybuilding, movie roles, and charisma, Schwarzenegger was swept into office, despite the fact that he had never held a public office or had any political experience.

In a televised public debate before the special election, political opponents tried to knock him down from his Number One perch. But Schwarzenegger proudly displayed the sine qua non of success—he was a successful entrepreneur. He criticized his Democratic opponent for never having signed the *front* of a check as Arnold had, an act reserved for the owner of a company. Meeting a payroll is a core component of the entrepreneurial spirit in business-dominated America. It has become the starting block for someone to run for a political office. But the further implication was that lowly persons who sign only the *back* of a check (a worker) cannot possibly be qualified to be governor.[9] Of course, Arnold has certainly signed the back of many checks in much larger amounts than most others would dream of, and that is really the underlying issue—I am rich. When Arnold displayed his economic bravado of signing the front of a check, voters thumped their chests and saluted with approval—right on, power to the people. But this is a new interpretation of power to the people for a public that defines success with an image of fame and entrepreneurship. Schwarzenegger is a symbol of today's image of success, elected based on fame and money to one of the highest offices in the land without having any experience in politics. But, he is a success in media and, as he emphasized, a successful entrepreneur. Consider the image for children of this "success story." See what you can accomplish if you are a famous actor? And make sure you run your own business. The fact that he was not even born in the United States adds the element of an immigrant success story that historically we cherish. There has even been banter that the Constitution should be amended so that the foreign-born Schwarzenegger can run for President.[10] Contrast this attitude with the vitriol of the immigration issue in politics today and the response toward poor immigrants who do not become successful bodybuilders or actors.

Following his whirlwind election, Schwarzenegger makes appearances in a windbreaker, and everyone wants his autograph and handshake. After all, it is a double thrill—he is a big name actor and a governor. The international press comes to Sacramento, just because it is Arnold. His campaign and election are now covered by the infotainment media such as E! channel and Access Hollywood. Appearing on *Hardball* with Chris Matthews[11] before a college audience, Schwarzenegger responds to questions often by correcting the questioner. "I'm not a politician," he asserts. This is quite a statement concerning the unprecedented special election that made him governor. No one seems to have said to him—you are now.

Schwarzenegger enjoys a teasing banter, using an adolescent phrase "girly man" (it is just a joke), but a reporter stumbles onto a financial report in 2005. It seems that two days before he was sworn in as governor, he signed a lucrative $8 million deal with American Media, a company that owns *Fitness* and *Supplement* magazines, along with tabloids *National Enquirer* and *Star Magazine*. The contract also called for ongoing payments for articles or other services and even a percentage of the subsidiary magazine's annual advertising revenue, guaranteeing at least a million dollars a year.[12]

But this news of the governor's entrepreneurialism draws a reaction typical of today's normative narcissism. Quickly, staff responds—so what is the big deal? Schwarzenegger's free agent signing as he is about to be a governor is no problem, even though he subsequently vetoed a bill that would have restricted the selling of supplements. No conflict of interest here! Republican talk show hosts and Republican pols in Sacramento are perplexed—what is the problem? He has supported this industry all along; the money he received is not going to change his decision or stance on the issue. In other words, it would only be a problem if he took money and changed his position on an issue. Why not capitalize and profit as governor on his existing viewpoints?

Staff for the governor point out that he is not taking his $175,000 salary, and deals like this allow him to do so, thus, saving taxpayers a lot of money. The justification and rationalization has become a common one: Side deals or profit from other sources outweigh regard for rules and regulations. The attempt is made to redefine the manipulative behavior by countering with a behavior that offsets it. When CEOs are on trial for fraud, their contributions to charity and to the community are always highlighted. In the new cultural view of entrepreneurialism, boundaries and limits, which when crossed were once referred to as a conflict of interest, are no longer reasonable.

The assumption here is that the public is better served by the money saved because a wealthy person refuses a salary and has other entrepreneurial ventures that would better themselves financially. Many states do not allow governors to take extra income from anywhere, but California is not one of them. So, technically in this case no laws were broken. Under public pressure, Schwarzenegger cancelled the contract but did not return any of the money he already received.[13]

After a few years as a politician, Arnold's popularity as reflected by ratings had noticeably declined. He received a setback when he called a special election in 2005 in which millions were lost putting forward propositions favorable to him that the voters rejected.[14] So, in 2006, he ran for reelection with a different course. By touting the environment and some workers' issues, he took issues away from his Democratic opponent and easily won a legitimate election for a second term. So, it seemed the social psychology experiment was ending, but Schwarzenegger displayed enough self-correction through the political process to get reelected.

During his reelection campaign in 2006, there was bare mention of the negatives cited above, from the magazine deal to previous reports of his grabbing women, for which he had issued an apology in 2003.[15] It would be one thing to say that his opponents brought these things up and they did not work, but these past issues were never even raised. The public, still enamored with a famous candidate and caught up in cultural narcissism, totally ignored negatives that have destroyed other politicians' careers. For example, in the same intense media market, Los Angeles Mayor Antonio Villaraigosa has been hounded and followed by press after he separated from his wife and dated a news reporter who had interviewed him.[16] How did Schwarzenegger avoid fallout from any critique of character or behavior? Why was he treated differently than other politicians? Because today a famous and rich media candidate epitomizes the cultural narcissism we cherish. In comparison, the other pols are boring, have been lowly workers, or even ghastly lawyers or engineers. How could someone in these professions understand what people want?

Post-2006 and his reelection, the trend continues. Schwarzenegger is one of the first governors to use election or campaign funds to give his key staff a bonus. His personal assistant was given $20,000 to add to his $85,000 salary, and his communications director was given $13,000 to add to his salary of $123,000. (The justification for these bonuses was the long hours, travel, and personal commitment to the job.) Their regular salaries are paid by state taxpayers and the bonus amounts to money collected from corporations and special interests and then funneled back to staff.[17] The governor irked his own party when in 2006 he hired Susan Kennedy, a Democrat with Kennedy-family relations, as his chief of staff.[18] He rewarded her handsomely in 2006 with $92,000 in campaign funds as a bonus to her state salary of $131,000. In an interview earlier, the *Los Angeles Times* reported that Kennedy said she needed the money to pay her mortgage.[19]

Schwarzenegger epitomizes what the public want in their life and in their leaders. His media image is a perfect fit for what the public admire. If the average person could buy gloves fit for Arnold, they would do so in a heartbeat and wear the gloves every day in hopes to become like him. To that end, his negatives, which would have buried other pols, are minimized.

In 2008, Schwarzenegger has come full circle. When he ran against Gray Davis in the recall of 2002, he blasted Davis's proposed increase in the car tax. In movie-star style, he announced the car tax was gone—"hasta la vista baby." But to respond to the economic meltdown he called an emergency meeting of the legislature in November 2008. He needed to fill a huge budget gap. One of his proposed solutions—an increase in the car tax.[20] The problems only got worse. In 2009, Schwarzenegger was embroiled in resolving a huge $26 billion state deficit. But Schwarzenegger has to be acknowledged. He utilized his success and seized the day. Schwarzenegger was not lucky, his type of success and image fits the cultural moment, and he was there to recognize it. Still, it would be a strain to argue that he is an example of productive narcissism. It will be quite interesting to see how his years as governor are analyzed and critiqued.

## RELIGION AND CAPITALISM

While the religious wars are prominent in every election, religion has become fused with today's supercapitalism and our culture of excess. The business world has adopted the Reagan philosophy of the marketplace as a religion. Social critic Thomas Frank documented the development of the formula in the late 1990s. In *One Market Under God*, Frank culls the writings of social critics and lists the passionate dogma of success: privatization + deregulation + globalization = turbo-capitalism = prosperity.[21] The value-laden success formula is fused with the intensity of goodness and religious values. While religious values can be used for marketing, they can also be used as a defense when capitalistic excess rages out of control.

The story of Richard Scrushy, CEO of HealthSouth Corporation, is an interesting case in point. Scrushy was indicted and tried for fraud, but was acquitted in June 2005. The Feds lost this case and it is believed they gave away get-out-of-jail-free cards to other executives who testified against Scrushy. This led to a jury that would not convict him. Scrushy was a huge figure in his hometown of Birmingham, Alabama, which played to his advantage. During 2000 to 2002, HealthSouth filed so many false entries that new auditors could not figure it all out until the time the trial was closing in 2005. HealthSouth then filed the honest results to the SEC, that profit during this time was overstated by $1.23 billion and revenues were overstated by $1.87 billion. This seems like quite a mistake.[22]

But the shrewd defense and manipulation accurately depicts today's culture of excess and the fusion of religion and financial success. When the SEC first filed charges, HealthSouth fired Scrushy in March 2003. He then embarked on capitalizing on the fusion and equality between the marketplace and God. Scrushy, who is white, left his suburban evangelical church and joined a mostly black congregation in a blue-collar neighborhood. He also bought a half-hour local TV program featuring himself and his wife, and black ministers as guests. Prayer groups worked daily to ask God to acquit Scrushy. The Guiding Light Church ordained him as a "nondenominational Christian minister." On the jury of twelve, seven were African Americans. It all worked.

After his acquittal, Scrushy appeared with his third wife in a photo op of free market heaven on earth. "God is good," he said, and after referring to "two years of torture," asked out loud, "What happened to the compassion in this world?"[23] Is it normal to expect compassion when the company you run has more than $3 billion in accounting discrepancy? Experts estimate Scrushy will keep more than $200 million from the fraud. And all the other CEOs and executives going to trial are certainly scrambling to find the "guiding light" Scrushy found. HealthSouth will not take him back, guiding light or not, and the company paid a paltry $100 million to settle SEC fraud charges in June 2005.

There was a report that Scrushy wanted to run for public office. But what goes around comes around. In 2007, a federal judge sentenced Scrushy to almost seven years in a very controversial political case. In this case, he was accused of arranging a $500,000 loan to a foundation for the former governor of Alabama in exchange for a seat on a state hospital regulatory board.[24]

Scrushy's case and outcome is remarkable. By using religion, he garnered enough support to avoid an objective assessment. Just as fame and fortune shielded Schwarzenegger from his negatives, religious favoritism protected Scrushy from his serious manipulative behaviors. The cultural trend to talk about and strongly display one's religious values ties in with the grandiosity of narcissism in our culture. If a leader conveys that he is strongly religious, the public rewards him with a blind faith, sparing him from critique, no matter how disturbing the person's decisions or behavior may be. Loudly proclaiming your religious values seems to guarantee you have a following, and the support of a religious community can make a big difference. The HealthSouth story sounds way out there, and many will not consider the case representative of what goes on in business, or will give the "so what" empty response that Scrushy is simply a bad apple and there are bad apples in every bunch. But, of course, the endless list of CEOs investigated and indicted has desensitized us to it all.

In today's manic marketplace, the promotion of religious values is good business. During the mortgage refinance heydays of anything goes, I was besieged with several snail mail and e-mail offers a week to refinance. But one e-mail offer caught my eye. This one was advertised as a "Christian" family loan. What exactly is a "Christian" mortgage loan? Does it offer a lower interest rate from God? I would certainly be disappointed if the rate were higher, in other words, if it cost extra to have contact with God. I have not seen any corollaries, for example, "Jewish loans" or "Hare-Krishna" loans (Muslim loans would not be a seller).

The marketplace and business are fused with religious terms, and one of my favorites is the "angel investor," a person with a lot of money who will fund your start-up company. So, if a person with a lot of money to invest is an "angel" coming down from heaven, then what is a person without money—the devil?

## COOKIN' THE BOOKS

The collective manipulation of Wall Street corporations takes entrepreneurial narcissism to an interesting level, beyond just that of CEOs. A story in the March 2002 edition of the business magazine *Investors Business Daily* cited a research report that took the top 100 NASDAQ companies and totaled what they reported to the SEC and what they reported to investors and the public. To the SEC these 100 NASDAQ companies reported losses totaling $19 billion. But to the public and investors the same companies concurrently reported a total profit of $82 million.[25] The latter spin utilizes the business concept of *pro forma earnings*, those onetime costs that will not happen next year, subtracted from the balance sheet. So, results to the SEC (and undoubtedly the IRS) show a loss. Reports on corporate profit or losses depend on who you are talking to, and this example illustrates a trend that is not anecdotal or just another bad apple. Involving the top 100 NASDAQ companies, the pattern is pervasive and systemic. This is the way business results are reported. This is the way it is done. To the business world and the outer limits of the accounting profession, there is nothing wrong with this.

The practice is a result, in part, of a cultural change. In a culture of excess, the auditors have lowered the standards. Accountants used to be those boring bookworms who were very conservative. In college, we referred to the business fraternity as "the typewriters." But no more. They are now active advisors, trying to help the company constantly avoid taxes, and fostering an entrepreneurial approach that contributes to the manipulation and growth of cultural narcissism. "Creative" accounting seems readily accepted by the boards of directors who in today's free market hypnotic trance are more apt to say defiantly: "What's wrong with that?"

The first evidence and breakthrough of accounting standards was Enron, and nowhere was this change more evident. In the Enron scandal, the new standards resulted in a historic accounting icon, Arthur Andersen, going out of business. Auditors abandoned long-held conservative standards for purely economic reasons. In 2000, U.S. corporations spent $3 billion on auditing and $6 billion on consulting. Enron spent $23 million on auditors and $29 million on consulting.[26] Clearly, consulting is more profitable than auditing. Of course, in today's environment it is OK for one company, like an Arthur Andersen, to do both. The estimated cost of investor loss from Enron was $140 billion.[27]

Further evidence of the depth of manipulation throughout the financial system comes from how major banks aided and abetted the Enron scandal. A congressional report and inquiry was undertaken about Citigroup's role in helping Enron cover up. Follow the bouncing ball. Enron, with great help from banks, used a financing mechanism called a prepay, which involves one party paying another for a service or product to be delivered at a future date. Citigroup engineered many Enron prepay schemes, raising $4.8 billion over six years. There were 14 transactions. Competitor J. P. Morgan, not to be outdone, made 12 transactions raising $3.7 billion. Let us take one of the prepay deals. An entity was created called Yosemite. Citigroup assisted in helping Yosemite issue some $800 million in bonds, which were purchased by private investors. Yosemite then lent the money to an entity called Delta Energy, which was controlled by Citigroup. The location of Delta Energy was listed as the Cayman Islands. Or at least that is where it was on paper. Delta Energy and Enron then struck another deal, another prepaid contract. This contract was based upon the spot price of crude oil at a future date. Delta Energy paid Enron the $800 million up front. Making a long story short, a series of hedging transactions cancelled each other out. And when the maturity date of the contract was reached, poof, the $800 million was recycled back to Yosemite.

During this process, Enron paid $29 million to Delta Energy every six months. Delta then turned around and paid Yosemite, which returned a 7.25 percent annual interest-rate return to Yosemite's bond investors.[28] Do you think this example fits the manipulation criteria of narcissism? The end conclusion of all this is that Enron was able to borrow money without showing it as debt on the company's books. (The slogan for Citigroup is "Citigroup never sleeps.")

So, Congress is not interested in all this except that the deal did not allow investors or analysts to see Enron's true level of debt. In other words, this whole elaborate process is designed to manipulate or circumvent the rules and regulations for a public company. Like the pro forma earnings example, this process became established as an ongoing business practice. Two years later, the SEC rendered a verdict—a fine of about $300 million for Citibank and J. P. Morgan for their supporting role in Enron's mass economic homicide. But there were civil suits; all the retirement groups and other investors who lost big money took action in what is the biggest nemesis to God and the marketplace—class action lawsuits. Four years later, Citigroup agreed to pay $2 billion to Enron shareholders. Of course, they admitted no wrongdoing. And it was not just one bad apple bank, as other financial behemoths had to kick in too. Merrill Lynch paid $80 million to the SEC, Bank of America paid $69 million to Enron investors, Lehman Brothers $222.5 million to the University of California and investors, and finally rival J. P. Morgan won the contest, settling only a few days after Citigroup in June 2005 for $2.2 billion, a little more than

Citigroup.[29] Sounds like J. P. Morgan had bad lawyers. No admitted wrongdoing for anyone, and a small price to pay for all the gains made by these large corporations. After all, they did nothing wrong, they were only conducting financial transactions and business as it is done today.

It seemed obvious that such a fiasco like Enron would lead to self-correction and increased regulation. But it did not. Despite passing the Sarbanes-Oxley bill,[30] lack of adequate accounting or auditing could not begin to cope with the excessive risk-taking of the 2008 failures of some of the largest Wall Street firms—Bear Stearns, Lehman Brothers, or AIG Insurance. Other banks and financial firms that did not fail outright were teetering on the edge. Everywhere excessive risk-taking was the norm. New financial paper inventions, like "credit default swaps," have added a new importance to that old saying that the deal is not worth the paper it is printed on. Cookin' the books was the only desperate strategy left to try to control the excess, to cover over the lack of corporate self-control.

## DEREGULATION

A child cannot develop and grow without limits and boundaries. Put another way, balanced regulation is necessary for healthy growth and development. If parental boundaries are too loose (nonexistent) or too rigid, child development is impaired. The end result can be complex in the internal world of a young adult. But put very simply, impaired development may produce a young adult who lacks self-control and direction, or has an overcontrolled obsessive style. The same principle applies to markets. Adequate and balanced boundaries (regulations) are necessary and *required* for growth and maturity.

Yet economic deregulation has grown dramatically in the past 20 years, an important social movement and powerful trend that allows for the rise in excess, narcissism, manipulation, and the crossover into antisocial behavior of fraud. Deregulation has become the mechanism and the vehicle for the narcissistic manipulation of persons and businesses to prevail in any manner possible. In deregulated environs, only the strong survive is replaced by only the manipulative survive.

History seems to be irrelevant when it comes to the "me-first" and profit-only mission that supports deregulation. The American public seems brainwashed. From the Great Depression to the junk bond crisis to the savings and loan scandal to the recent economic collapse of multiple financial institutions, there seems to be no lesson learned. In his book,

*Everything for Sale*, economist Robert Kuttner presents broad evidence of the effects of deregulation.[31] Kuttner presents example after example from a historical and industry perspective on the "virtues and limits of markets." He fully documents the misconception of deregulation and its negative effects on the banking, airlines, and telecommunications industries. He also points out the disturbing end result of deregulation—that the big corporations survive the intense competition, and then use their hegemony to crush smaller, more efficient competitors who try to come along. In other words, undoing or minimizing regulatory agencies and mechanisms is tearing down what made our marketplace as successful, powerful, and resilient as it is today.

Nevertheless, social and cultural forces are constantly at work to tear down regulation. In the end, the overall message becomes simple: Regulation bad, deregulation good. And we pay the price, which includes not only the obvious financial destruction and loss but increased competition, stress, and daily conflict. The deregulated philosophy even filters down to an impact on children. The tremendous financial growth in the toy and entertainment industry results in programmed children who play with branded toys.

In 1984, the Federal Trade Commission deregulated children's television, allowing products tied to TV programs to be licensed. The resulting partnerships led to the branding of toys. In 2002, nine of ten best-selling toys were advertisements for a TV program, a movie, or a video. A typical example is "Care Bears" by American Greetings, in which educational materials were sent to 25,000 preschools nationwide to help kids learn how to care.[32] Interactive toys are the rage and a toy has to talk or do something human, until its effect wears off and another interactive toy is bought. When I recently bought a Monopoly game for an eight-year-old, it was stamped with a Sponge Bob/Square Pants label, indicating some sort of infiltration of the successful brand into the game of Monopoly. Child experts are very concerned that this branding leads to a type of programmed play that lacks creativity. The precision-like guerilla marketing results in what consumer and economic expert Juliet Schor calls "commercialized children." In *Born to Buy*, Schor provides an analysis of the negative effect of rampant consumerism on childhood development. Her statistical analysis shows a clear relationship between consumer involvement and psychological distress in children.[33]

Deregulating as a course of action allows an anything-goes business culture and has led to a hostile environment. An angry public has demanded more rules. Consumers have besieged Congress to pass a

"Passenger Bill of Rights" after airline customers spent more than six hours stuck on a plane with no options (among other examples of poor treatment). But it has not become law. Likewise, an effort to pass a "Credit Cardholder Bill of Rights" was put forth after consumers had their interest rates increased several points for no apparent reason. Finally, after another huge political battle, President Obama signed the Credit Card Accountability, Responsibility, and Disclosure (CARD) Act in May 2009.[34] Congress wrestled with and did pass a "Patient Bill of Rights" in health care. The impact of deregulation has created a stressful and hostile business environment. What does it say that consumers who fly on an airplane, have credit cards, and try to obtain adequate health care are seeking legal action and regulation to guarantee "rights" so that they simply will not be abused? Why do we live this way—creating such stress in necessary day-to-day activity? Health care actually poses an interesting example, as the "rights" movement arose against overcontrol by the private sector. For-profit health care giants used managed care, one of the most regulated mechanisms ever invented, like a club and battering ram to keep patients from specialists, limit hospitalization, and supposedly control costs. In other words, when the private sector uses regulation for profit and gain, it is good. But government regulation for safety, fairness, or fraud protection is bad.

Deregulation forces must overpower the main source of regulation— the government. This is not hard. In 2005, it was reported that the number of lobbyists had doubled since 2000 to a whopping total of 34,750. Dividing this number by 535 (435 representatives and 100 senators) you get almost 65 lobbyists per member of Congress. In the spirit of marketplace mania, the amount charged to clients also increased by 100 percent.[35] Of course, lobbyists constantly work against any governmental regulation of the special interests they represent. Many organizations actively work to deregulate. For example, the Heritage Foundation, a prominent supporter of Republican business interests, maintains a nonprofit status despite spending 30 million plus to prevent regulation. They publish materials like their report "How to Close Down the Labor Department."[36] Former SEC Chairman Harvey Pitt was actually a prominent lobbyist for the accounting industry before being named its top regulator. When Pitt assumed the SEC chairmanship, he announced and embarked on a kinder and gentler role for the SEC. This did not exactly fit with the rapid misdeeds of Enron, WorldCom, Tyco, and Global Crossing. Amidst controversy that he was biased, too friendly, and had a conflict of interest in SEC cases, he resigned.[37] Likewise, deregulators seek to have someone head the Department of Labor who does not believe in the minimum wage, or a leader of the Environmental Agency who will not try too hard to enforce existing regulations and does not believe in global warming.

Probably the most incredible and superficial concept proposed is the phrase "voluntary regulation," used by the deregulators who are unfamiliar with what an oxymoron is. Deregulation is the linchpin for the culture of excess and nothing represents a culture of excess more than the active deregulators. But the deregulators are out of control, always hammering away until there is destruction, like a guy who hammers a nail in a board, but then keeps hammering until the board breaks.

Rather than the term deregulation, we need a new term that would describe a process of reducing unnecessary administration and waste while increasing efficiency and balancing the protection and fairness of the marketplace with pro-business growth. This is in contrast to just throwing out all the old rules. Unfortunately, today's competitive deregulation rat race is really one big power grab. More important, deregulation fuels cultural excess and narcissism. In the end it affects childhood development and self-control, just as if a child grew up without parents who provided limits and boundaries enabling her to grow in a healthy and normal way. Meanwhile, we pay a heavy psychological price for unfettered deregulation, living in perpetual conflict and with a belief in unlimited growth.

This fear that something might limit our possibilities is constant. A classic example of this fear is the complaint that CEOs are overpaid, but yet an unwillingness to regulate their salaries or options. The gap between a CEO salary and the wages of the average American worker is well-known, having increased to a factor of more than 500. Graef Crystal, an executive pay consultant, statistical expert, and critic of CEO pay, has utilized a complicated formula to evaluate total pay packages for executives. He reports in 2003 that the average CEO's total compensation was $12 million, and that 60 percent of that was in stock options. Crystal also reported that when a CEO's pay was above average, 86 percent of the difference was not explained by either the size of the company or performance.[38] So the full story of what a CEO makes is underreported and has little relation to performance. Although the public frequently complains about CEOs' exorbitant pay, executive salaries are still considered to be an area where regulation or limits by the government would interfere with economic and market development. Somehow, the argument is even put forth that businesses would not be able to find skilled leaders if CEO salaries were lowered or restricted. It is hard to imagine having difficulty finding candidates if a salary is reduced from $20 million to $10 million. This is even giving the benefit of the doubt that a CEO is really that skilled anyway. And the idea that companies or CEOs will self-regulate or deal with this area seems implausible. One can hardly imagine a CEO going to a board meeting and announcing, "I think the company is paying me too much." While athletes and entertainers are grossly overpaid too, sports have developed a compromise that business should look over. Sports leagues have set in place a salary cap, not allowing a team to exceed an upper limit. This regulation sets a boundary for all teams, trying to insure that one rich owner cannot simply buy up all the good players.

Finally, the often repeated argument against regulation and for deregulation is the famous dictum that the free market will self-correct if you just leave it alone. The self-correcting and laissez-faire defense is a wonderful narcissistic ploy. The underlying attitude is "leave me alone and get off my back," an attitude that resonates with defiance and adolescent opposition. The list of companies and financial institutions that have self-corrected and failed continues to grow. Finally, some acknowledgement has surfaced. In testimony to Congress in October of 2008, former Federal Reserve Chair Allen Greenspan, guru and sage of free market heaven, was subdued. The *New York Times* reported "a humbled Mr. Greenspan admitted that he had put too much faith in the self-correcting power of free markets and had failed to anticipate the self-destructive power of wanton mortgage lending."[39] Of course, this is only one part of the problem, and does not include the failures of major financial institutions. Later, he also conceded in response to his lifelong ideology: "Yes, I've found a flaw. I don't know how significant or permanent it is. But I've been very distressed by that fact."[40]

There are a couple reasons the self-correct model does not work. First, you have to be objective and honest to self-correct. And you must recognize there is a problem or conflict in order to examine it. By definition, cultural narcissism results in an inability to admit or recognize a conflict of interest. Deregulation becomes the mechanism of denial and ignoring any possible conflict of interest. The second reason involves the systems approach. In order to self-correct, a system has to be healthy. Then an automatic process or homeostatic mechanism returns a system to normal. That is the way our body works. But today's business system is dysfunctional, even simply from the perspective that CEOs and top management are so overpaid that the entire balance of the company's financials is out of whack. Throw in the killer that CEOs receive bonuses even if their companies do not make a profit, or are paid huge amounts just to resign.

A system cannot self-correct if it is dysfunctional. Make it functional, then maybe it can self-correct and even have built-in mechanisms to do so. Many times if we get sick we will get better just with time and a little rest. But if our illness is serious, we go to a doctor, and try to get an accurate diagnosis and treatment. Today's marketplace would respond well to a prescription of regulation. For a diagnosis of marketplace mania, perhaps a dosage of lithium, closely monitored for side effects.

## ROBOT QUALITY ASSURANCE

Tony Soprano is kvetching to his therapist. He reports on calling a business and being put on hold. Mimicking the recorded "your call is important to us," he tells his therapist that if the call is so important, why doesn't someone pick up the phone? In an intense marketplace of competition and sales, even if we do not need a bill of rights, we need a lot of patience to deal with what business likes to call "quality assurance" or customer service. By providing quality assurance, companies supposedly are backing up their products and services. Technology now sets this up, often with a toll-free number. But usually, to get to a real person, you must listen closely and check off several options—and then wait.

My friend relates his wife's experience trying to resolve a conflict with a phone company. "Don't even say it," she tells the customer service representative, cutting him short from reading the time-consuming mantra about providing excellent service and that her call is important. Posted on the wall or on a dummy card in front of the representative, the mantra is read to each customer with the proviso that the call is taped. But when the caller has a special or unique problem, such as receiving a bill that is not theirs, the "system" fails. Robots can handle routine matters, but the exceptions fall through the cracks.

A system is only as good as how it handles the exceptions, the cases that do not fall within the general guidelines of customer service training. And customer service training is big business, teaching people how to talk, but not really listen, and—like robots—to repeat the same message to all customers. This is the golden rule. The people robots read and respond in a "standardized" way without fully listening to the customer. They must continue to offer options to the caller of how to add services, no matter what the purpose of the call is.

"Telemarketing" is a fine art of nonsense, with sugar-coated people reading off cards. Ironically, the "telecommunications" companies are the worst. Calling many companies is an exercise in inefficiency, plowing through numerous phone options to get the right area or person to handle your call. At each step is the reminder to buy something else. Honest phone telemarketers will tell you they try to sell people products that they do not need. Once on the line, they think they have you—a ready target to sell anything they can. The system is designed that if you push the option for new services, an actual person quickly responds. Calls for complaints or billing questions go into a different holding bin—those can wait. The echolalic message—your call is important to us—is missing the underlying caveat: if you are purchasing new services.

What effect does this overcontrolled sales training have upon the employee and the caller? The caller wastes time and has to fend off sales attempts, and the customer service industry has an incredibly high rate of turnover. Of course, who would want to be reading the same message for each and every call and have all their calls taped? "Who wants to be a robot?" is not the same question as who wants to be a millionaire. If I call a customer service line and a representative asks how they can provide me with excellent service, I tell them to be quiet and just listen.

Why do we dehumanize the workers we hire for quality control? What can be more degrading than being trained to be a robot? The mistreatment and overcontrol to increase sales and profits leads to employees and *customers* who grow more frustrated every day. And does all this training really work anyway? Probably not. Gallup analyzed results over seven years and found that only one company out of twenty had customer satisfaction scores that showed any evidence of a consistent improvement.[41]

Quality assurance is at the other end of the spectrum of marketplace mania, driven by money, fast profit, and constant activity. But quality assurance yields no immediate reward or opportunity for unlimited growth. So, we mechanize it into a robotic interaction. It is interesting how you are put on hold and that the message is always that the calls are taped. But really, the underlying message is thanks for buying our product, and unless you want to buy something else—get lost. We have little patience if we are not immediately yielding a profit. So, in the end, on both ends of the call, we are all going through the motions. Acting super nice and reading scripts, customer service people exude a sense of rigidity and detachment. The intense marketing and competition puts a sell first, worry about service later approach as standard operating procedure. And the service workers simply detach, withdraw, or burn out.

This psychological process is evident throughout today's culture of excess. After the mania and the "success" of fast sales and profits, we relapse, withdraw, and become disconnected. Somehow, the feeling of entrepreneurial success does not keep us connected with others. Excess, overindulgence, and mania cannot be constant and ongoing. The feeling of success dissipates, and when the dust settles, something seems missing, not real, not quite right. The mania of today's marketplace has worn us out.

Today's fast pace, deregulation, and excess are all parts of cultural narcissism, underneath which exists a cauldron of disillusionment and despair. How does an individual who tries to grow, develop, and improve oneself and skills still maintain boundaries of self-control? Can everyone be an entrepreneur? To maintain professionalism and high standards in one's chosen career and profession is a psychological battle, a mental war, against the powerful external forces that define a culture of excess. The continued growth of collective narcissism in our culture does not always reward professionalism, productivity, continuous quality improvement, or loyalty. As a result what we experience as success does not always feel right.

The definition and attainment of success comes at quite a psychological price. A true self must develop to maintain our perspective, our boundaries, and a healthy balanced lifestyle. Only the self-sustained and integrated person can cope, adjust, recoup, and maintain a true self, underneath the false self needed to survive in an era of cultural narcissism.

## NOTES

1. Bogle, J. (2005). *The battle for the soul of capitalism* (p. 122). New Haven, CT: Yale University Press.

2. Financial Dictionary in Forbes's *Investopedia*. (n.d.). Retrieved December 20, 2008 from http://www.investopedia.com/terms/u/uptickrule.asp. Pozen, R., & Yaneer, B. Y. (2008, November 18). There's a better way to prevent bear raids. *The Wall Street Journal Opinion*. Retrieved November 29, 2008 from http://online.wsj.com/article/SB1226974100 70336091.html. There has been much discussion to reinstate the uptick rule. It is likely that it could be placed back into law in 2009.

3. Labaton, S. (2008, October 3). Agency's '04 rule let banks pile up new debt, and risk. *The New York Times*, p. A1.

4. Numerous ads advertising MBA programs with flexible schedules are in newspapers and print media. This ad occurred in the *LA Times* in 2002–2003.

5. Purcell, J. (2007, August 16). An expanding world of business opportunities. *Birmingham Evening Mail*. Retrieved November 29, 2008

from http://www.highbeam.com/doc/1P2-12580934.html. Stinson, J. (2007, June 7). More U.S. students go abroad for their MBAs; they get their degree—and a vacation too. *USA Today*. Retrieved November 29, 2008 from http://www.usatoday.com/money/perfi/college/2007-06-06-euro-mbas-usat_N.htm.

6. Person, E. S. (1986). Manipulativeness in entrepreneurs and psychopaths. In W. Reid, D. Dorr, J. Walker, & J. Bonner (Eds.), *Unmasking the psychopath* (pp. 256–273). New York: W. W. Norton.

7. Public policy professor Richard Florida has provided voluminous data on workers and urban policy. His data reports surveys of technology workers who list challenge and responsibility followed by flexibility as what today's worker wants. He also points out with U.S. Labor Dept. data that claims we all want to be self-employed are exaggerated. See Florida, R. (2002). *The Rise of the Creative Class* (pp. 88–101 and pp. 106–109). New York: Basic Books.

8. Raasch, C. (2003, October 10). King-makers emerge on late night TV. *USA Today*. Retrieved December 20, 2008 from http://www.usatoday.com/news/opinion/columnist/raasch/2003-10-10-raasch_x.htm.

9. Schwarzenegger stated this in debate of September 24, 2003.

10. Schneider, B. (2007, January 18). President Schwarzenegger—a potential blockbuster. CNN.com. Retrieved December 20, 2008 from http://www.cnn.com/2007/POLITICS/01/15/schneider.schwarzenegger/index.html.

11. Delgado, R. (2005, March 16). "Hardball College Tour" brings Gov. Schwarzenegger to farm. *Standford News Service*. Retrieved December 20, 2008 from http://news-service.stanford.edu/news/2005/march16/hardball-031605.html.

12. Salladay, R., & Morain, D. (2005, July 23). Before and after; supplements in the picture; Schwarzenegger stays connected to an industry he helped build; ethics issues arise. *Los Angeles Times*, p. A1. Rau, J. (2005, July 20). Governor's deal ignites larger debate; limits on outside work and tightened rules on income disclosure for statewide officials are discussed. *Los Angeles Times*, p. B1.

13. Rau. Governor's deal ignites larger debate.

14. Carlton, J. (2005, November 10). Defeated, governor acts nice. *The Wall Street Journal*, p. A14.

15. Sanchez, R., & Booth, W. (2003, October 3). From Schwarzenegger, an apology: Candidate says he is "deeply sorry" for his behavior towards women. *The Washington Post*, p. A01.

16. Fresco, A., and agencies. (2007, July 6). News anchor suspended after affair with L.A. mayor. *Times Online*. Retrieved December 5, 2008 from http://www.timesonline.co.uk/tol/news/world/us_and_americas/article2036694.ece.

17. Nicholas, P. (2006, December 28). Election funds go to gov's aides. *Los Angeles Times*, p. B1–9.

18. Nicholas, P., & Vogel, N. (2007, February 1). Governor's campaign reports $2 million debt. *Los Angeles Times*, p. B5.

19. Nicholas. Election funds go to gov's aides, p. B1–9.

20. CA's car tax may be on the road again. (2008, November 11). *Los Angeles Times*, editorial page.

21. Frank, T. (2001). *One market under God: Extreme capitalism, market populism, and the end of economic democracy* (p. 17). New York: Anchor Books. Frank is actually quoting another author named Luttwak, who wrote this formula as part of a larger quote. Frank has the terms/formula in all capitals in Chapter 1, p. 17.

22. Romero, S., & Whitmine, K. (2005, May 31). Scrushy on trial: Class, race and the pursuit of justice in Alabama. *The New York Times*. Retrieved December 21, 2008 from http://query.nytimes.com/gst/fullpage.html?res=9E02E2DC1F39F932A05756C0A9639C8B63&sec=&spon=&pagewanted=all. Kinsley, M. (2005, July 3). The Lord and Mr. Scrushy. *The Washington Post*, p. B07.

23. Mulligan, T. (2005, June 29). Ex-CEO cleared in 2.7 B fraud. *Los Angeles Times*, p. A1.

24. Carns, A., & Bauerlein, V. (2007, June 29). Scrushy gets nearly 7 years in bribery case. *The Wall Street Journal*, p. A-3.

25. Wise, C. (2002, March 25). Profit folly: How firms convert red ink to black via pro forma. *Investors Business Daily*.

26. Bogle. *The battle for the soul of capitalism*, pp. 34–35.

27. Black, W. (2004). Enron: We slept through class. *Ethical Perspectives*. Santa Clara University Markkula Center for Applied Ethics. Retrieved August 7, 2008 from http://www.scu.edu/ethics/publications/ethicalperspectives/enronclass.html.

28. Hamilton, W., & Sanders, E. (2002, July 23). Citigroup aided Enron, panel says. *Los Angeles Times*, p. C1.

29. Hamilton, W. (2003, July 29). JP Morgan, Citigroup settle in Enron probe. *Los Angeles Times*, p. C1.

30. The Sarbanes-Oxley Act of 2002, intended to protect the public from accounting errors and fraudulent practices, defines which records a business must store and for how long. Financial records and electronic records (e-mails) are included. The legislation was enacted in response to the Enron and WorldCom financial scandals. See http://searchcio.techtarget.com/s Definition/0,,sid182_gci920030,00.html.

31. Kuttner, R. (1997). *Everything for sale: The virtues and limits of markets*. New York: Alfred A. Knopf.

32. Linn, S. (2004). *Consuming kids: The hostile takeover of childhood* (p. 73). New York: The New Press.

33. Schor, J. (2004). How consumer culture undermines children's well-being. In *Born to buy: The commercialized child and the new consumer culture* (pp. 167–175). New York: Scribner.

34. The White House, Office of the Press Secretary. (2009, May 22). President Obama signs the Credit Card Accountability, Responsibility, and Disclosure Act. Retrieved August 1, 2009 from http://www.whitehouse .gov/the_press_office/Fact-Sheet-Reforms-to-Protect-American-Credit-Card-Holders/.

35. Bimbaum, J. (2005, January 22). The road to riches is called K Street. *The Washington Post*, p. A01.

36. Reported in Callahan, D. (2004). *The cheating culture: Why more Americans are doing wrong to get ahead* (p. 163). New York: Harcourt Books.

37. Farrell, G. (2002, November 6). Harvey Pitt resigns as SEC chief. *USA Today*. Retrieved December 1, 2008 from http://www.usatoday.com/ money/companies/regulation/2002-11-05-pitt-resigns_x.htm.

38. Crystal, G. (2007, March 15). SEC's Cox turns executive pay into hieroglyphics: Graef Crystal. Retrieved July 28, 2009 from http://www .bloomberg.com/apps/news?pid=20601039&sid=akvSUpMPv6wY. Herring, H. (2003, August 17). Bulletin Board: At the top, pay and performance are often far apart. *The New York Times*.

39. Andrews, E. (2008, October 24). Greenspan concedes error on regulation. *The New York Times*.

40. Greenspan quoted in response to probe by Henry Waxman in same Congressional testimony. Quoted in same article in the *New York Times*.

41. McEwen, W. (2005). *Married to the brand: Why consumers bond with some brands for life* (p. 12). New York: Gallup Press.

# Chapter 3

# DIGITAL COPING: LOSS, REALITY, AND SELF-DECEPTION

Failure is not an option.
> —Gene Kranz, Mission Control Flight Director, Apollo 13
> April 1970

People told me, "You can do it all. Just stay the course, get your education and you can raise a child, stay thin, be in shape, love your man, look good and raise healthy children." That was a lie.
> —Michelle Obama, *LA Times*
> August 22, 2007, p. A13

Anshe Chung is the well-known avatar for Ailin Graef, a Chinese entrepreneur who has dominated the land market in the virtual world game of Second Life. Created in 2003, Second Life has more than 15 million accounts and at any given time an average of 38,000 people are online and participating.[1] One major aspect of this virtual world community (and there are many others) is the creation and trading of virtual property. Because so many people play these games, the virtual property accumulated can be sold for real dollars and money. Second Life has its own online currency called Linden dollars.

Anshe Chung has been so successful at the game that CNN called her the "Rockefeller of Second Life."[2] But just like today's real-life manipulation and entrepreneurialism, there is controversy. When she was interviewed live on CNET news, "griefers" interrupted her interview by interjecting animated flying penises. The interview was disrupted and in a terrible tragedy was continued offline.[3] Seems some object to Anshe Chung's "inflexibility on land pricing," among other activities. She also began her success in Second Life as an escort with erotic services. Ethical dilemmas abound in virtual worlds, too. Anshe Chung Studios now employs 60 people and holds accounts with *Fortune* 500 companies.[4] It is a real business. Welcome to a new reality, where if you "work" hard enough, anything is possible.

The Sims is a "strategic life simulation computer game" that came out in 2000. By 2002 it was the best-selling personal computer game in history. Now in advanced versions, more than 16 million copies of Sims have been sold worldwide.[5] Players design their own characters or adopt another pre-developed one, controlling all aspects of the character or family. Pop culture critic Chuck Klosterman sums up an analysis of playing the game with his six-year-old niece. He observes that when a child plays with actual real toys, she will create a story with full-blown creativity, but not on a screen. There, in a virtual game, the rules are actually fixed. He concludes: "Clearly, video technology cages imagination; it offers interesting information to use, but it implies that all peripheral information is irrelevant or off limits. Computers make children advance faster, but they also make them think like computers."[6]

More than 80 percent of teens play online games. More than 50 percent download music and more than 75 percent get their news online. More than 40 percent have made purchases online.[7] Multiplayer online games (MMORPGs), role-playing fantasy games in which players "connect" with others using fictional characters and adventures, are the rage. World of Warcraft (WoW), considered the most popular MMORPG, has 11 million subscribers worldwide.[8] Countless other games are available with huge followings. It is hard to understand how all this time spent in online virtual worlds cannot detract from our psychological development, a sense of who we are in relation to others and the world, and affect our external capacity for self-control.

Online activity changes communication and self-disclosure too. E-mail allows someone to challenge and confront you, but when you ask them to meet or talk directly, they suddenly disappear. In other words, many people are willing to let their aggression and feelings out electronically, but not in real life. This is especially so for feelings of frustration and anger. Likewise, in the story about the sting set up by the TV program *Dateline*, adults seem to believe they can express blatant sexuality and fantasies online that will remain private or unknown to others. Technology also alters family dynamics. A mother reports that if she asks her teenage daughter how her day was, the teen says OK. But if she texts her, she receives much more information back about her day.

More than self-control is changing. Americans' decline in self-control and increase in indulgent acts must reflect an inner psychological condition that has also changed. Today's virtual worlds are a major component of Generation Me. Use of technology has disrupted access to our inner world, where we need privacy and boundaries to think, to heal from trauma and to respond effectively. It is difficult to objectively assess this change in the boundaries of self-control and expression, but the expansion of ways to "communicate" a message or a video, and omnipresent recording devices, has a psychological effect on our ability to cope.

No matter what you call it—Virtual Reality, New Reality, False Reality, or Modern Reality—technology has dramatically altered our perception of what is real and what is "possible," and has changed child development and character development. Today's sense of reality is characterized by immediacy, illusionary expectations, inflated self-concepts, a demand for a perfect image, and loss of privacy and access to our inner world. All of these factors contribute to narcissistic tendencies and make us more psychologically vulnerable. In the end we are less stable in mood and behavior, and more defended. One significant result is the hindrance of our natural development of growth through coping with loss and pain.


REALITY AND LOSS

Jane, in her early twenties, acknowledges in her initial interview she has been depressed and does not know why. She is doing OK and finds that nothing is so seriously wrong that she should be depressed. In listening to her development and history, she reports casually that last year her grandmother died. I inquire if she was close to her grandmother and she answers strongly that she was and that her grandmother was instrumental in raising her in her early years. I inquire if she feels that this is a factor in her depression. Startled, she looks up and says: "Do you think so?" For the remainder of the session, she talks about her grandmother, describing the funeral as a very quick process with a statement that "we wanted to remember her as she was."

In her 1986 book, *Necessary Losses*, Judith Viorst, accomplished children's writer, broadens the concept of loss and develops the theme that "central to understanding our lives is understanding how we deal with loss." She elaborates further "that the people we are and the lives we lead are determined, for better and worse, by our loss experiences." Viorst subtitles her book "the loves, illusions, dependencies, and impossible expectations that all of us have to give up in order to grow."[9] Central to coping and continuously working through loss as we mature and age is an individual's battle to be true to oneself, to keep track of what we are and what we display to others and the world. But when we lose the battle and adopt a presentation of ourselves as always trying to win and influence, to get attention and praise, we develop what psychoanalyst D. W. Winnicott calls the False Self. As Viorst notes, the False Self seems to be saying, "I'll be what you want me to be."[10] Psychoanalysts focus the individual back to childhood, where Winnicott refers to the True Self, which develops from the early attachment and bond with mother.

But contemporary economic and technological forces have altered the playing field. In other words, cultural forces may be more influential than a strong parental bond and may create a false self in a child's developmental years. Parenting styles, responding to these strong cultural forces, unwittingly help foster that false self. Just to survive psychologically in today's society, good, healthy people find they must cultivate a false self. "I can sell anything," "You'll have it tomorrow," "I can do the job," "I have hands-on experience," and countless other exaggerated assertions are made as we develop our children to go out there and knock 'em dead—a no-holds-barred philosophy that has no upper limit. At the professional level, these exaggerations are put on our resumes. When you keep adding up and increasing the number of false selves, the total makes up a false society.

The cultural and economic forces that disconnect us from our feelings and lead to a false self is most evident when it comes to the media bombardment of traumatic events. The operating media principle today is that if it bleeds it leads.[11] Cameras are everywhere—in cell phones and hanging on walls—making immediate and public viewing possible. Often the images shared focus upon our tragedies and personal losses. The media voyeurism overwhelms our ability to cope, grieve, and integrate our inner feelings of loss. It leads us to the misperception that there is more crime and violence than ever before. This belief feeds upon itself and we have heightened anxiety that trauma will happen to us.

Out of this overexposure to trauma and violence springs a more subtle form of ambulance chasing—trauma response. Initially well-intentioned, trauma response has become a huge industry with far more players than potential victims. In the mid-1990s, paramedic Jeffrey Mitchell developed a procedure called Critical Incident Stress Management and trained 40,000 students a year in the Mitchell method. Another entrepreneur, utilizing Mitchell's help, developed Crisis Management International, taking the "method" to the wealthy private sector. In an effort to help their employees after violence or a trauma, and also to minimize lawsuits, employers paid thousands a day for crisis interventions, never really questioning the effectiveness.[12] As you can imagine, the copycats followed with their own models of grief counseling, and free market forces and capitalism began to profit from all our tragedies.

But public monies have few limits, too. For example, in 1991, a Maryland school provided trauma assistance for students at a school building that had caught fire, even though the fire was on a Sunday evening and no students were present or injured. The federal government spent $371,000 for North Dakota residents to receive crisis counseling for a record rainfall and crop disease. Not to be left out, the Boston Public Library invited in counselors for their librarians suffering a loss when a basement flood destroyed a large collection of books and maps.

Trauma response services are certainly needed and employers duly respond to their ethical responsibility. But in actuality, today's media invasion has made public our grief process and integrative healing. Media immediately seeks out victims for an interview. In some cases, one wonders if the intent on human contact is more so for the counselor than the victim. Shortly following the attacks of September 11, 2001, approximately 9,000 grief and crisis counselors swarmed New York City, and many were not invited. After only about two days, New York City's commissioner of mental health was begging the assistant attorney general in Washington, D.C., to stop sending any more counselors. The invasion of counselors pursuing victims often interfered with the work of the Red Cross, historically the organization that provides this type of assistance from professional *volunteers*. In fact, there were not enough victims to go around, so grief counselors were reported to be counseling each other.[13]

As research evolved, the claims of the effectiveness of critical incident stress counseling were shown to be exaggerated.[14] The standards and procedures used by "counselors" in trauma response were interesting. I recall going to a Mitchell model class in the early 1990s as the phenomenon was growing. I was struck with how elemental and general the process was, and how an active effort was made to play down the process for professionals, as presenters would not allow anyone's degree or title to be put on a name badge. There was an active attempt to present a generic, easy model that anyone could deliver—a sort of McDonald's-like approach to a process that is really quite complex.

The growth of trauma response, whether intentional or not, forces upon others a model way to respond to a loss. The larger issue is: How does one deal with loss under such a public barrage? If a family suffers a loss of a loved one, the news media and crisis counselors bombard them for the story and to offer "help." But the essential grief and healing process is internal, takes time, and involves processing and integration. "Leave me alone" might be the healthiest response one can give following a trauma. Without a respect for the comprehensive importance of dealing with all levels of loss, how can this process develop and occur in a society that overresponds and invades privacy?

The invasion of our private world results in the loss of the inner place necessary to grieve. We then lose our ability to cope with loss. When this happens, our psychological development is burdened. In addition, our sense of inner reality is impaired. Cultural forces may redefine reality for you, suggesting that you have a loss or trauma when you may not really have one. This includes exaggerating a situation into convincing you that you have had a trauma. If it really is a life-threatening crisis, will others respond? Comedian Dennis Miller put it well when he told his audience that if the police or someone is beating him up, he hopes people will put down their cameras and help him.

## RIGIDITY AND SELF-DESTRUCTION

Narcissistic tendencies increase our vulnerability to resolving experiences and conflicts that require us to adjust and cope. We become more defensive and as a result react more negatively to critique or feedback for improvement. To cope with the normal travails in our lives, we seem to need to take refuge from the powerful external forces that bombard us and drive us into thought patterns that hinder our natural response. Our coping mechanisms may tighten up, like a code red alert, ready to defend and aggressively respond to an impending attack. We then may become fixated or become strangled in our development, maturity, growth, and adaptation, or our recovery and ability to work through a conflict. And often, we cannot integrate. Our minds and bodies freeze up, become rigid, and we become obsessive, controlling, or demanding. (People like to describe this type of person as "anal.") We then develop a single-minded focus—to survive as unharmed or perfect and to succeed at any cost. But the rigidity and perfectionism can kill us.

Rudolph Zurick had been a corrections officer at Union County Jail in New Jersey for 15 years. Affected by his mother's death, a few months later he encountered a problem at work. Two inmates had escaped by burrowing through a cement wall. They left behind a mocking note thanking Officer Zurick by name for "the tools" needed and for being "a real pal." An automatic investigation ensued, in which the prosecutor indicated there was no concern that Zurick had been involved, and a routine interview was scheduled. Zurick had a lawyer to assist him. But a few hours before the scheduled interview, Zurick was found dead at home, a suicide completed by a gunshot to the head. His lawyer reported: "Rudy was a perfectionist. I think the pressure got to him." Describing his client's spotless record, he added: "I think the idea that people thought he did something wrong, it made him very depressed. I just hope the real story gets out." Zurick was 40 years old, married, and had a 4-year-old daughter.[15]

Yale psychologist Sidney Blatt has documented the occurrence of sudden and unexpected suicides in highly successful people who were perfectionistic.[16] Usually, when someone commits suicide, we can identify life stressors such as divorce, loss of job, illness or injury, depression, or a combination of all of these. But Blatt cites three cases gleaned from the news where no one noticed any of these indicators. In all cases, the persons were highly successful, had attained high levels of success in their fields, and their suicide was sudden and unexpected. The most notable case cited was that of Vince Foster, former White House counsel. Hillary Clinton reported that Vince Foster was the last person she ever thought would commit suicide. Below is an excerpt from Foster's commencement speech to Arkansas Law School graduates a few months before his suicide:

> The reputation you develop for intellectual and ethical integrity will be your greatest asset or your worst enemy ... Treat every pleading, every brief, every contract, every letter, every daily task as if your career will be judged on it ... I cannot make this point to you too strongly. There is no victory, no advantage, no fee, no favor which is worth even a blemish on your reputation for intellect and integrity ... Dents to the reputation in the legal profession are irreparable.[17]

Blatt also reexamined data from a huge study of depression conducted by the National Institute of Mental Health. He discovered that those depressed persons who were not helped by psychotherapy or who also dropped out of treatment often had perfectionistic tendencies. In other words, perfectionism is more likely to result in a poor clinical outcome.[18]

Psychological researchers Paul Hewitt and Gordon Flett have been at the forefront of definitive research on perfectionism. Breaking the concept down into three subtypes, they have conducted research to show that two of the subtypes are related to suicide attempts. The perfectionistic person continues to drive and attain success, maintaining incredibly high standards, and is often on a straight and meteoric career path, without encountering any failures or setbacks. The drive to attain and maintain success is so intense, for perfectionistic persons, that researchers describe them as "vulnerable to an experience of failure."[19] Sort of like the bigger you are the harder you fall, a successful and driven person drives on, until a failure or setback occurs, and then, vulnerable to such an experience of failure, commits an abrupt act of self-destruction. You do not have to look too far to see that the destruction may also be toward others. Unexplained family murder-suicides leave us at a complete loss, especially when we hear what seems like a standard response from family and neighbors that nothing seemed amiss. Overall, psychological vulnerability makes a person more susceptible to overresponding to setbacks when the defense system finally breaks down.

The increase in perfectionism has caught the attention of researchers. One estimate indicates a 300 percent increase in research in this area, or what has been called the "perfection infection."[20] A new scale, *The Almost Always Perfectionism Scale*, is now being used to quantify the tendency in children.[21] But perfectionism is not all bad. Like the presentation of the concept of productive narcissism, perfectionism is a characteristic and major contributor to getting things done. How many times I have wished some of the people I was working with were more perfectionistic. So the differential becomes determining a perfectionism that encourages achievement versus a perfectionism that is self-destructive. Of course, a key difference comes in noticing the response when a person does make a mistake. Can they move on, improve if required, and avoid overresponding with tremendous guilt and self-punishment?

One major contributor to the perfectionistic drive is the general acceptance of the often heard statement "failure is not an option." This overused quote was initially made famous on the Apollo 13 flight by the Mission Control leader. Under great duress, his statement exuded determination and strength. The story of how the troubled NASA flight survived and landed safely is historic and used as a case study in leadership.[22] But the confidence exerted by a leader in extreme crisis is different than day-to-day endeavors. We need to just plow through everyday conflicts. An emphasis on basic competence and doing very good is healthier than the drive for "excellence" and that failure is not an option. A Google search for this phrase yields almost a million hits, and a perusal of the results shows the phrase used to advocate for career success, educational attainment, and creativity. The recent economic bailouts support a popular view—anything but allowing a failure.

On the other hand, today's immediate dissemination through media technology of a failure increases one's shame and guilt and makes it much harder to respond in a responsible manner. Instead, we live on a heightened alert to avoid mistakes. This leads to more cover up, denial, and partial rationalizations (excuses), and over time a more rigid personality. So, like most everything, it is a matter of balance and moderation. There is an old saying in personality theory that an exaggeration of your strength becomes your weakness. So, if you are a self-confident person, that certainly is a strength, but if you are too self-confident, you certainly will underestimate something and then your strength becomes a weakness. If you are too perfect, it can become a weakness that can be self-destructive.

Today's intense cultural pressures and competition lead to young people who feel they have to be at least near perfect. Parents may acknowledge that their demands for success should not be too intense, but strong social trends combat them. Parents often go to great lengths to get their child in the best schools and start the competitive process at an early age. The intense competition to succeed, often at any cost, now fosters perfectionism as an ingrained and normal part of childhood development. In other words—it is a given—it is baked in the cake. This is the way to be, driven for success and with an attitude that no one should hinder or stop you. Failure is not an option.

Of course, without failure we have no mistakes. And without mistakes, how can we learn? In 1999, I presented a paper at an FBI symposium concerning the increase in suicides among law enforcement personnel. I presented the research cited above, drawing the generalization that perfectionism must be a factor in the high rate of suicide in law enforcement populations.[23] The data was certainly striking: Among reports that showed a glimpse of different law enforcement agencies and periods of time, in all cases more law enforcement personnel died from suicide than from active duty.[24] (The September 11 tragedy, a onetime catastrophic event, may make this not completely true, but overall, the trend was prominent in major police departments. However, the problem remains today.)

Colleagues also told me anecdotal stories about successful professionals, some even referred to as "rising stars," and others who unexpectedly committed suicide. Does stress enter in? Obviously, a law enforcement job is quite stressful. To answer that question, researchers Hewitt and Flett examined levels of stress along with measuring perfectionism in persons who had reported suicidal thoughts and ideas. Defining perfectionism as "an active striving to be flawless," they found that two of the three sub-types of perfectionism were able to discriminate suicide groups and serve as a moderator variable between high stress and suicidal ideation.[25] In other words, simply having high levels of stress did not lead to suicidal thoughts, but when perfectionism is added in, suicidal thoughts are much more likely. The results are similar to what Blatt reported earlier about depressed persons who were also perfectionistic. So, it is not simply the stress that contributes to suicide, but rather the rigidity and perfectionism of a person who cannot afford to make a mistake or have a failure, and psychologically has no other way out when a failure does occur.

Making a mistake in law enforcement can mean you or someone else ends up dead. So, training programs are conducted on a basis whereby mistakes cannot be allowed. In my presentation and paper, I posed these questions to law enforcement personnel: Does training in law enforce-ment prepare a candidate for the possibility of experiencing difficulties or mistakes during their career? Or instead, does training produce a candi-date who has no expectations of difficulties or failure, and is expected to maintain a career-based perfectionism for the next 20–30 years? If the latter question is true, then some decent people will simply break down and snap. Following my presentation, many law enforcement professio-nals commented to me with examples and emotional stories about situa-tions in their departments that reinforced the self-destructive trend of perfectionism.

In other occupations as well, stress alone does not seem to lead to self-destruction. Rather, the intense drive for immediacy, perfection, and suc-cess leads to a rigidity that has no allowance for making or acknowledging a mistake. The higher the profile position, the more this seems to be true. An unwritten rule prevails: Never publicly admit a mistake. Call the lawyer and ask for advice and it comes back quickly: Do not admit it was your fault, or that you or the company did anything wrong. No matter how much we work with children to teach responsibility, the real work world and the pressures in such a competitive society make today's workplace a different environment. Admitting mistakes and accepting responsibility is avoided.

In the paper presented at the FBI symposium, I also argued that an approach was needed that was more comprehensive and integrated. Law enforcement, just like society in general, looks for a quick and simple fix. The prevalence of stress management programs in law enforcement is based on the idea that occupational stress is the main cause of career maladjustment. The belief is that if I can just learn to control the stress, I will cope effectively and survive. But consider how a perfectionistic and rigid person would approach a stress management program. Focusing on external control, they try even harder to control external stress, much of which is really beyond their control. The stress management program may be like putting gasoline on a fire, urging a perfectionistic person to be even more controlling and perfectionistic. Besides, if stress management programs are so abundant in law enforcement, why has the suicide rate continued to increase? When problems are encountered, society in general—not just law enforcement—looks outward for a solution. But the countless programs on stress management concentrate on the external realm, and in doing so may be offering us a disservice rather than having a positive effect. The solution is not to try for more external control, but to look inward and change one's view and perception of the world and others.

Today's powerful supercapitalism directs us outward, not inward, and we respond to the external demands with more external solutions for doing things better and faster. Sometimes, we may even self-destruct, within a range of reactions from a mild withdrawal to apathy, or the repressed anger of depression. Of course, we can lash back, with interpersonal violence and scathing verbal attacks and insults. All you have to do is put on the radio or TV to experience that. Every day the circle of behavior continues, as the rants and negativity on talk radio breed anger, counterresponse, and hostility. Unfortunately, those who become really good at the scathing can become quite successful and even media stars and heroes. This confounds the psychological perspective, as now it is rewarding and healthy to be extremely critical. Until, at least, it gets turned back on you, and the vicious circle continues.

The external forces of intense competition, media invasiveness, and immediacy, overconsumption, and the drive to be perfect, all come together. They dramatically provide us with a different perspective for assessing what is real in our world. Our coping mechanisms try to respond and prevent us from sinking into a physical or psychological state of hypervigilance and overdrive, or defensive rigidity. In either continuous state, human beings are developing in mind, body, and soul in a totally different way than 20 years ago. Our adaptation involves accepting as real an environment that bombards us with hype, exaggerations, and outright falsehoods. Once adopted, once accepted or subconsciously assimilated, we become official members of the false society. What is real, what is reality, is now in reality false.


## THE REALITY OF SELF-DECEPTION

The development of a false self inherently involves self-deception. What we tell ourselves has to be related to how we portray ourselves to others and the world. Manipulation or "lying" in the external world, when excessive, must contribute to fissures in one's internal integration and self. By lying, one manipulates the world to one's advantage. The subtleties of deception and lying have many levels and lead to many an arcane argument.

St. Augustine listed eight types of lies, ranking them by their seriousness and capacity for forgiveness.[26] Today, we sometimes can distinguish lying from just plain bullshit. The surprising popularity of moral philosopher and scholar Professor Harry Frankfurt's book, *On Bullshit*, shows the awareness of this issue in our society. Frankfurt states his reason for the short work, a six-by-four-inch pocketbook of only 67 pages:

> One of the most salient features of our culture is that there is so much bullshit. Everyone knows this. Each of us contributes his share. But we tend to take the situation for granted.
>
> Most people are rather confident of their ability to recognize bullshit and to avoid being taken in by it. So the phenomenon has not aroused much deliberate concern, nor attracted much sustained inquiry.[27]

Most persons do not lie outright, because it is too easy to get caught; instead, they deceive by not telling the full story or exaggerating and embellishing to get their way. Everyone may argue whether this deception is "lying." A case in point is President George W. Bush's State of the Union address in which he referenced a connection between Niger and WMD (weapons of mass destruction). Defenders said the questionable statement amounts to only 16 words—indicating no big deal—the rest of the speech was accurate. Of course, you can lie in one word (e.g., "Did you sleep with that woman?" answer: "No"). The defensive after talk is always amusing. As the saying goes, the cover up is what always gets a pol in trouble.

Lying, exaggeration, and bullshit are primary operating mechanisms of communication in our culture that pose a tremendous internal conflict and dialogue. The resulting deception and self-deception have redefined attitudes toward actual cheating. Somehow the ethical line and boundary is formulated in one's mind, and as noted earlier the CEOs who have gone wrong were not previous criminals or cheaters. Lying could be viewed as *consciously* presenting something as reality to attain a goal. The degree of distortion or exaggeration is what we argue about—is it a lie or "just bullshit." Our society runs on advertising, public relations, and marketing. All of these present their reality to us to achieve their goal. The better the spin, combined with repetition, the greater the probability we will accept their reality and make it our own.

It is hard to document or measure whether actual cheating has increased over the years. Intuitively, it certainly feels like it has. And we are a law and order society. In fact, we know that the United States has more people in prison than anywhere else.[28] But this is usually related to aggression and violence, and as noted earlier, corporate fraud (cheating) is considered nonviolent. Like research on any behavior in the natural environment, it is impossible to determine a cause-and-effect relationship, and so we settle for what data we can analyze. David Callahan, author of *The Cheating Culture*, has provided the most comprehensive documentation of cheating and the cultural changes that are at its roots. Callahan lists three overall cultural forces that increase cheating. These include "new pressures, temptations, and trickle down corruption."[29] Everyone is caught up in these cultural trends and excuses. But what *overall* impact does the cheating culture have on our psychological development and character development? Is the result and impact of a cheating culture creating adults who have deception and manipulation as a normative part of their development? Will we no longer be able to tell the difference between right and wrong, or will the ethical boundary be so porous that moral development and character development cannot even take place?

One source of an ongoing survey of youth comes from the Josephson Institute of Ethics, a nonpartisan, nonprofit organization in Southern California, which conducts an extensive youth survey every two years.[30] A survey of 12,000 high school students in 2002 produced alarming results. Students admitting that they cheated on an exam at least once in the past year increased from 61 percent in 1992 to 74 percent in 2002. But consider the data on a survey question related to the workplace. Those students admitting they would be willing to lie to get a job rose from 28 percent in 2000 to 39 percent in 2002. The 2002 survey results also showed that students who attended "private religious schools" were more likely to cheat on exams (78% to 72%) and lie to teachers (86% to 81%). Further, students who participated in varsity sports cheated on exams more so than students who did not play varsity sports by a 78 percent to 73 percent margin.

Percentages can be hard to put in perspective for social issues in comparison to economic figures. Although the Josephson data shows small increases between groups that are probably not statistically significant, note the overall high levels. More than 80 percent of students lie to teachers. More than 70 percent cheat on exams. The norm is to be dishonest; the norm is to be deceptive. And why would students in private schools have slightly higher numbers? A possible rationale may lie in the competitive drive mentioned previously and how early it starts with parents fighting to get their kids into the best preschools. Parents make unbelievable sacrifices to have their children attend private and religious schools, or even to homeschool their children to avoid the highly criticized public schools. The survey results suggest that parents' efforts may have unintended consequences.

Michael Josephson, president of the Josephson Institute of Ethics, adds a strong summary:

> The evidence is that a willingness to cheat has become the norm and that parents, teachers, coaches and even religious educators have not been able to stem the tide. The scary thing is that so many kids are entering the workforce to become corporate executives, politicians, airplane mechanics and nuclear inspectors with the dispositions and skills of cheaters and thieves.[31]

That quote was from 2002. The Josephson Institute conducted a larger follow-up in 2004, increasing the sample size to 24,763 high school students. All in all, 85 schools were involved, and the breakdown was 45 percent public schools, 40 percent private religious schools, and 15 percent private nondenominational schools. Josephson reported that for the first time in 12 years, reported rates of cheating and theft actually declined. But a closer look raises some doubts. Students reported a very high endorsement of the importance of character and honesty in themselves and others. These results were described by Josephson as "almost unanimous," but the same students also were quite cynical about whether someone can be ethical and succeed. He describes these results as a "troubling inconsistency between words and actions." Later surveys address this issue. Is this an inconsistency, or is it a realistic assessment? Our students may be right on, stating that character development is very important, but when you get out there in the "real world," well, let the games begin. This recognition could be a positive, an awareness of a conflict that with much discussion can be used to enhance moral development. The question becomes: Can you maintain character and ethical behavior and still be "successful" in today's business environment?

The improved 2004 results showed that 62 percent admitted to cheating on exams, and 22 percent stole from someone in the past 12 months. A considerable percentage at 40 percent admitted lying to *save* money. It would seem logical to conclude, as Josephson does, that student cynicism about success comes from the continuous reporting of business fraud. But this same conflict exists for adults: Does looking at other successful leaders who are not always ethical become a justification for "cheating" because that is how you get ahead? The exact data and questions show that 59 percent of students agreed that "in the real world, successful people do what they have to do to win, even if others consider it cheating." This is an interesting way of framing the question, indicating that "consider it cheating" may be open to opinion and interpretation. In response to the statement "a person has to lie or cheat sometimes in order to succeed," 42 percent agreed. Herein lies the internal processes and conflicts mentioned earlier about the distinction between lying and bullshit. This is where the psychological battleground is.

Here is more proof. Finally, 22 percent agreed with the statement that "people who are willing to lie, cheat or break the rules are more likely to succeed than people who do not." Note the drop from 59 percent above when it is stated that "people do what they have to do to win." So, where is that boundary from the view that "considers" it cheating and actual definite cheating? It seems clear that manipulation and "doing what you gotta do" is certainly an internal mantra.

Josephson sums up the 2004 report:

Though the Report Card on the Integrity of American Youth continues to contain failing grades, there is reason for hope. For the first time in 12 years the cheating and theft rates have actually dipped downward and the stated devotion to ethics is the strongest we've seen. While this results in a troubling inconsistency between words and actions, character education efforts should be able to build on the fundamental appreciation of ethics, character and trust to achieve continuing improvements in conduct. Still, it can't be comforting to know that the majority of the next generation of police officers, politicians, accountants, lawyers, doctors, nuclear inspectors and journalists are entering the workforce as unrepentant cheaters.[32]

Josephson improves the survey each time out, and in 2006 had an even larger sample of 36,122 high school students. The 2006 results are very close to that of 2004 in the percentages of stealing and lying statements. However, the most recent survey in 2008 shows increases from 2006. Stealing increased in both boys and girls (32% to 35% and 23% to 26%), along with lying (39% to 42%) and cheating (60% to 64%). The rate of cheating was highest in religious schools. But now data is reported that reflects the disjoint between actually being honest and student's self-image or self-assessment of their ethics. A huge 93 percent of teens said they were "satisfied with their personal ethics and character," while 77 percent reported that "when it comes to doing what is right, I am better than most people I know." The psychological conflict is profound for today's teen: The normative standard is dishonesty, while more than 90 percent are satisfied with their ethics and character.[33] This internal discrepancy is accepted. I am satisfied with my character and better than most others, but I will lie, cheat, and steal to be successful. That's the way it is.


## PARENTS AND REALITY: DELAYED ADULTHOOD

With increased awareness of the "real-world" cheating among successful people and considerably greater public emphasis on religious values, adolescents are under pressure to respond. In effect, they may be put in a vice in which they feel they have to be more honest than others, and be viewed as honest by their parents. We know that in general a self-serving bias exists on surveys or self-assessment scales. (The self-serving bias is reflected in the survey results that show teens believe they have higher ethical standards than others. This would not surprise social psychologists. More about this in Chapter 4.) Josephson has his own internal check on the validity of the results by asking the survey takers if they had answered all items honestly. Josephson reports that the 2008 results are probably *underreported*, as about 1 in 4 respondents admitted to not being fully honest on more than one item.

Data reported on parent-teen communication and relations are also noteworthy. Indulged with materialism and burdened with today's high cost of living, teens may find it harder to individuate and become independent from their parents. Teens and young adults have a moral conflict. The desire to be emotionally close to their parents and perceived as having high character competes with what they actually have to do to respond to social and career pressures. But look at the 2004 data on parent-teen interactions. While the 2004 numbers are improved (unless the improvement is negated by a positive bias), 82 percent admitted they lied to a parent in the last year about "something significant." Then, 57 percent admitted lying two or more times. Are these results a decline in respect for authority, or a reflection of their actual behavior and their parents' perceptions and expectations of them? It may also be an indicator of their separation and individuation from their parents—to have a private self and world.

Typically, when teens go off to college, they interact less with parents than in high school. Or do they? Trends in the difficulty of separating are observed on the college campus. It seems the parent-child relationship for an 18-year-old has changed. Parents are more involved than ever before. In a 2006 survey, eight of ten young adults (ages 18 to 25) reported they talked to their parents in the past day. About 75 percent reported they see their parents weekly, and half see their parents daily.[34]

Some parents continue as strict managers for their children's entry into college, and colleges are responding. Nine out of ten four-year schools have special orientation programs for parents, and many have staff to handle the newly created "parent relations" department. In California, San Diego State, USC, and Stanford have up to three staff persons to handle parental inquiries.[35] Counselors report the most humorous of phone calls, realizing quickly it is the parent—not the teen—who needs someone to talk to about the separation and individuation. Parents call to change their child's academic schedule while sounding as if they are changing their own schedule. Parents often read and critique their child's research papers for class requirements. At USC, a camera is placed in the student union square so parents can observe their child and what they might be wearing. When asked why they want such scrutiny, some parents express that they are paying huge amounts of money for the education and they are making sure their "investment" is not going down the drain.

Perhaps teens seem to have less inclination to be independent because it also means some separation from the ever-flowing materialistic goods they get. Stricter laws result in teens getting their driving licenses later than they used to, a right of passage that I recall as significant for my independence. It is also curious to wonder how teens feel to have their parents call the school. I could not imagine my parents calling my college to talk about a schedule change—I would have died from embarrassment.

College transition years and social patterns are actually obvious and clear to educators. The close relationship between teens and their parents is so strong, individuation and adulthood is delayed. Developmental experts have added an additional phase to Piaget's last stage called Formal Operations. This new stage is called Post Formal Operations. In a provocative article in *Psychology Today* in 2004, Hara Estroff Marano described today's parenting style as "Hothouse Parenting."[36] In this style, parents are so overconcerned, protective, and overinvolved that they even try to make sure their child does not fall or that any injury is minimized or negated. When ready for college, parents actively intervene to improve their child's SAT scores, even finding professional documentation that allows special "accommodations," that is, extra test time for the SAT. And all a child has to do is alert their parent of impending conflict, and parents immediately respond with the helicopters and a DEFCON level 3 response. Developmental experts agree, a child must fall, and in a broader way, experience failure to develop and be ready for adulthood. Protection from injury and failure hinders development. Marano predicts the end result is the title of her article—"A Nation of Wimps." Marano sums up her observations:

> No one doubts that there are significant economic forces pushing parents to invest so heavily in their children's outcome from an early age. But taking all the discomfort, disappointment and even the play out of development, especially while increasing pressure for success, turns out to be misguided by just about 180 degrees. With few challenges all their own, kids are unable to forge their creative adaptations to the normal vicissitudes of life. That not only makes them risk averse, it makes them psychologically fragile, riddled with anxiety. In the process they're robbed of identity, meaning and a sense of accomplishment, to say nothing of a shot at real happiness. Forget, too, about perseverance, not simply a moral virtue but a necessary life skill. These turn out to be the spreading psychic fault lines of 21st century youth. Whether we want to or not, we're on our way to creating a nation of wimps.[37]

But today's culture of narcissism and drive for "success" is more important than development. Development is no longer a natural process of maturation, but geared, designed, and controlled for success. "I only want the best for my child," a statement no one would dare disagree with, now has a different meaning in the context of cultural narcissism.

## SELF-DECEPTION: THE PRIVATE RELIGIOUS BURDEN

Josephson's survey data about higher rates of cheating in religious schools puts forth an interesting but unwanted dilemma. Does religion contribute to self-deception? Gregory Paul, a paleontologist who has studied dinosaurs, reports that in his profession he has had to deal with the creationism/evolution debate for years. But Paul embarked on an interesting research endeavor. He culled research and survey data from multiple sources to compare data in prosperous democracies that were secular and religious. Publishing his findings in the *Journal of Religion and Society*, the compiled data compared included homicide rates, abortion, suicide, and teenage pregnancy.[38] Paul points out that the United States is the only "prosperous nation" that has a majority of people who believe in a creator and where evolutionary science is not popular. Two-thirds of the U.S. population strongly believes in God and half of society supports creationism. Paul's comparative data showed a clear pattern. When compared to 17 more secular democracies such as Canada, France, Germany, and Japan, the United States had higher murder rates, the highest juvenile mortality rates, shorter life span, the highest abortion rates among countries where abortion is legal, and the highest sexually transmitted disease rates. Paul reports:

> Indeed, the data examined in this study demonstrates that only the more secular, pro evolution democracies have, for the first time in history, come closest to achieving practical "cultures of life" that feature low rates of lethal crime, juvenile-adult mortality, sex related dysfunction, and even abortion. The least theistic secular developing democracies such as Japan, France, and Scandinavia have been most successful in these regards.[39]

Certainly, there are many reasons for crime, and the comparative data does not mean religion is the cause. But the data also shows that strong religiosity does not mean less violence or social dysfunction. It certainly does not seem to support a belief that it leads to healthier living in the United States.

This is an intense issue. Just as with the economic scandals, constant examples emerge of religious deception and fraud. William Lobdell covered the religion news for the *LA Times* from 1998 to 2006. Covering the sexual abuse stories from the Catholic church and scandals at other religious organizations, Lobdell burned out. He was an evangelical

Christian who in a front-page story reported he was giving up the religious beat and had become a "reluctant atheist." He is writing a book about his experiences and the impact upon him. His article drew 2,700 email responses, considered a record response for one story. An article that draws 300 responses is considered remarkable. His wife bound the e-mails and put them in five sets of books.[40]

Today, this intense internal conflict for youth is heightened by the cultural pressure to display and pronounce their religious values in public. This seems to be an expressed counterforce to help cope with the looming conflict of attaining success and still maintaining one's moral and character structure. Everywhere you look are discussions of religious values and their importance. The 2008 election continues the pressure—a candidate better declare how important their religious values are or they are quickly toast. Both Barack Obama and John McCain welcomed a chance to debate at megapastor Rick Warren's Saddleback Church in Lake Forest, California. Interviewing each candidate separately, Warren asked both of them: "Does evil exist, and if it does, should we ignore it, negotiate with it, contain it, or defeat it?" Obama gave a thoughtful answer, that evil exists in many places, describing how he views it. When McCain was asked, he responded simply and strongly: "Defeat it." The crowd burst into applause.[41] It seemed like a macho and simple answer, but that's what we want today, a leader who will immediately stamp out evil, at least in front of a religious audience. The candidate's minister or pastor better be likeable too. The correct religious attitude today is one of certitude, bravado, and swagger.

Today, parents try hard to opt out of the public school system in favor of private religious schools. Since private schools are expensive, homeschooling has arisen as an alternative. While homeschooling is difficult to research, more than one million students were reported to be homeschooled in 2003. This was an increase of 29 percent from 1999 data.[42] Every indication is that this current trend continues.

Notable support for homeschooling has come from the religious right. A multitude of surveys show several reasons parents make this decision. Besides religious reasons, academic and teaching methods of the public schools are cited along with general dissatisfaction of the public schools. Within this disdain for the public schools is the fear of a negative peer influence. In addition, parents also cite categories described as "family reasons" and "lifestyle choices."[43] While it is logical to lament the public schools, all of the above reasons do suggest a unique "my kid is special" philosophy. And homeschooling can avoid these negative public school influences and teach values that match one's "lifestyle." But the underlying reasons for the homeschooling craze still point in the direction of cultural narcissism. At some point, doesn't a child have to live in a public world? Note the composition of the schools sampled in Josephson's 2004 data of almost 25,000 teens surveyed. The sample consisted of 40 percent private religious schools and 15 percent private nondenominational schools. That totals 55 percent private schools with the remaining 45 percent for public schools. In this sample, the majority of schools surveyed were private.

The survey data also reflected a very high and even unanimous emphasis on importance of character. Children attending private schools and those able to redirect tax dollars to homeschooling are pursuing this course from parental direction that most surveys indicate involves putting religious values first. Of course, the belief is also that the education is "private" and better. While the schools are private, the proclamation of religious values is not. The popularity of faith-based schooling has become a public statement of the importance of religion. The fusion of religion with the free market, as discussed in Chapter 2, is quite remarkable. Today's New Economy must include some set of religious values, in effect, a new modern code for day-to-day behavior. Traditional religious beliefs and codes may appear anachronistic to today's youth, because the economic and social cultures have changed so dramatically.

As a child and growing up Catholic, I was an altar boy. (For the record I was not sexually abused.) I had to memorize the eight Beatitudes. That is, a code for character and conduct, something to memorize and internalize for meaning and purpose in character and behavior. It is hard to read the Beatitudes without contrasting their powerful spiritual meaning and purpose to today's free market and fast-paced society. Think of your neighbors, community, schools, and business partners and dealings, and try to identify those youth or adults you would describe as being "rich in spirit," "pure in heart," or "merciful." When we talk about "moral values," you do not get the feeling these virtues have a place in today's competitive workplace. How could they? What I also learned as a youth was that to be humble was sort of a good thing, as in the third Beatitude which reads: "Blessed are the meek; for they shall inherit the earth." Children, programmed for success, have no time to be meek and humble. Is there another code or guidelines that have emerged to take its place? (I have found the eighth Beatitude is a comfort to me personally, as a liberal Democrat who is continuously persecuted on earth, I am destined for heaven.)

Politically, the claim is intense and prominent that people of faith get no respect and that the Ten Commandments should be displayed in the public schools. At Christmas, the media loves to portray stories of companies or places that will not use the word Christmas and are somehow denying religious expression. Despite the tremendous magazine headlines and media coverage of religion in the past few years, those advocating religious values are constantly complaining that a cultural bias exists against them. But you can readily observe what must be a new code of behavior and religious mentality that is developing for teens. A code based upon proud public expression that leads to success.

Evidence is all around us. The evangelistic Harvest Crusade comes to Orange County, California every year, a conservative county south of Los Angeles County, and home to Saddleback Church pastor Rick Warren, author of the megaseller, *The Purpose Driven Life*.[44] One of the wealthiest counties in the nation, Orange County represents religious cool, wealth, complacency, and extreme individualism. In 2005, a three-night gathering of thousands for a public Christian rally is reported on the headline page of the *Los Angeles Times*. The first paragraph reports:

> Sumo wrestling for Jesus, religious motocross stunts and a dose of Christian testosterone. That's a sampling of the lineup this weekend as a trio of large-scale Christian events descend upon Anaheim and Los Angeles.[45]

This seems all for the good. The Christian sumo wrestlers may be a very healthy alternative to World Wrestling Entertainment. In this league, "wrestlers" throw each other around and break chairs over each other's head. The Three Stooges would be proud. The entertainment for the Crusade is free—no admission charge. That is, unless you attend a separate event by the Promise Keepers, which is $89 a ticket (only $69 if you are under 18). The theme for the 2005 event: "The Awakening: An Unpredictable Adventure." The 2006 event did do away with the thrill-seeking and substituted "quality religious music."

But in today's business marketplace it is important to realize that one of the most successful marketing methods is religion. That is the idea behind Christian loans and Christian motocross or Christian Monster Truck Shows. Religion is a basis for politicians getting elected and entrepreneurs rising to the top. The coup de grace comes from a recent story about labor unions. Divided and conquered by market forces, unions have lost membership and influence. So the AFL-CIO decided to use the marketing strategy that works. They hired about three dozen "aspiring ministers, imams, priests and rabbis to spread the gospel of union organizing across the nation this summer." The AFL-CIO is paying the people-of-faith consultants $300 a week to organize workers ranging from security guards to carpenters to meatpackers. The consultants are critical of management, quoting scripture and telling management to be more Godlike in how they treat workers.[46] This a strategy that will probably work. In fact, it will probably lead to an entire new industry—people-of-faith business consulting. You can be certain that as it succeeds, the $300 weekly cost will skyrocket.

How does the fusion of religion and faith with marketplace profit and consumerism develop into a code of behavior that helps a young person show integrity and character? What is the code? The Ten Commandments seem far too general and nonspecific, and clearly, the Beatitudes are no longer a code or set of guidelines. It may be that the strong emphasis on character without a well-developed code beyond "be honest" simply results in greater pressure and conflict for a young person. Such pressure may be unrecognized as the new public proclamation of the importance of faith and image becomes all consuming.

The new blend of religion, faith, and marketing for profit is another component of a society that contributes to a false self and a false reality. This fusion defines a new Holy Trinity: Consumption, Proclaimed Religion, and the Marketplace. The cycle repeats continuously as we consume, proclaim our religion, and reenter the marketplace.

For today's youth, the religious emphasis and fusion with consumerism may be a conflict that is quite an emotional burden. Parents enroll their children in private religious schools, more to help them succeed and get ahead, perhaps, than for their spiritual and moral development. The additional pressure in development of society's religious burden is carried dutifully on a young person's back. And when asked, the young adult can only respond: "It ain't heavy—it's my religion."

Evidence abounds to cause serious concern about a decline in ethics coupled with an increase in self-deception, both in our youth and adults. But the Josephson data on youth from 2002 to 2008 are a cause for concern that things are going into an ethical free fall, replaced by a powerful economic and social structure that empowers an unmitigated drive for self and success with few boundaries and forgotten conflicts of interest. The powerful psychological effects of these forces are changing human development. Adults unwittingly reinforce the new rules and the new definition of success, at the cost of inhibiting their children's normal maturation. The media bombardment of both children and adults and the dramatic speed of technology increase our anticipation and anxiety toward anything negative that may happen. When we experience a loss or trauma, our privacy is often invaded, preventing the normal coping and developmental processes to unfold. We may withdraw into rigid self-obsessive and compulsive behavior, in a psychological attempt to control the environment and control others. But over time, that does not work either.

Today's young adult must cope with the societal burden to have "moral values" while religion is used for marketing and profit and the new definition of success. The conflict is heightened with private schools, homeschooling, and the dramatic emphasis on test scores. In addition, the impact of screen media and virtual reality impacts how we think, solve problems, and make decisions. Our capacity to analyze and interpret information has been altered, making it difficult to make meaningful comparisons. As a consequence, today's youth have dramatically different expectations and a different view of attaining success and of what is meaningful and real.

NOTES

1. *Wikipedia, The Free Encyclopedia.* (n.d.). Retrieved December 15, 2008 from http://en.wikipedia.org/wiki/Second_Life.

2. Sloan, P. (2005, December 1). The virtual Rockefeller: Anshe Chung is taking in real money in an unreal online world. *CNNMoney.com.* Retrieved December 12, 2008 from http://money.cnn.com/magazines/business2/business2_archive/2005/12/01/8364581/index.htm?cnn=yes.

3. Terdiman, D. (2006, December 20). Virtual magnate shares secrets of success. *CNETnews.com.* Retrieved December 1, 2008 from http://news.cnet.com/Virtual-magnate-shares-secrets-of-success/2008-1043_3-6144967.html.

4. Ibid.

5. Walker, T. (2002, March 22). The SIMS overtakes Myst. *Gamespot.* Retrieved December 15, 2008 from http://www.gamespot.com/pc/strategy/simslivinlarge/news_2857556.html.

6. Klosterman, C. (2004). *Sex, drugs, and Cocoa Puffs* (pp. 16–17). New York: Scribner.

7. Hansen, J. (2007). The Haves, Have-nots, and Don't Wants, Table 3.3. In *24/7: How cell phones and the internet change the way we live, work, and play* (p. 43). Westport, CT: Praeger Publishers.

8. Blizzard Entertainment. (2008, October 28). World of Warcraft® surpasses 11 million subscribers worldwide. Retrieved December 23, 2008 from http://www.blizzard.com/us/press/081028.html.

9. Viorst, J. (1986). *Necessary losses: The loves, illusions, dependencies, and impossible expectations that all of us have to give up in order to grow.* New York: Simon and Schuster.

10. Viorst, J. (1986). The private "I." In *Necessary losses: The loves, illusions, dependencies, and impossible expectations that all of us have to give up in order to grow* (pp. 55–56). New York: Simon and Schuster.

11. Data shows high percentage of network news devoted to crime, a theme often expressed by media critics. See Kerbel, M. R. (2000). *If it bleeds it leads: An anatomy of television news.* Oxford, United Kingdom: Westview Press. Moore, M. (Producer). (2002). *Bowling for Columbine* [Motion picture]. United States: United Artists.

12. Kadet, A. (2002, June). Good grief. *Smart Money*, 108–114.

13. Ibid., 111. Also, Groopman, J. (2004, January 26). The grief industry. *The New Yorker*, pp. 30–38.

14. Response by expert Richard McNally and researchers: "Most people who receive debriefing endorse it as helpful . . . But this does not mean that it prevents post traumatic mental disorders. These reports that the method is helpful may reflect little more than polite expressions of gratitude for attention received." See McNally, R., Bryant, R., & Ehlers, A. (2003). Does early psychological intervention promote recovery from posttraumatic stress? Psychological science in the public interest. *American Psychological Society*, 4 (2): 45–79.

15. Jones, R. (2008, January 3). Guard mocked by escaped prisoners is found dead. *The New York Times*. Retrieved December 15, 2008 from http://www.nytimes.com/2008/01/03/nyregion/03elizabeth.html.

16. Blatt, S. J. (1995). The destructiveness of perfectionism: Implications for the treatment of depression. *American Psychologist*, 50:1003–1020.

17. Blatt, S. J., Quinlan, D. M., Pilkonis, P. A., & Shea, M. T. (1995). Impact of perfectionism and need for approval on the brief treatment of depression: The National Institute of Mental Health Treatment of Depression Collaborative Research Program revisited. *Journal of Consulting and Clinical Psychology* 63:125–132.

18. Blatt, S. J., Zuroff, D. C., Sanislow, C. A., & Pilkonis, P. A. (1998). When and how perfectionism impedes the brief treatment of depression:

Further analyses of the National Institute of Mental Health Treatment of Depression Collaborative Research Program. *Journal of Consulting and Clinical Psychology*, 66:423–428.

19. Hewitt, P. L., & Flett, G. L. (1990). Perfectionism and depression: A multidimensional analysis. *Journal of Social Behavior and Personality*, 5:423–438. Hewitt, P. L., & Flett, G. L. (1991). Perfectionism in the self and social contexts: Conceptualization, assessment, and association with psychopathology. *Journal of Personality and Social Psychology*, 60:456–470. Hewitt, P. L., Flett, G. L., Donovan, W. T., & Mikail, S. F. (1991). The Multidimensional Perfectionism Scale: Reliability, validity, and psychometric properties in psychiatric samples. *Psychological Assessment: A Journal of Consulting and Clinical Psychology*, 3:464–468. Hewitt, P. L., Flett, G. L., & Donovan, W. T. (1992). Perfectionism and suicidal potential. *British Journal of Clinical Psychology*, 31:181–190. Hewitt, P. L., Flett, G. L., & Weber, C. (1994). Dimensions of perfectionism and suicidal potential. *Cognitive Therapy & Research*, 18:439–460.

20. Kirwan-Taylor, H. (2007, February 23). The perfection infection: More virulent than bird flu, perfection infection is decimating society, causing irrational rages, depression, and even suicide. *The* (London) *Evening Standard*, Magazine Section, p. 23.

21. Vandiver, B., & Worrell, F. (2002). The reliability and validity of the Almost Perfect Scale-Revised with academically talented middle school students. *Journal of Secondary Gifted Education*, 13 (1): 108–119.

22. Failure is not an option, originally by Gene Kranz, Mission Control Flight Director, on Apollo 13 flight, April 1970. Search conducted December 13, 2008 from http://www.google.com.

23. Slosar, J. R. (2002). The role of perfectionism in law enforcement suicide. Paper presented at FBI Quantico Symposium on Law Enforcement Suicide on September 23, 1999. In Sheehan & Warren (Eds.). *Law Enforcement & Suicide* (pp. 539–549). Quantico, VA: FBI Academy, Behavioral Sciences Unit.

24. Fields, G., & Jones, C. (1999, June 1). Suicide on the force. *USA Today*, p. A1–A2.

25. Hewitt, P. L., Flett, G. L., & Weber, C. (1994). Dimensions of perfectionism and suicidal potential. *Cognitive Therapy & Research*, 18:439–460.

26. Slater, T. (1910). Lying. In *The Catholic encyclopedia*. New York: Robert Appleton Company. Retrieved August 10, 2008 from http://www.newadvent.org/cathen/09469a.htm. BBC. (n.d.). Philosophers on lying. In Religion & ethics—ethical issues. Retrieved July 6, 2008 from http://www.bbc.co.uk/ethics/lying/lying_3.shtml.

27. Frankfurt, H. (2005). *On bullshit* (p. 1). Princeton, NJ: Princeton University Press.

28. Liptak, A. (2008, April 23). Inmate count in U.S. dwarfs other nations'. *The New York Times*. Retrieved December 23, 2008 from http://www.nytimes.com/2008/04/23/us/23prison.html.

29. Callahan, D. (2004). Everybody does it. In *The cheating culture: Why more Americans are doing wrong to get ahead* (pp. 1–28). Orlando, FL: Harcourt Books.

30. Josephson Institute Center for Youth Ethics. (2002). The ethics of American youth: 2002. Retrieved December 23, 2008 from http://charactercounts.org/programs/reportcard/2002/index.html.

31. Josephson Institute Center for Youth Ethics. (2004). The ethics of American youth: 2004. Retrieved December 23, 2008 from http://charactercounts.org/
programs/reportcard/2004/index.html.

32. Josephson Institute Center for Youth Ethics. (2006). The ethics of American youth: 2006. Retrieved December 23, 2008 from http://charactercounts.org/programs/reportcard/2006/index.html.

33. Josephson Institute Center for Youth Ethics. (2008). The ethics of American youth: 2008. Retrieved December 23, 2008 from http://charactercounts.org/programs/reportcard/2008/index.htm.

34. The Pew Research Center. (2007). *How young people view their lives, futures and politics: A portrait of Generation Next*. Washington, D.C.: The Pew Research Center for the People and the Press.

35. Silverstein, S. (2004, November 28). Colleges are learning to hold parents' hands. *Los Angeles Times*, p. A1.

36. Marano, H. E. (2004, November/December). A nation of wimps. *Psychology Today*, 37 (6): 58–68.

37. Ibid., p. 67.

38. Paul, G. (2005). Cross national correlations of quantifiable societal health with popular religiosity and secularism in the prosperous democracies. *Journal of Religion & Society*, 7:1–17.

39. Ibid., p. 7.

40. Reem, C. (2008, May 8). The man who learned too much. *OC Metro*, pp. 32–38.

41. (2008, August 16). Saddleback Church Forum on the Presidency: Obama and McCain with Rick Warren. Retrieved December 23, 2008 from http://trevinwax.com/2008/08/17/obama-mccain-with-rick-warren-at-saddleback-forum-video/.

42. Collom, E. (May 2005). The ins and outs of homeschooling: The determinants of parental motivations and student achievement. *Education and Urban Society*, 37 (3): 307–335.

43. Ibid.

44. Warren, R. (2002). *The Purpose Driven Life*. Grand Rapids, MI: Zondervan.

45. Rivenburg, R. (2005, July 15). Christian events to take center stage in L.A. and Anaheim. *Los Angeles Times*, p. B3.

46. Simon, S. (2005, July 17). Labor and religion reunite: The AFL-CIO is sending forth seminary students to shore up waning clout of unions by reviving the connection with a traditional ally. *Los Angeles Times*, p. A1.

# Chapter 4

# (UN)MEANINGFUL COMPARISONS

We're lost, but we're making good time.

—Yogi Berra

We're losing a dollar on each widget, but we hope to make it up in volume.

—Anonymous dot.com executive

In March 1997, *U.S. News & World Report* conducted a poll of a thousand Americans, in which people were asked how likely they thought different celebrities would go to heaven.[1] Those who were thought "very likely" or "somewhat likely" to go to heaven included Oprah Winfrey (66%), Michael Jordan (65%), and, before her death, Princess Diana (65%). President Clinton weighed in at 52 percent, as in general, the American public finds it hard to imagine a liberal Democrat going to heaven, even if he is the President. Dennis Rodman came in at 28 percent, and O. J. Simpson had low ratings at 19 percent. Mother Theresa came in second place at 79 percent, but the survey participants saved first place for someone special—themselves. A whopping 87 percent rated themselves as likely to go to heaven.

Social psychologists refer to this as a self-serving bias, and it is more pronounced in individualistic cultures like ours.[2] Of course, if our own sense of self is inflated, the greater the self-serving bias will be. Today's excesses and narcissistic currents inflate our self-view and contribute to greater evidence of a self-serving bias.

Although this often can seem humorous, the magnitude of the self-serving bias has serious consequences. The concept has profound implications for any type of self-report or self-assessment and also obliterates what used to be perceived as a conflict of interest. Self-serving bias makes it very difficult in our culture to make a meaningful comparison—a comparison that is accurate, unbiased, and more likely to be correct—because we often use ourselves as the basis of comparison. A meaningful comparison implies the ability to take in some information and make a decision or establish a point of view. Psychology uses and promotes the term critical thinking, which aims in helping a student see all sides of an issue.

The cultural impact of narcissism on personality development also affects changes in cognitive development. Declining self-control impedes analytical thinking and effective decisions. This is not because information is not available. With just a few clicks we can obtain mountains of information. But reading and integrating this information is another matter. Relying on screen media, we often cannot separate what is accurate and what is not. Or, we will not take the time and focus to do so. In combination with our strong biases, we often lose the capacity to be objective. In the end, we make terrible decisions with poor outcomes.

The loss of objectivity compounds further. We actually may avoid analyzing data, preferring not to think in a systematic way. Complaints abound that the public demands simplicity and information without substance, or "dumbing down." The lack of analytic ability and focus is reflected in our dismal national student test scores in math and science. Our culture does not like math and spurns the time-consuming, systematic, and analytical thinking required. There is a clear end result of this lack of interest. Tech companies cannot find an adequate talent pool for jobs and must import workers from India and other countries. An increase in Ph.D. degrees awarded in the United States in 2006 was attributed to degrees for *non-U.S. citizens*. China graduates six times the amount of engineers than the United States does. This is going to continue. Incoming college freshmen in 2006 chose business followed by social sciences and then education as the most popular majors. Experts have been warning for years that the decline in math and engineering degrees will result in the United States losing a competitive edge and economic position in the world.[3] Many do not believe they are good at math and science, and besides they are not a form of what we are enthralled with—novelty and entertainment.

We seem to be far more interested in a personal story than analysis or quantitative thinking. The immediacy and the power of a personal story hold our interest. But this creates confusion when we try to make decisions—should we base a decision on an individual case or anecdote or examine group data? A doctor has a patient who has one foot in a refrigerator and another in an oven. He calculates the average temperature. He concludes the patient feels fine. (Today's health care marketplace would probably say that the patient had no medical necessity.) But actual day-to-day decisions are often based more on experience than training or information. The whole basis of an individual appointment with a doctor is that she will listen and evaluate our particular case and symptoms. But researchers and decision makers like to analyze group data. Like the analogy of being able to see the forest from the trees, the issue becomes the importance of an individual evaluation versus group data for making a decision.

When we use group data, sometimes we only rely on an average. In this case, we do not get a handle on the most important factor in making a meaningful comparison. That factor is the variability of the data. So the evaluator must go back and forth between the two. Is it helpful to have group data or information in making an individual evaluation? For example, is it helpful to know that a certain percentage of teenagers experience suicidal thoughts? It is. The information helps frame an issue and should lead to a better decision. But the actual decision of whether that particular teen will attempt or commit suicide is another matter. Applied clinicians recognize the dilemma as that between statistical and clinical significance. Treating a patient involves clinical significance. One heart attack is too many, especially if it is you. We can proudly report that a suicide rate has declined—but one suicide is too many, and a clinician must assess the risk of that one person sitting in front of him or her.

Of course, other business decisions are not as urgent, but their outcome may still dramatically affect our lives. One hopes that data is clear and demonstrative, but it usually is not so. We are bombarded daily with information. We hear and read summaries, research reports, and expert analyses. People actively search the Internet for data and information. Yet we would much rather read or hear the personal story of recovery or success.

## APPLES AND ORANGES

You can probably recall a math teacher stating "you can't compare apples and oranges." Yet the number of educated people who shun the research process and mathematical comparisons is striking. The mere mention of the word "statistics" can immediately engender anxiety in just about anyone. But it is even more elemental than that. It is not uncommon to hear adults beg off from computing something in their head if they do not have a technological device at hand. Their attitude is—why would you want to think about that? At the beginning of a research methods class I teach, I ask students to rate from one to ten how worried they are about the class. I want to know who the tens are. My experience has told me they stew in their own anxiety, do not do well in the class, and influence the interactions or mood of the entire class. By addressing them, I alleviate their concerns, lower barriers, and sometimes even see a dramatic change in the students' receptivity. I then state my goal in the class: Students will learn to make a meaningful comparison. I point out that throughout society others are constantly trying to influence how they look at data and to reinforce an intended viewpoint.

In the standard scientific method, academics seek large samples and groups to arrive at statistical significance and convincing results. They state the probability of their findings with 95 or 99 percent confidence. The main point of this statistical procedure is to test a hypothesis and, if proven, to be able to generalize the findings. The cumbersome cause-and-effect model has many assumptions, such as random sampling, that often are impractical and cannot capture the tremendous rate of change and movement in today's society.

Although we crave a personal story, the value of a *systematic* case study or individual case is not as well appreciated in today's computer-generated sources or statistical analyses. An unstructured discussion of a case study is most common. By looking at human development and mistakes made, we can learn what to do and not do. Freud extensively used the case study method, presenting clinical cases and describing treatment methods. Similarly, in business we may examine a company as a case to learn from its ups and downs. Enron became a significant case study.

Another type of individualized research is less popular as it systematically collects well-defined data for more than discussion purposes. From an opposite theoretical position than Freud's and psychoanalysis, the behaviorists developed this methodology called the single subject research design. In this design, behaviorists meticulously observe, collect data, and *measure progress* on one case/person and follow that subject for an extensive period of time. By establishing a baseline (the business term is benchmark), an intervention can be introduced and compared against the baseline to see if it works. This method contrasts with traditional scientific methodology which would put people in a group, add up and average their scores or output, and compare the groups by statistical analysis. But few people understand the scientific method, few people are willing to try to understand it, and worse yet many people are just plain turned off by it.

The single subject research design is more rigorous than a case study, and can be quite powerful. Many great discoveries have been made by one case, which then is replicated again and again as being true, accurate, and factual. Claude Bernard, a nineteenth-century investigator,[4] made discoveries utilizing one case and then verifying and generalized his results with direct and systematic replication. Bernard, considered one of the originators of biochemistry, is credited with discovering the vasomotor system; the action of curare, carbon monoxide, and other poisons; the functions of the pancreas in digestion; and the glycogenic function of the liver. (Bernard performed his work on one subject at a time—and his subjects were sheep.)

From Bernard's work and that of behavioral researchers, the single subject research design was standardized and developed. Unfortunately, today the method is not widely adopted as it is too detailed and time-consuming for today's electronic world. The precision, carefulness, and replication used by Bernard are replaced by innovative technologies that are supposed to provide these features. Although technology has dramatically increased our capacity to collect data and use statistical analyses, the nitty-gritty of observation and recording takes too much time. (Even if we use video to film everything, we have to systematically analyze the data.) In the end, a valuable aspect of capturing human behavior may be lost. Besides, it matters what goes in to the computer, if you remember the classic saying—"garbage in, garbage out."

Within a design that involves a systematic method, the importance of variability emerges more clearly. A health care researcher reports that 30 percent of Medicare expenses are for 6 percent of persons who are in the last year of their lives.[5] This meaningful comparison tells us that a significant percentage of expenses involve the last year of life, and the number of persons in the last year of life is small. The data really does yield meaningful information, even without giving us a baseline or benchmark of exact figures upon which to make a comparison. We know that total health care expenses for Medicare are huge, and the numbers indicate that a disproportional percentage involve the last year of life. Usually, percentages are not so friendly. In this case, the slice of data helps us realize the tremendous efforts that are made to sustain life and to have the courage to look ahead and consider preparing a living will. Living wills allow health care professionals to avoid dramatic life-sustaining efforts out of fear of being sued for failing to do everything possible. They also lower health care costs. This example also demonstrates that we can use data to make some comparisons based on variability—how much of the proverbial pie is taken up by what services. Of course, statistical models analyze variability in infinite detail, but the professionals must explain the results to the public.

Other popular methods for dissecting variability are designed for business, including gap analysis and Six Sigma.[6] The latter became well known after Jack Welch used it to turn around General Electric.[7] These methods are healthy attempts to look deeper at variability and determine ratios or formulas for success, often referred to as being in "the zone." Optimum performance results from finding the zone and staying there. Successful diets are based on staying in the zone of a balance between proteins and carbohydrates. If you maintain the proper ratio and stay in the zone, you will lose weight. When Michael Jordan burst into the National Basketball Association (NBA), he was scoring 40 and 50 points a game. But there was a problem—the team was not winning. Coaches had to convince him to go along with a "triangle offense" to increase efficiency in offense and scoring. In a famous exchange, coaches told him there was no "I" in team.[8] But Jordan snapped back that there was an "I" in win. Jordan did convert to the offense and lowered his point total. The team was well on its way, and one season won 72 games, still an NBA record. Even during this run, sometimes Jordan had an exceptional game and scored 40 or more points, and when this happened, the team usually lost.

Finding and staying in the optimum range of variability also requires sustained attention and a specific level of arousal. But our performance is best under conditions of moderate rather than either low or high arousal. This comes with a proviso that a new and difficult task is accomplished more effectively under low arousal in which one can be attentive but still relaxed. Well-learned or easy tasks are actually accomplished more readily when one is highly aroused.[9] Staying in the moderate range of arousal is best overall, but you can be too aroused and not do well on those important tests or decisions.

The velocity and volume of information today, the speed of the Internet, and a heightened arousal state certainly impede making meaningful comparisons and decisions. Self-control of one's behavior is the same process needed to have self-control of one's thinking and decision making. The lack of self-control and impulsivity leads to increased mistakes and poorer performance. Discovering our own optimal range of variability and arousal in which we function best becomes more difficult. The outward symptom observed is the inability to make a meaningful comparison and a good decision. The dramatic technological changes in how we gather information hinder systematic thinking and sanction quick thinking.

An overstimulated and aroused mind cannot maintain focus to analyze data, and worse yet we get anxious when we try.

## DON'T SUE ME

Examples abound for how easily we are fooled. To no one's surprise, media strongly influence false beliefs. An example is the widespread belief that everyone will sue anyone over the smallest offense and win huge financial awards. The idea is that the prevalence of lawsuits is a major barrier to business. The resulting anti-lawsuit position is a prominent representative factor of today's pro-business, unlimited profit basis of entrepreneurial narcissism.

But the facts show a different picture. In a survey of 35 states by the National Center for State Courts, the number of lawsuits filed declined by 4 percent from 1993 through 2002.[10] This is incredible when you consider that during this period of the emergence of the Internet, our country sustained the most dramatic economic activity and growth ever. In other words, more people, more activity, less lawsuits. The U.S. Department of Justice reported that in the 75 largest counties in the United States, the median court award in 1992 was $63,000 (adjusted for inflation). This compares to a median award of $37,000 in 2002.[11] But you would never know it from any conversation you would have with friends or business associates.

If it financially bleeds, it also leads. A plaintiff award is front-page news. Most people are unable to look beyond the newspapers or the nightly news broadcasts to discover that most dollar awards are seldom realized in actual amount, and many are overturned.[12] Just because you win a judgment does not mean the loser just sits down and writes you the check. Invariably, the verdict, if not overturned, is greatly reduced as parties settle for an "undisclosed amount." Settlements could take quite a while and may involve the winner agreeing never to disclose the amount. Don't forget those who lose will often only settle when stated in writing there is "no wrongdoing" on their part.

These final outcomes are seldom reported as prominently. Research studies of media reporting show that when ten newspapers report a front-page plaintiff award, only two or three will use the front page to report the verdict has been overturned.[13] A 1999 study by Rand Corporation's Institute for Civil Justice showed an extreme bias in media reporting of plaintiff awards or verdicts in contrast to when the defendants won the lawsuit.[14] We want to see the big award and winner, like winning the lotto or becoming a millionaire. It is that one big deal—why can't it be me?

Successful business lobbying, not hard to do on this issue, has led to tremendous legal restraints by states concerning how lawsuits can be filed and the amounts that can be awarded. The pro-business forces are aided by rampant Internet rumors of unjust and extravagant lawsuits that never occurred. Major media, including CNN, reported the following *nonexistent lawsuits*:

1. Merv Grazinski who sued Winnebago for an accident and won $1.6 million causing Winnebago to rewrite their owner's manual.

2. A woman was awarded $1.6 million in Portland, Oregon for a botched liposuction surgery. The award was against a phone directory that published and allowed a dermatologist to advertise as Board Certified when he was not.

3. Amber Carson of Lancaster, Pennsylvania argued with her boyfriend at a restaurant and slipped and broke her tailbone after throwing a drink at him. News reports stated she won $113,500.

4. Kara Walton in Delaware went to a nightclub and tried to avoid a $3.50 cover charge by climbing through a bathroom window. She fell and broke a couple teeth, the story goes, and won a judgment of $12,000 and dental bills, of course.[15]

Is it possible that pro-business profiteers could pitch so many explicitly phony stories to gullible media to make the public and trial lawyers look bad? If so, the scheme has worked. The conclusion is that juries in state awards are too generous. So, in February 2005, President Bush signed a federal law that makes it harder to file class action lawsuits in a state court.[16] Seems these suits must be directed into the federal court system—so much for advocating for states' rights.

Similarly, Bush and others have cited medical malpractice lawsuits as a major factor in rising health care costs. But, in fact, the actual data shows a very minimal impact of lawsuits on health care costs.[17] A pol can rack up a lot of points by bashing lawsuits. Engage someone in this conversation and watch the veins bulge about "frivolous lawsuits." And, of course, some lawsuits *are* frivolous. Being sued or involved in a lawsuit is stressful and exhaustive. Once it happens, especially if it is frivolous, it is hard to not be angry and resentful. The anger and resentment is comparable to those of crime victims, and any lawyer who abuses this part of the legal system should be disbarred.

What many also do not realize is that lawyers refuse to pursue some truly egregious lawsuits that would involve huge dollar amounts because of state-imposed limits on jury awards. In these few cases, the true victims and the worst victims are actually unable to sue. These include people who have even lost limbs or are paralyzed. California has been successful in containing medical malpractice suits and keeping malpractice premiums affordable by placing a limit on the amount that can be awarded for noneconomic damages ($250,000).[18] Believe it or not, this limit was imposed in 1975 when Democrat Jerry Brown was governor. But the limit has never been increased, and in the high cost legal arena today, lawyers refuse cases due to the economic restraint and cost/benefit outcome.

It is certainly not politically correct to express the opinion that lawsuits are a viable course of action forcing our overexuberant market system into response mode. But one lawsuit can be far more effective in problem-solving and less costly than the long road of passing legislation and then enforcing that legislation. Consider a 1997 Supreme Court decision on sexual harassment.[19] The workplace environment was immediately and drastically changed when the Supreme Court ruled an employer was responsible for any sexual harassment in the workplace even if the employer was unaware of the incident or systems imposed to prevent such harassment had not worked. Employers' immediate response was to establish specific sexual harassment policies and supervision, making employees fully aware of the rules and consequences. This made for a better workplace environment for all workers, a direct consequence of a lawsuit.

Lawsuits are an important part of our market system, more cost-effective and immediate than legislation, and involve dealing with values a free market system often ignores. To lose the right to sue puts one in an unfair and helpless business environment. But today the emphasis is always on deregulation and profit and anything seen as a cost or barrier to profit and gain is wrong and unfair. At least that is the politically correct position—one that is hard to challenge.


DON'T SHOOT ME

Some topics are so emotional, critical thinking seems impossible. In this type of an issue, frequency data is especially problematic for meaningful comparisons. In a well-known book, *More Guns, Less Crime*, author John Lott presents the following data. Stating the premise that children are much less likely to be accidentally killed by guns than most people think, he reports that there were 1,400 accidental firearm deaths in 1995. Of these, 30 deaths involved children up to four years of age, and 170 more deaths involved five- to fourteen-year-old children. In a comparison, he points out that 2,900 children died in auto crashes, 950 children died from drowning, and more than a thousand children died from fire and burns in the same year.[20] Lott, who is described as a "Fellow" in Law and Economics from the University of Chicago, concludes that more children die in bicycle accidents each year than die from all types of firearm accidents.

First of all, what is the comparison here? The comparison not made has to do with opportunities. We must know the full range of data on exposure to accidents to make any kind of a comparison. Behaviorists would call this data a baseline and business productivity experts refer to it as a benchmark. How many times does a child ride in a car? Certainly, several times a day for most children. How many times does a child ride a bike? What is the comparison with this frequency to how often a child comes in contact with a gun? The frequency comparison is meaningless. One would certainly guess that since we constantly drive our kids everywhere, the opportunity for a car accident would make the 2,900 figure seem incredibly good. Yet, data examples like Lott's are often cited in the emotional debate about gun control. One frequently hears that more children die from auto, bike accidents, and fires than accidental gun deaths. Not to mention that this data does not pertain to gun deaths of youngsters by intentional means, such as drive by shootings, another significant comparison to consider. One wonders how an economist entered the fray about social policy and guns.

So consider another one of Lott's views or recommendations. Citing sophisticated study after study from data he analyzed from different states that more guns mean less crime, he concludes later in his book that "at least" permitting school employees access to guns would seem to make schools less vulnerable to mass shootings.[21] Yet such a conclusion from his data would send trembling fear among parents who imagine school personnel having access to guns to respond to school violence. Those whose jobs require carrying guns can readily report how difficult it is to use them under stress or in the moment. In fact, accidents in training exercises for law enforcement personnel are not uncommon, and even trained professionals can misuse their weapons or have an accident.

Further analysis of Lott's book and data shows a larger problem.[22] Several researchers have reported problems with his methodology and errors in data, and have stated that his claims are unsubstantiated.[23] The criticism fueled a huge political war as many backed Lott and others attacked him. Critics wanted data from an earlier survey that Lott was not able to produce.

The controversy centered around whether Lott had published data in a peer review process or not. It also involved the emotional issues surrounding think tanks. Lott had been working at the American Enterprise Institute, a well-known conservative think tank. These agenda-determined centers allow data to be presented that is designed to win and influence and often escapes traditional peer review. Peer review, revered by academics, serves to filter articles for validity and credibility. Most articles do not make it through the peer review process. In fact, major peer reviewed journals in psychology accept only 10–20 percent for publication.[24] Seldom is an article published as submitted on the first try. If it makes it through the review process, changes and the review process take months or even a year or two. But in the end, the data is deemed valid and credible. But in the world of think tanks and popular media, who wants to go through that long scientific process? Easier to self-publish your own data and let it fly. Then you can make the impact first, before critical analysis can occur, and become an "expert." Today's rapid projection of data and information into the public realm, especially with the ease of the Internet, produces volumes of what appears to be believable data that has not been fully evaluated. The equivalent in the business world would be hiring someone for an important position before they were fully vetted.

Lott's story and the challenge to his findings have continued for years, even involving—yes—lawsuits. Lott sued the publisher and authors of *Freakonomics*, who reported that other researchers could not replicate his findings.[25] While he lost this suit, a second defamation suit was settled when the defendant admitted making some false claims that Lott's research had not been published in peer reviewed journals.[26]

But the big splash had been made and the culture war was on. The National Academy of Sciences entered the fray with a huge review of the research in 2004. In that report, the NAS could not determine any impact on lowering crime from either gun control policies or from possessing a gun.[27] Both sides, consequently, claimed vindication. The band plays on.

NOT ME

Even in critically important matters, numbers are presented with little analysis of magnitude or comparison, a phenomenon that rings true for a culture of excess. We lose perspective. Secretary of State Colin Powell in his famous speech to the United Nations stated that there was evidence that Saddam Hussein had "one-hundred to five-hundred tons" of chemical weapons.[28] So, let's use the middle of the range, say 300 tons. Three hundred times two thousand pounds (it is best to use a calculator) comes out to be 600,000 pounds. That is a lot of pounds—wouldn't it be easy to find the large storage space needed to house that many WMD? I was fascinated also to hear others report that many of these WMD were gases or vapors—how could something that is close to weightless amount to 600,000 pounds? Likewise, many said the WMD could be very small and easy to hide. If they were small, they would not weigh much and there would have to be a whole lot of them stored somewhere to weigh 600,000 pounds. If I told you I was going to deliver 10,000 or 100,000 or 300,000 pounds of anything, wouldn't you wonder where on earth you would put it?

Although the debate centered on the lack of veracity of the existence of the WMD, the magnitude of the distortion should have immediately drawn skepticism. We cannot forget another factor here in the presentation of data and making meaningful comparisons. Secretary of State Powell certainly had credibility.[29] So, when an authoritative source has high credibility, we simply do not look further—we do not even try to make a meaningful comparison. We trust the source. But today's authority figures and experts are under the influence of a culture of excess.

A picture speaks a thousand words. A January 2003 photo shows the board members of Haemonetics, a company that markets blood-filtering equipment, ringing the opening bell on Wall Street.[30] In the photo is Dr. Harvey G. Klein, a top expert in blood transfusion from the National Institutes of Health (NIH). As shocking as a punch in the nose, the photo draws openmouthed disbelief. Who does Dr. Klein work for? Later, Dr. Klein is reported to have accepted $240,000 in fees and 76,000 stock options from several companies during the last five years. Of course, today's cultural zeitgeist opens the door, and he is not alone. Dr. H. Bryan Brewer, Jr., NIH expert who established new cholesterol guidelines, earned $114,000 in fees from 2001 to 2003 from four companies making cholesterol medications.[31] This included one drug named Crestor, which later was connected with a serious side effect called rhabdomyolysis, a breakdown of muscle fiber that can cause kidney failure and death. Eight cases were reported in clinical trails of Crestor, but marketing prevailed, reassured by Dr. Brewer's report in the August 2003 *American Journal of Cardiology* that Crestor was safe. Later, the FDA reported 78 cases of the side effect reported during Crestor's first year on the market. Among the 78 cases, two people died.[32] The bravado of the Wall Street picture is one glimpse in time. Another biomedical company, Lipid Sciences of Pleasanton, California, actually listed Dr. Brewer with title on its company Web page, including video clips of Dr. Brewer and his entrance to work at the NIH Clinical Center![33]

Drs. Klein and Brewer have had their activities reported in the press, but all told, at least 530 NIH scientists have taken stock, stock options, or consulting fees from biomedical companies from 1999 to 2003.[34] And the disclosure and information did not come easily. The House Energy and Commerce Committee realizing they were probably being stonewalled by NIH directly sent a letter to 20 companies asking for information. Responses showed more than 130 consulting arrangements that did not appear to have approval of NIH. The standards were loosened per the explosion of the stock market boom and a different business and cultural attitude toward professionalism and conflicts of interest. Finally, since 2005, regulators are now starting to enforce rules and meting out consequences to professionals for probable conflicts of interest.

Scientists were insulted—threatening to quit—as if they were being prevented from making a living. In a pure example of entrepreneurial narcissism, in November 2004, two hundred NIH scientists sent a letter to the NIH director informing him that a permanent ban on industry consulting would make them "second class citizens in the biomedical community."[35] Just a sidebar, the salary range for NIH scientists is between $130,000 and $200,000 a year. There is little likelihood a scientist will receive any consequence for a conflict of interest violation. Prior to all this moonlighting, the last NIH scientist prosecuted and convicted for a conflict of interest offense was in 1992. Facing a maximum sentence of 20 years in a federal penitentiary, Dr. Prem Sarin repaid $25,000 to a pharmaceutical company in Germany that was doing AIDS research. He received two months of community service.

The entrepreneurial activities at NIH are a serious problem in the larger issue of trust in public information, public policy, and safety. What if the referees for the Super Bowl disclosed they were paid last year as consultants for one of the teams in the championship game? The referee would have to state publicly that as a true professional, his judgment and decisions would be unaffected, as today's business leaders or scientists proclaim. And that is ludicrous. A study of medical students in 2001 asked them if they thought gifts from the drug companies influenced their colleagues. Eighty-four percent said yes. When asked if the gifts would influence them, only 16 percent said yes. Numerous studies have shown people cannot overcome their biases, even when offered a reward.[36]

Separate from the NIH scientists, the profound issue of distorting science and false or minimized data is of serious concern to the scientific community. In July 2004, about 4,000 scientists which included 48 Nobel Prize winners and 127 members of the National Academy of Sciences publicly proclaimed and accused the Bush administration of distorting and suppressing science for its own political agenda.[37] Unfortunately, the problem goes deeper than that.

Sources are established as experts to provide technical information and to protect us. The scientists and professionals have status, expertise, and countless years of dedicated training we trust and rely upon. But today, that knowledge and expertise are up for sale. Is it good data if the experts say it is? Today's culture of narcissism devalues science. It uses science in manipulative ways for the entitlement of success through the pursuit of wealth. The lack of boundaries necessary to avoid a conflict of interest and evaluate data permeates all levels of society. The realization that experts cannot be trusted adds further to the negative response and anxiety about statistics and numbers. Worse yet, it leads to a disbelief in science.


## POLITICS: UNMEANINGFUL COMPARISONS

Nowhere is the spin and manipulation of information greater than in politics. In this arena, whoever manipulates the data most effectively wins the power and control of the country. So the prize is the biggest there is. Consider the common perception of how the two political parties spend money.

Learning often occurs by forming associations, and the association of Democrats as big spenders and Republicans as business experts who control spending is emblazoned in our brain cells. This association seems to be as strong as red means stop and green means go, but historically it just is not so. Before George W. Bush was declared President in 2000, the previous 24 years included 12 years of Democratic presidents (8 years for Clinton, and 4 years for Carter), and 12 years of Republican presidents (8 years of Reagan, and 4 years of Bush senior). *Los Angeles Times* columnist John Balzar researched data from the U.S. Census Bureau and Treasury Department to report the data for spending and budget deficits for each year, and then averaged the Republican years and the Democratic years.[38] His results showed that under Republican presidents, the average government spending was 22 percent more than revenue, but under Democratic presidents, deficits averaged just 7 percent. In other words, under a Republican president, deficits averaged more than three times that of Democrats. More specifically, average deficits were as follows for each President: Clinton, 4.4 percent; Carter, 13.23 percent; Bush senior, 21.75 percent, and Reagan, 21.87 percent.[39]

Acknowledged Republicans to whom I have pointed out this data have stated flat out they did not believe the numbers, laughing that Congress, not the President, controls spending. Republicans have successfully argued that when a Democratic majority exists in Congress, big spending occurs. This argument seems kind of a self-fulfilling prophecy, indicating that Reagan and Bush were powerless to stop Congress from spending while Clinton and Carter were able to hold spending to a lower level.

Nevertheless, the data continues to repeat the trend. After eight years of George W. Bush, we hit the largest budget deficit ever recorded, though the deficit continues to worsen. The Congress also was Republican until 2006. Defenders of the deficit cite the effect of the September 11 attacks, arguing that there was no choice but to create the huge bureaucracy of Homeland Security. Once an association is made, it is hard to undo the conclusion, no matter what the data say. We could use a Detective Joe Friday from the 1960s' *Dragnet* program, with his classic line: "The facts ma'am, just the facts."

Simplistic conclusions about "red" states and the "blue" states also prompt associations that deny facts. The complexities and social issues of states are far more complex than mere voting patterns. Although the public associates Republican red states with religious values and Democratic blue states with permissive liberal attitudes, factual data on several social variables clearly do not support this dichotomy. For example, in 2001, the top eleven states in divorce rate were all red states. Red states had a total of 572,000 divorces, while the blue states reported a total of 340,000. The per capita rate of violent crime in red states was 421 per 100,000 people, while in blue states, it was 372. The top five states in teen pregnancies and alcohol dependence and abuse were also red states.[40] The behaviors among the population in red states compared with blue states do not reflect the common simplistic association of red states being more religious and blue more permissive. Substantive research on the difference between liberal and conservative ideologies helps us look beyond this simplistic association. Two factors found that help differentiate the differences are "attitudes toward inequality" and "attitudes toward social change vs. tradition."[41]

No discussion of political manipulation of data can omit the fury about global warming. In 2006, the *National Journal* asked Republican senators and representatives: "Do you think it's been proven beyond a reasonable doubt that the earth is warming because of man-made problems?" The response was 23 percent yes and 77 percent no. In the following year, an international report came out in which 90 percent of 2,000 scientists answered the same question affirmatively. Consequently, considerably more attention and evidence for man-made global warming entered the public discourse. Yet in 2007 when the Republicans were asked the same question again, the number responding yes declined to 13 percent.[42] In other words, the more evidence that was presented, the stronger the established position against man-made global warming became. Harvard psychologist Daniel Gilbert suggested that if we could infuse the issue with moral energy, movement might follow. Perhaps, he noted, if we could only prove that gay sex caused global warming, the urgency to act would create a solution.[43]

Politics is about power and control, but what a tremendous disservice it is not to allow meaningful comparisons and debate on the important issues of our times. The stunting effect divides us into ideological camps, contributes to the dumbing down of political discourse, and delays or prevents effective solutions. To adopt a predetermined viewpoint and perspective is to ignore the evidence, no matter the data. No growth or development in thinking can take place. The hardheaded positions are similar to the defensive, obsessive, and perfectionistic patterns of a narcissistic personality, discussed in Chapter 3, and the rigid thinking that goes with it can be destructive.

## SUMMATION: AN EMPTY HOLE

Developmental psychologists K. Warner Schaie and Shelley Willis began a longitudinal study in 1956 in which they used standardized tests of mental abilities.[44] The pair tested more than 5,000 individuals at seven testing cycles through 1998. The study uses a cross-sectional design, adding the younger generation as a new set of subjects in each new test period, while continuing the subjects who are now older. In the category of numerical abilities, a decline in scores began in the 1950s and continued; today's cohort or generation does not score as well on numerical tests than the now older cohorts did. Could something be said for the methods of teaching the older cohort?[45]

The cohort effect—differences attributed to experiences unique to a particular generation—is an important concept to this type of longitudinal research.[46] This data does not mean younger people today are dumber or less intelligent than those of the older cohort. We know that today's technology handles numerical abilities for us. Today's clerk does not have to count out the change as those in the 1950s. Calculators and computers rule the day. But use it or lose it, and the ability to make calculations in one's head declines. The inability of the current and future generations to manipulate and compare numbers mentally may pose a huge problem. The overreliance on technology to make speedy computations eventually may erode underlying mental construct or mechanisms, and limit the ability to make important numerical comparisons. The demand for fast and immediate numerical answers also may correlate with impulsivity and premature decision making. In other words, our minds just do not think in this numerical way anymore—why should they?

Considerable evidence has been presented that U.S. students are far behind those in other countries in math and science. The reasons for the low performance are generational and related to cultural factors. Today's young student is simply not interested in math and science, at least when it comes to choosing a profession in which they may become famous. Our efforts to help overcome the deficiency are hopeless when put in the perspective of a culture of excess.

Except for Denmark, the United States spends more on education per child annually than any other country.[47] Yet, this does not translate into success. The *average* 10-year-old in Singapore is ahead of the top 5 percent of U.S. 10-year-olds in math.[48] The United States ranks 18th among the 24 wealthiest nations in math and science scores of 14- and 15-year-olds.[49] Although these comparisons are strained due to factors such as the age of starting school and standardization of the testing, the consensus is still that we are plenty behind the rest of the world. Domestic studies also show deficits and declines in history, science, math and less interest in the fine arts.[50]

Systemic cultural differences are a major factor in educational achievement. The above comparison showing a high level of spending for education in the United States is based on averages, but considerable variability exists across the nation. The amount spent per child can vary from $3,000 to $15,000, just by changing zip codes.[51] The result is poor schools and good schools. In Japan, one of the highest-ranking countries in math and science, a nationwide educational system and national curriculum prevents the extreme variability in spending the United States has. Almost all Japanese children attend public school, and if a child moves and switches schools, the system and curriculum will be the same. The result is very low absenteeism, and, in fact, less than 2 percent of students drop out of school.[52] This would be a statistic that educational reformers in the United States would die for.

The cultural differences in system design reflect parental attitudes. Harold Stevenson and colleagues have conducted five cross-cultural studies comparing U.S. students with students in Japan, China, and Taiwan. The gap found in academic scores is lowest in first grade, as might be expected, and highest in eleventh grade. But the research provides a more direct explanation. Asian teachers spent significantly more time teaching math in the early grades than U.S. teachers. Asian students were more likely to do their math homework and receive parental assistance than U.S. students. But what was most striking was the researchers' report of parental attitudes. Mothers in Japan and Taiwan were more likely to attribute their children's math achievement to effort; U.S. parents were more likely to attribute it to innate ability.[53] So, to American parents, a child either has it (math ability) or he does not. I see this attitude constantly among younger students as well as adult students who openly proclaim: "I have never been good at this." The avoidance and anxiety follow. They believe they just do not "have it." They believe they will never be good at it (math), and when a problem comes their way, they give it to someone else who does "have it."

Experts long have noticed a low point in learning in the United States, beginning around age 11. What seems like a big hole is a trend that is noticeable in declining grades. The first year of middle school marks this low point.[54] The emergence of puberty and sexuality immediately comes to mind as a possible factor. Then, why is a decline in preteen scores not seen in other cultures also? The answer may lie in the cultural differences surrounding this life stage. Emerging puberty seems especially difficult in the United States, a culture with tremendous social and economic pressure. The social pressures have been linked simply to the actual transition to middle school. U.S. students encounter what is referred to as the top-dog phenomenon,[55] occurring when a student moves from a top position in a smaller elementary school to a lower position in a middle or junior high school. Charting the transition from sixth to seventh grade, researchers found that the perceptions and worldview of seventh graders changed. Now in the seventh grade, students reported they were less satisfied with the quality of school life, less committed to school, and had less favorable response toward teachers. This decline was found even in students who had performed well academically.[56]

If these cultural trends are not enough, we return again to our elevated sense of self and the self-serving bias. We all must do well and believe we are doing well, which affects objective evaluation of student progress. Grade inflation prevails. From 1965 to 1973, grade point averages at 134 colleges rose an average of .404 points. Surveys conducted through the 1990s found that college students attended class less often and spent less time studying than previous students but received the same or higher grades.[57] Getting an A and receiving "honors" today is easy and common. In 2001, a report found that 91 percent of Harvard graduates received honors.[58] With this kind of percentage, how must it feel to graduate from such a prestigious school without honors?

A broader investigation showed that grade inflation was a problem at Harvard, but it exists everywhere. Educators bow and buckle to intense lobbying from students and the proliferation of A grades continues. Professors fear the lower ratings they receive from students if they maintain high standards and stricter grading.[59] In today's society, nothing less than an A or excellent will do—and the attitude is "you're gonna give it to me." The pressure is readily noticeable when I teach college classes. Students approach me in a manner that I would never have contemplated when I was a student, both because of respect for my professors and because I would have felt like an arrogant idiot. But I have had students inform me they have all As, as if to remind me not to spoil their record. Students who receive a B will tell me they are not a B student. The implication is that if you did not give them an A, something must be wrong with you. A deluge of requests for extra credit follow my giving back test results. Other adult students frequently tell me they need an A to go on to another school or program or that their employer will not reimburse them unless they get an A. Instructors who fail to award the highest scores should be prepared for the petitions and contests that follow. I sat at a faculty meeting in which a department chair lamented receiving an appeal from a graduate student who was unhappy with an A minus.

At the beginning of some classes for adult students, I ask students to list three things they would like to get out of the class. I want to get a handle on their expectations and what they want to *learn* in the class and to be able to adapt my teaching to adult students' diverse backgrounds. I also assume, as older students taking an evening class, they are oriented toward learning practical and applied information and that getting an A might not be as important. But many students list an A among their three priorities. I have revised my request and now state when passing out the form that I assume everyone wants to get an A, so do not list that as an item.

Grade inflation and the pressure to evaluate everyone as excellent devalue the educational system. Students' attitudes toward teachers and professors have changed; students are far more likely to lobby for an A, and less likely to receive feedback for improvement.

Social and cultural forces, including declining self-control, inflated sense of self, and competitive pressures, have impacted our thinking and cognitive development. Lower scores in math and science are a result. We have even reached the conclusion we are innately poor at math. The long-term impact on our society is tremendous. The number of students choosing engineering and math as a career has declined and employers lack an adequate talent pool for important technical jobs. Workers from other countries will perform the important and serious jobs that determine our country's economic development and defense.

This trend is not because Americans are not smart enough, but because we have become uninterested in the type of thinking required for math and science. A culture of excess dominated by screen media directs us outward to novelty, fantasy, and entertainment. Math cannot compete. Someone who majors in math or science will not become Arnold Schwarzenegger.

The cumulative effect of declining math and analytical ability creates psychological symptoms—we avoid this type of thinking because it engenders anxiety from expected failure. The process filters down to difficulty in making meaningful comparisons and effective decisions. As a consequence, we are prone to developing false belief systems and terrible policy decisions. The development of our health care system provides a poignant example.

NOTES

1. U.S. News & World Report. (1997, March 31). Oprah: A heavenly body? Survey finds talk show host a celestial shoo-in, p. 18. David Myers, prominent author of psychology textbooks, suggests this example in support materials from McGraw-Hill as a way to introduce the self-serving bias.

2. Myers, D. (2005). The self in a social world. In *Social Psychology* (8th ed., pp. 66–72). New York: McGraw-Hill.

3. See U.S. Department of Education, National Center for Education Statistics. (2008); *Digest of Education Statistics, 2007* (NCES 2008-022), Chapter 3; National Science Board—Digest of Key Science and Engineering Indicators 2008: http://www.nsf.gov/statistics/digest08/start.htm; Baiggori,

M. (2008, July 15). Math and Engineering Education and Labor Information: Number of U.S. Science, Engineering graduates stagnate. http://news.medill.northwestern.edu/washington/news.aspx?id=94961; Lee, B. (2007, April 16). Hire anxiety: Faced with lack of engineers, tech firms press H-1B issue. *Los Angeles Business Journal.*

4. Bernard, C. (1957). *An introduction to the study of experimental medicine.* New York: Dover Publications (original work published 1865; English translation published 1927).

5. Fuchs, V. (1993). *The future of health policy.* Cambridge, MA: Harvard University Press. Fuchs cites a now outdated study about Medicare, which is Lubitz, J., & Prihoda, R. (1984). The use and cost of Medicare services in the last two years of life. *Health Care Financing Review,* 5 (3): 117–131.

6. Six Sigma is a quality management method that strives for near perfection. The method, a way to control for manufacturing defects, was originally developed at Motorola and then used at General Electric by CEO Jack Welch. "Sigmas" are a refined measurement of variability and standard deviation. Welch used the method but also his direct and personal leadership training to create incentives and turn GE around. Six Sigma training follows a karate model, issuing a Black Belt for those who become experts. Gap analysis is defined as business resource assessment tool that enables a company to compare actual performance with potential performance.

7. Byrne, J. (1998, June 8). How Jack Welch runs GE. Cover story, *Business Week.*

8. This exchange has been reported widely in sports coverage. Retrieved December 27, 2008 from http://www.inspirationalquotes4 u.com/jordanquotes/index.html.

9. Psychology textbooks refer to this as the Yerkes-Dodson Law. See Santrock, J. (2005). Motivation and emotion. In *Psychology 7* (pp. 426–427). New York: McGraw-Hill.

10. Galanter, M., Bosshard, J., & Bosshard, R. (n.d.). Misleading anecdotes about lawsuits. New York: Center for Justice & Democracy. Retrieved December 20, 2008 from www.centerjd.org/archives/issues-facts/stories/MB_2007anecdotes.php.

11. Levin, M. (2005, August 14). Legal urban legends hold sway; tall tales of outrageous jury awards have helped bolster business-led campaigns to overhaul the civil justice system. *Los Angeles Times,* p. C-1.

12. Ibid. See also Stella Awards: Six outrageous-but-real lawsuits show-case the need for tort reform. Retrieved December 27, 2008 from http://snopes.com/legal/lawsuits.asp.

13. Levin, M. (2005, August 15). Coverage of big awards for plaintiffs helps distort view of legal system; in most such cases, the verdicts are either later rejected or the amounts are severely lowered. *Los Angeles Times*, p. C1; Glaberson, W. (1999, June 6). The $2.9 million cup of coffee; when the verdict is just a fantasy. *The New York Times*. Retrieved December 27, 2008 from http://query.nytimes.com/gst/fullpage.html?res=9F06E4 DB1439F935A35755C0A96F958260&sec=&spon=&pagewanted=1.

14. Rand Corporation survey as cited in Levin, Coverage of big awards for plaintiffs helps distort view of legal system, p. C1.

15. Kurtz, H. (2003, June 23). A little snag in those frivolous suits. U.S. News's examples were "myths." *The Washington Post*; Mencimer, S. (October 2004). False alarm; how the media helps the insurance industry and the GOP promote the myth of America's "lawsuit crisis." *The Washington Monthly*.

16. Bush wants more litigation limits; the President signs a bill shifting most large class-action suits from state to federal courts. (2005, February 19). *Los Angeles Times*, p. A-23.

17. Researchers report: "The cost of defending U.S. malpractice claims is estimated at $6.5 billion in 2001, only 0.46 percent of total health spending. The two most important reasons for higher U.S. spending appear to be higher incomes and higher medical care prices." See Anderson, G. F., Hussey, P. S., Frogner, B. K., & Waters, H. R. (2005). Health spending in the United States and the rest of the world. *Health Affairs*, 24 (4): 903–914.

18. The California law called MICRA passed in 1975 when Governor Jerry Brown responded to malpractice insurance crisis. The law, which limits noneconomic damages to $250,000, is considered to have solved the crisis and to having controlled malpractice insurance premiums in California since that time.

19. The case was *Faragher v. City of Boca Raton*, decided in June 1998. In this case, female lifeguards quit their jobs and filed a suit against the city for sexual harassment by male supervisors. The case questioned whether employers are always responsible for employees' behaviors, even if the employer is not fully aware of behavior or if efforts or procedures in place to curb misbehaviors did not work. The original decision holding

the employer responsible was reversed on appeal. The U.S. Supreme Court upheld the original decision and reversed the appellate court. The lack of a policy on sexual harassment and its dissemination to employees was a factor. Employers are now fully aware that such policies are needed and that all employees must know the policies and consequences. This is part of what is called an affirmative defense, which limits liability.

20. Lott, J. (1998). *More guns, less crime* (p. 9). Chicago: University of Chicago Press.

21. Ibid., p. 115.

22. Hemenway, D. (1998). More guns, less crime: Understanding crime and gun-control laws / Making a killing: The business of guns in America. *The New England Journal of Medicine* (27): 2029–2030; Ayres, I., Donohue III, J. (2003). Shooting down the "More Guns, Less Crime" hypothesis. *Stanford Law Review*, 55 (4): 1193; Glenn, D. (2003). "More Guns, Less Crime" thesis rests on a flawed statistical design, scholars argue. *The Chronicle of Higher Education*, 49 (35): A18. Retrieved December 27, 2008 from http://chronicle.com/weekly/v49/i35/35a01801.htm.

23. Mooney, C. (2003, October 13). Double barreled double standards. *Mother Jones.*

24. Santrock, J. (2005). Chapter 2. In *Psychology 7* (p. 42). New York: McGraw-Hill.

25. Higgins, M. (2006, April 11). Best seller leads scholar to file lawsuit: Defamation allegation targets U. of C. author. *Chicago Tribune.*

26. Glenn, D. (2007, August 10). Dueling economists reach settlement in defamation lawsuit. *The Chronicle of Higher Education*, 53 (49): 10.

27. Vines, V., & McDonald, H. (2004, December 16). Data on firearms and violence too weak to settle policy debates; comprehensive research effort needed. (Press release for the report *Firearms and violence: A critical review.*) Washington, D.C.: National Academy of Sciences. Retrieved December 27, 2008 from http://www8.nationalacademies.org/onpinews/newsitem.aspx?RecordID=10881.

28. Hanley, C. (2003, August 11). Powell's case for Iraq war falls apart 6 months later. *The Associated Press.* Retrieved December 22, 2008 from http://www.commondreams.org/headlines03/0811-09.htm.

29. Demonstrated effectiveness of source credibility or perceived expertise and trustworthiness in the field of social psychology. See Myers,

D. (2005). Persuasion. In *Social Psychology* (8th ed., pp. 250–252). New York: McGraw-Hill.

30. The issue was followed closely in a series of articles, Case study; Dr. Harvey G. Klein. See Willman, D. (2004, December 22). Public pays for blood expert's advice, and so do firms. *Los Angeles Times*, p. A-27.

31. Willman, D. (2004, December 22). The National Institutes of Health: Public servant or private marketer? *Los Angeles Times*, December 22, 2004, p. A-1.

32. Willman, D. (2005, March 10). Three researchers in NIH controversy are leaving. *Los Angeles Times*, p. A-14.

33. Ibid.

34. Willman, D. (2006, August 10). Congress to probe policies at NIH. *Los Angeles Times*, p. A-14.

35. The sick NIH. (2004, December 23). *Los Angeles Times, Opinion* section, p. B-12.

36. Harvard psychologist Daniel Gilbert, author of *Stumbling on Happiness*, cites the medical resident study and sums up the research in this opinion column. See Gilbert, D. (2006, April 16). I'm OK, you're biased. *The New York Times*. Retrieved December 27, 2008 from http://www.nytimes.com/2006/04/16/opinion/16gilbert.html.

37. Philipkoski, K. (2004, February 18). Scientists: Bush distorts science. *Wired Magazine*.

38. Balzar, J. (2002, January 11). Debunking the big spender myth. *Los Angeles Times*, p. B-17.

39. Ibid.

40. American Prospect Staff. (2004, December 20). Dossier: Red state values; what really goes on in morally elite states, p. 7. Retrieved December 21, 2008 from http://www.prospect.org/cs/articles?articleId=8971.

41. Research in this area by John Jost and others at New York University includes the importance of how ideology develops, what motivates people to act on ideology, regional differences, and underlying psychological differences between liberalism and conservatism. See Jost, J. (October 2006). The end of the end of ideology. *American Psychologist*, 61 (7): 651–670.

42. Cohen, R., & Bell, P. (2007, February 3). Congressional insiders poll. *National Journal*. Retrieved December 27, 2008 from http://

syndication.nationaljournal.com/images/203Insiderspoll_NJlogo.pdf; Chait, J. (2007, March 25). Why the GOP goes nuclear over global warming. *Los Angeles Times, Opinion,* p. M-2.

43. Gilbert, D. (2006, July 2). If only gay sex caused global warming. *Los Angeles Times, Opinion,* p. M-1.

44. Schaie, K. Warner. (1996). *Intellectual development in adulthood: The Seattle Longitudinal Study.* New York: Cambridge University Press.

45. The researchers describe the data this way: "On the other hand a curvilinear cohort pattern has been found for Number skills reaching a peak with the 1924 birth cohort and negative slope thereafter." See Schaie, K. Warner, Willis, S., & Caskie, G. L. L. (June 2004). The Seattle Longitudinal Study: Relationship between personality and cognition. *NeuroPsychology Cognition,* 11:304–324.

46. Cohort effects are a result of a person's time of birth, era, or generation but not the result of actual age. The effects are particularly important in assessment of adult intelligence as in Schaie, *Intellectual development in adulthood.*

47. Berger, K. S. (2006). The school years: Cognitive development. In *The developing person: Through childhood and adolescence* (7th ed., p. 375). New York: Worth Publishers.

48. Trends in math and science, 2003 international study (as cited in ibid.). See also http://timss.bc.edu.

49. Ibid.

50. Bauerlein, M. (2008). Knowledge deficits. In *The dumbest generation: How the digital age stupefies young Americans and jeopardizes our future* (pp. 17–26). New York: Jeremy P. Tarkin/Penguin.

51. Stevenson research (as cited in Berger, K. S., 2006, pp. 378–379).

52. Information on Japanese schools (as cited in Berger, K. S., 2006, pp. 378–379).

53. Stevenson research (as cited in Berger, K. S., 2006, pp. 378–379).

54. Berger, K. S. (2006). Adolescence: Cognitive development. In *The developing person: Through childhood and adolescence* (7th ed., pp. 469–470). New York: Worth Publishers.

55. Santrock, J. (2007). Achievement, work, and careers. In *Adolescence* (pp. 389–390). New York: McGraw-Hill.

56. Ibid.

57.  Gordon, M. (2006, August 11). When B's are better. *The Chronicle of Higher Education*, 52 (49): B1.

58.  Healy, P. (2002, June 6). 91 percent to graduate with honors. *Boston Globe*.

59.  Schultz, D., & Schultz, S. E. (2006). Performance appraisal. In *Psychology & Work Today* (9th ed., p. 132). Upper Saddle River, NJ: Prentice Hall.

# Chapter 5

# HEALTH CARE: WASTE, EXCESS, AND BROKERS

*STEWART:* Are you saying the American public shouldn't have access to the same quality health care that we give to our better citizens?

*KRISTOL:* To our soldiers? Absolutely. [*Crowd boos*]

*KRISTOL:* explaining that soldiers get paid less, but "one way we make it up to" them is by giving them "first-class health care." "I feel like you trapped me somehow."

*STEWART:* I just want to get this on record—Bill Kristol just said that the government can run a first-class health care system.

*KRISTOL:* Sure it can. [*Crowd applauds*]

*STEWART:* And a government-run system is better than a private health care system. [*Kristol backtracks*]

*STEWART:* [*summing up*] So what you are suggesting is that the government could run the best health care system for Americans, but it's a little too costly, so we should have the shitty insurance company health care.

> —*The Daily Show*, July 28, 2009. Jon Stewart interview
> with Bill Kristol, editor of *Weekly Standard* and avid
> conservative opponent to government health care.[1]

Nothing irritates conservatives more than when Michael Moore refers to free health care. Obviously, health care is not free, and the distraction only fuels the antiliberal attacks against Moore. Unfortunately, the political attacks do not allow us to get down to a comprehensive cost-benefit analysis comparing today's health care "system" with a proposed national health care plan.

The dramatic insistence on free market principles and competition determines the way health care is delivered today. The entire process exemplifies the culture of excess and cultural narcissism. The excess comes from the tremendous waste of money and resources. This is coupled with the ability of brokers and corporate entities to overcharge and take out money at everyone else's expense. These are the entitled "me" in the equation. The rest of us continue to pay more and more and even get less and less. Or, many just cannot afford health care at all. Facts and meaningful comparisons are dismissed and not considered by the fear of an alternative labeled as Socialism.

The health care issue splits the positions of both political parties. The Republicans bash "government-run health care" even though their party led the fight to pass the Medicare bill in 2003. This bill was passed in the middle of the night, with the grossly unethical behavior of the leadership who kept the vote open for several hours while they woke up President Bush and lobbied members of Congress to change their votes. Controversy followed. Accusations flew and investigations ensued from charges that the bill's costs were tremendously understated and that arm twisting transpired to get yes votes. But the bill did pass, considered by many to be a huge endowment to Big Pharma.[2]

On the other hand, the Democrats propose mixed models, described as a "compromise," in an attempt to preserve the godlike free market and profiteering of the major health care players. Those who propose health care reform are always shut down by those arguing against "government-run" programs and so-called socialism. While the government Medicare program provides health care benefits for a dramatically growing population who are aging and living longer, the rest of the working folks pretty much need to rely on their employers for health care coverage.

But the number of people privately insured is not as big as you might think. In fact, about 60 percent of health care is *publicly* funded.[3] As an example, in California, 60 percent of deliveries are paid for by the government-run Medi-Cal system. More than half of pregnant women in California receive care from this basic and poorly funded medical program.[4]

The barriers to reforming health care in the United States are political ones, and many have advocated an incremental rather than a comprehensive approach. Hillary Clinton is still lampooned for putting forward a government-run health care plan. But after about 20 years of social/economic experiments within the free market, it is hard to imagine that anything else can be tried. The Kaiser Family Foundation in 2005 reported that premiums for health care for family coverage have increased by 59 percent since 2000.[5] That is six times the rate of inflation. The upward trend continues unabated. Health care costs rose 7.2 percent in 2004 and another 6.9 percent in 2005, an increase that was heralded as a success, since it was the smallest increase since 1999.[6] The 2007 data shows an increase of 6.1 percent from 2006. The health share of GDP is expected to hold steady in 2006–2007 before resuming its historical upward trend. Experts predict that health care spending will reach 19.6 percent of GDP by 2016.[7] The nation spent $2.4 *trillion* on health care in 2008, or about approximately 17 percent of GDP. This amount is 4.3 times greater than what is spent on national defense. Average cost per person is now a staggering $7,421 and rising.[8] In addition, increased costs are simply passed on to the patient. In 2006, out-of-pocket expenses increased 3.3 percent for patients. This was followed by another 5.3 percent increase in 2007.[9] All of this with 46 million or more still uninsured.

And here is the kicker. Comparative outcome studies of U.S. health care with that of other industrialized countries show Americans do not live longer or have better health.[10] In 2006, a major comparative study with Great Britain reported results that Americans at every income level had more illness than the Brits.[11]

The staggering growth figures in health care come after years of "managed care," which free market advocates touted as a silver bullet for controlling costs. The amount of waste and inefficiency is truly staggering. But the human "costs," and the consequential larger ethical and moral issues, far exceed any rationale for insisting on a free market health care design.

Most health care professionals realize the battle was lost a long time ago. The insurance industry has won. Wall Street companies completely control health care delivery and they profit handsomely. Today, many doctors are paid lower rates of reimbursement for their services than 10 years ago. Worse, more is expected of them. Mental health care professionals receive the same rate of reimbursement for an outpatient mental health session as when managed care first started 20 years ago. In some cases even less. Keep in mind that the economic stagnation for health care professionals has occurred against a backdrop of the greatest economic growth our country has ever seen in the middle to late 1990s. But not for doctors, hospitals, and health care professionals. Meanwhile, there are huge profits year after year for the conglomerates that dictate health care. It should be no surprise that doctors are retiring early, and trauma/emergency rooms are closing and becoming few and far between.[12] Despite an economy that is always evaluated on whether there is job creation, and a constant critique that there are not enough jobs, we have a nursing shortage.[13] Why wouldn't the laws of supply and demand solve the problem of a nursing shortage when there is an active demand for job creation? Morale and professionalism in health care are waning, choked by a free market culture that dictates price controls and what doctors and health care professionals are paid. Despite these attempts to control the cost of health care, costs continue to increase.

Managed care was supposed to be the mechanism to control health care costs. What is so remarkable is that there was *never* any solid evidence that it worked. But that did not stop the marketplace from the irony of having the private sector *regulate* health care. Even as far back as 1989, the Institute of Medicine established a task force to investigate utilization management by third parties. Their publication reported that:

> It is an unfortunate reality, however, that most cost containment strategies eventually disappoint its supporters and evaluators to some degree; even when strategies seem to reduce costs initially, projections do not appear to show an appreciably lower increase in total cost over the long run.[14]

Notice the particular wording and reference to "the long run." Everyone gets excited when initial savings appear, but over time—well, that's another story. The verdict is in. Over time, managed care has failed. Unfortunately, the conclusion by the Institute of Medicine has been ignored, and other government studies have never been integrated into decision making. In a comprehensive investigation of managed care by employers, the General Accounting Office (GAO) in 1993 issued a report finding "little empirical evidence" of cost savings to employers.[15] The GAO report cites the difficulties in determining true cost savings. The tremendous diversity in types of claims, frequent switching of plans by employees and employers, the size of the physician network, and even the geographic location of the managed care plan were variables that made meaningful comparisons nearly impossible.

But managed care and "utilization review" rolled on in the marketplace. In the 1990s, before the battle was lost, many professionals tried to point out the glaring conflict between for-profit health care and optimum patient care. Managed care companies sprang up everywhere and business and corporations loved them. During this time, managed care focused on not just medical services but also mental health care. Experts reported that managed care was probably spending about half of what they should have on mental health care. Drastic cutbacks in care and medications ensued with not just declining outcomes but horror stories.[16] Eventually, the drastic procedures of managed care led to the passing of the Mental Health Parity Act in 1996. This federal law forces insurance companies to provide adequate care to serious diagnoses, including major depression. But the draconian managed care in the 1990s made these companies the darlings of Wall Street. They were the hot companies you wanted in your portfolio. Here is an example of one managed care company, Foundation Health, as described in *Money* magazine in 1996.

*HMO Phenom Foundation Health* (ticker symbol: FH; NYSE, $38; no dividend).

This $3 billion provider of managed health care, based in Rancho Cordova near Sacramento, is betting big on California. Residents already account for about half of Foundation's 1.3 million HMO members. New HMO contracts commencing later this year will double the state's membership to 1.3 million, some 68 percent of the total. In April, moreover, the firm landed a five-year deal with the Defense Department to supply group health services to 720,000 military retirees and dependents located largely in California. Foundation also derives about 13 percent of revenues from workers' comp insurance sold mostly in the state. This concentration in California's expanding employment pool helps create the economics of scale crucial to sustaining profit growth. Analyst Bill Jacobs of Chicago's Harris Associates, which owns 6 percent of FH's stock, sees profits rising 15 percent in calendar '96 to $3.15 a share, a price/earnings multiple of 13, and another 17 percent in '97. That looks like a steal to him—and me—compared with the 22 P/E that $3.6 billion U.S. Healthcare, an East Coast HMO chain, commanded when it agreed in April to be acquired for $8.9 billion by $13 billion insurer Aetna. What could FH's $38 stock fetch in 12 months? "I'm aiming for $62, or more than 60 percent," says Jacobs.[17]

An HMO "phenom," Foundation Health was raring to go. HMOs were the rage and known for limiting treatment for mental health and even depression—one of the costliest and most pervasive problems in our culture today.[18] Note the excitement about this in *Money* magazine. The juxtaposition above shows the perverse incentives for health care in a Wall Street model. If a health care company announces they will curtail mental health care, eliminate vaccination shots or preventative screenings for its subscribers, the analysts will love it and recommend the stock as ready to go. In contrast, if a health care company announced it was going to add preventative screenings or increase mental health services, this company would be a bad investment.

The process or mechanism that kept health care alive and operating in the 1990s and into the twenty-first century was managed care. Free market proponents constantly cited how well it worked. Yes, it worked, but for the total benefit of the for-profit health care companies. In the late 1980s and early 1990s, a dramatic cost shifting occurred through managed care.[19] Instead of the health care dollars going to doctors and hospitals, they went to the "fiscal intermediary," or in effect, a middleman. These brokers redirected the money and thus the control of health care to private insurance companies.

No better an example of a middleman or brokerage for health care exists than the tremendous financial success of UnitedHealth Group (UHG). UHG rose to prominence under the leadership of CEO and physician William McGuire, whom *Forbes* ranked as one of the highest compensated CEOs in 2005 at a total compensation package of $124.5 million, derived primarily from stock options.[20] *Fortune* described UHG as one of their "most admired companies," due to McGuire's "innovation." By ratcheting down costs, contracts, delivery systems, and payments, UHG grew from a $600 million regional health plan to a $70 billion global giant. During McGuire's term, UHG grew at a rate that was 30 times greater than the Standard and Poor's Index. UHG produced a return on investment that was 8,453 percent.[21] No wonder he was so popular. All this "success" sprung not from developing new treatments or medications, but from acting as a middleman in the paperwork morass of health care delivery.

But in 2006, there was trouble in River City. McGuire had cashed in huge amounts of stock options, and in one of the crimes du jour of today's overpaid executives, he timed exercising his options for maximum gain. By illegally backdating when a stock option was granted to a day when the company stock was low, a person can ensure he receives the greatest gain when cashing in the option. The *Wall Street Journal* analyzed 12 of McGuire's stock option grants from 1994 to 2002, each timed noticeably to his advantage. The newspaper reported that if the options had been

randomly dated, the odds of these options occurring at such an advantageous time for McGuire would be 1 in 200 million.[22] This resulted in
one more countless executive investigation.

McGuire ended up settling with the SEC, the UHG special litigations
committee, and CalPERS, the powerful California Public Employees'
Retirement System. (CalPERS lost money when the stock price declined
amidst the controversy.) Reports stated that McGuire personally paid
$30 million in the class action suit involving CalPERS and UHG paid
$895 million. McGuire also surrendered 3,675 million shares of stock
options.[23] Again, in the culture of excess, note the magnitude of the "settlement"—$895 million by UHG. How much health care would that buy?
How many people ever see that much money?

The exact mechanisms involved in being a health care broker and
middleman involves controlling the contracts and rates. The UHG paradigm after McGuire continues. In February 2008, the New York State
Attorney General investigated Ingenix, Inc., whose parent company is
UHG. Ingenix is a company that forms databases to determine "reasonable and customary rates" for health care services. These databases are
then used to resolve disputes, especially when "out-of-network" services
are obtained by the patient. The investigation found that the process was a
scheme that ended up defrauding consumers. Ingenix provided data on
costs to the insurance companies that were much lower than the actual
cost of customary medical services. In other words, the process was
rigged. The end result was justification for the insurance companies to
deny portions of doctors' and hospitals' claims, and push the cost and balance down to all of us. Consumers had the pleasure of getting overcharged
for services they received that were "out of network." UHG settled in
2009 agreeing to pay $50 million to set up a new database for claims,
and another $350 million to the American Medical Association and other
health care providers.[24]

The excess of this brokering hurts all of us and there are many varia-
tions. Another interesting derivative of the middleman process in health
care is the practice of keeping prices steady while curtailing benefits
through the fine print, see-if-you-can-find-it details in an insurance policy.
Through this economic sleight of hand, managed care advocates point to
overall costs and say they were steady. Indeed, the cost of the policy
may be the same, but the profit margin is maintained by curtailing benefits, usually buried in fine print mailings that subscribers easily ignore.
Of course, this still goes on today but since health care is now in a crisis
mode, it is more noticeable. How often can benefits be curtailed and cut

before people notice? Even if we pay the same amount, we are getting less. Then when rates go up again, we are paying more *and* getting less.

It would be as if you went to the grocery store to buy your favorite can of vegetable soup. Noticing an increase in the price of some other cans of soup, you are pleased your favorite is the same price. But then when you take it home and sit down to eat, you notice something is wrong. It does not taste the same, because there are fewer vegetables and more water. The soup has been diluted. As the 1990s progressed, we continuously experienced a diluted health care system. Even today, many people have expensive policies that cover very little, falsely believing they are insured. In the free market of health care, all sorts of these broker activities are employed to reap huge profits. The entire manipulative process is a familiar paradigm of cultural narcissism.

## PSYCHOSOCIAL DESPAIR

The broker activities in health care lead to a devaluation of the professional health care worker. This is also part of a larger problem; that is, the larger problem of the exportation of jobs, and general devaluation of many skilled American workers. But in health care, many express little sympathy for doctors whom they believe are overpaid in the first place. And doctors and hospitals certainly brought managed care upon themselves by overcharging in a fee-for-service model, or actually a free-for-all-service model. The standing and image of doctors in the public eye has declined in unison with that of college professors and lawyers (especially trial lawyers). In the mind-set of a society immersed in wealth over ability, professionals are not as well respected, and can even be attacked. The attitude toward professionals today is more like "you owe me—I am paying for it," and when some professionals charge several hundred dollars an hour, a part of this attitude may be understandable. When our currency becomes devalued, experts and the government respond dramatically to the crisis. But no one responds to the devaluation of the professional worker with recommendations and solutions to the problem. In health care, there is little concern that a very well educated professional works harder and gets paid less.

The issue is one best described as psychosocial and not economic, because it involves our underlying philosophy of what is fair and what a community really needs. But today's marketplace makes it difficult for a well-educated, well-intentioned, and hard working health care professional to find full opportunity. Constantly struggling for a competitive salary or reimbursement, a professional today must have the inner strength to tolerate the ratchet down competition and to keep getting better at what they do. The spirit and drive of a professional worker to offer high-quality work has been crushed. Time and again doctors and other experienced professionals tell you they cannot wait to "get out," and to retire.

This devaluation and psychosocial despair has an impact on the quality of all of our lives, an effect that has just begun. A major characteristic of cultural narcissism will be fewer people seeking a professional career or vocation, and instead seeking the broker jobs where it is possible to get in the middle of large amounts of money and take out as much as you can for yourself. One or two big deals might do it and make you wealthy. Health care is a representative example of today's societal conflict. Should a doctor provide quality service or become a broker? How long can health care professionals take reimbursements that are the same or less than 10 years ago? Today's professional, educated, and skilled worker must show tremendous psychological capacity and integration to accept the economic fact that the more skilled they become, the less they are valued, the less they are paid. The ironic and negative impact of the current economic environment leads to what I call psychosocial despair, and I often wonder if this is the underlying root of such a high growth in depression.

Overall, the psychosocial despair is harder to stomach because it really is rooted in the hypocrisy of it all. The private sector's valiant and passionate desire to preserve the free market and avoid government-run health care has resulted in the sledge hammer regulation of managed care. But regulatory mechanisms and price controls do not allow the laws of supply and demand to work in health care. Instead of acknowledging that controlling costs is essential for the common good and for our nation as a whole, we deceive ourselves with a belief that health care operates in the free market system, and that is what is best for everyone. It is the American way. But it is only best for the big players in health care, and the doctors and hospitals are in quicksand. The more they move and try to get out, the deeper they sink.

Despite it all, we have mostly a public health care system already. The part that is private is highly regulated by the health care conglomerates through managed care. Managed care reflects a basic premise that processes and mechanisms proceed based on profit and unlimited success for a few, and not on any objective evidence of cost efficiency or containment. The proof seems finally evident, after 15 years of managed care, health care premiums are soaring. The false pretense of managed care may now be a bubble ready to burst. Managed care can now be evaluated as a social/economic or social psychology experiment gone awry. When business profiteers say it works, it reminds me of that old health care joke: The operation was a complete success, but the patient died.


## ADMINISTRATIVE OVERLOAD: PAPER COVERS ROCK

No one likes paperwork. If anything frustrates workers it is a job that day after day involves mounds of paperwork. In health care, electronic billing certainly helps and makes a profound contribution to the environment. Medicare now utilizes only electronic billing. Improvements, led by Newt Gingrich, have established efficient databases, speeded claims processing, and reduced medical errors.[25] But these efficiencies still ignore the elephant in the room: how health care is funded.

Health care advocates have stated the obvious for years. The amount of waste in the United States in health care bureaucracy costs more in dollars than it would take to provide health care coverage for all of the 40 million plus who are uninsured. In other words, pure administrative overload, if eliminated, could save enough money to solve the problem of the uninsured. In 2003, estimates of administrative expenses are at about $399.4 *billion*. That is 24 percent of the total health care expenditures for 2003, estimated at $1,660.5 billion.[26] (Others have estimated this figure to be as high as 30%.) Using these figures, 24¢ on each dollar in health care is spent not on direct services to patients, but on paperwork and administration. Compare this amount to the general rule that 10 percent is a ballpark figure for administrative costs for an ongoing business concern. Imagine the amount of people involved in this administrative process. In fact, the number of people employed in health care administration provides a counterargument to changing health care to a universal plan or streamlining the administration and eliminating waste. That is a lot of people who could lose their jobs. And in an era where all we hear is the importance of jobs, jobs, jobs, this is a major barrier to health care reform.

The Canadian government-run, "socialistic" health care system provides a stark contrast. The United States spends about $752 more per person per year than the Canadian system.[27] The data is cited by well-known health care researchers and doctors, David Himmelstein and Steffie Woolhandler, and was reported in the *New England Journal of Medicine* (*NEJM*) in 2003. Their study reported overhead costs for U.S. insurance companies at 11.7¢ per dollar,[28] mostly for underwriting and advertising. Canada's system reported overhead costs of only 1.3¢ per dollar. Interestingly, private insurance companies in Canada reported overhead costs of 13.2¢ per dollar. Overall, this study concluded that administrative costs in the United States are 31 percent compared with 16.7 percent in Canada.[29] These estimates do not include other categories, such as the advertising costs of drug companies or hospitals, the profits of the health care industry, or the time spent by patients filling out paperwork. We would *never* consider or try to calculate an economic value to all the time patients and their families spend trying to deal with health care administration. Like the low man on the totem pole, you are stuck with the worst—left holding the bag or the long forms to complete. The administrative overload is a constant complaint of doctors who report they have to hire several assistants to deal with all the paperwork and different insurance companies.

(Henry Aaron of the Brookings Institution responded to the August 2003 *NEJM* article with an editorial that stated the figures were exaggerated and that the administrative costs were not that high.[30] But even if Aaron is right, the figures and waste should be completely unacceptable.)

Basic business principles that would minimize the costs of doing business are not a standard in private health care. In order to maintain and squeeze a profit from the health care financial structure, many people need to be hired to implement managed care, and to enforce policy restrictions. While this siphons profits, the amount of money is so large, there is still plenty left over for the huge private sector players. In other words, it is OK to have huge and wasteful administrative costs if the end result is profit for the private sector.

I like to ask older students, especially those with work experience, to estimate Medicare's administrative costs. "It must be huge," one student responds. With coaxing, I get answers of from 10 percent to 25 percent. Although almost 60 percent of U.S. health care is publicly funded, the misconception that the private sector is more efficient than the public sector is widely held. This is another inherent belief and association of a culture that operates on for-profit entrepreneurial narcissism and not facts. For years, the public Medicare system has had administrative costs of around 3 percent. The *NEJM* article reported a figure of 3.6 percent.[31] Consider the implications, especially since it is *our* tax dollars, a statement that should be equivalent to it is "your money" or "my money." More than 96¢ of each dollar is spent on *direct* health care for Medicare recipients. The private sector and free market gurus must be totally embarrassed to realize the federal government is more efficient than the private sector in delivering health care.

Well, it is easy to see why. Medicare does not try to make huge profits. The head honcho or CEO equivalent makes six figures, but not millions with a golden parachute. Medicare does not have to advertise. It is designed to benefit everyone and to use tax dollars efficiently, rather than trying to squeeze out more profits.

The 2003 Medicare prescription drug provision for seniors pollutes this pure rationale because it includes private sector drug companies who can charge high costs for medications paid for by taxpayers. Soon after the controversial pork barrel bill was passed, the drug companies raised their prices.[32] Worse yet, with unbelievable hypocrisy, the regulations in the bill prohibit purchasing medications in bulk or by mail from Canada or any other country. (Many people do it anyway.) In other words, when free market Republicans passed a bill that tapped into tax dollars, they eliminated competition, a hallmark of an open and free market. No regulations or restrictions prohibit U.S. companies from outsourcing jobs overseas, but global competition to purchase drugs is not allowed! It is OK to outsource your job to another country for a lower wage and increased company profits, but as individuals we cannot profit or save money by purchasing high-cost medications from another country. The potential savings here for Americans is huge, as many widely used drugs sell for twice as much in the United States as elsewhere.[33] Again, keep in mind the significance of high costs to Medicare, already over strapped and burdened, and that this bill was passed at a time when we are experiencing the highest budget deficit ever. Medicare gets a bad rap, especially since it covers the high-risk population—the older person who is more likely to get sick. Medicare is tainted by the global opinion that government-run means inefficient and that the private sector and for-profit mode is always best.

The huge advertising expenditures in the private health care sector are considered a sacrament and never questioned. The way in which to spend one's money or profit, whether it is that of an individual or a company, is one of the strongest and most self-centered, private "rights" to be found. The mantras are: "It's my money—and you better keep your hands off it" and "It's my money—and I can spend it whatever way I want." Mantras are written in the scroll on business TV programs—"your money" or "it's your money." (When the market closes each day, commentators on business news ask: "Do you know where your money is?") More important than the Constitution or the Bible, these mantras, I believe, are more often repeated (outwardly or to oneself) than the often heard "no government bureaucrat is going to tell me what to do."

But let us follow the money in health care through one simple example. Say you are watching a baseball game on TV. As the pitcher peers in at the catcher you notice the backdrop. Banners are everywhere advertising a large health care company. Few have any qualms with this. The cost of such advertising is huge and a prominent ad like this can easily be five or six figures. Rotating boards allow exposure for many more advertisers and greater profits for the ball team. At the commercial break, a nostalgic advertisement for baseball shows a family going to a game and using their VISA card, so they will not miss out on those special moments just because the prices are so high. Follow the money. You and your employer pay very high health care premiums. Then the health care company uses this money to pay high advertising costs at a ball game. In turn, the team owners pay their players CEO-type salaries. So, Barry Bonds and many other players make millions, subsidized by advertising fees from health care companies. This is true America and cannot be questioned. If you question this process, you automatically get an indignant response of our ingrained cultural narcissism: So what? So what is wrong with that? They can spend their money anyway they want, and they are increasing their business. Press the point, and you may be labeled a communist. These issues are sacrosanct. But just remember, if you are micromanaged into diluted health care treatment, a generic medication, or denied a new medication that you want and your doctor recommends, or if you are forced to reduce frequency of mental health or physical therapy treatment—well, just remember all the health care spending in advertising, including the couple in their backyard hot tubs after having sex.

I am not against advertising, but in health care I see the important dollars we need for care transferred to entertainment. But maybe as a free market advocate you believe that productivity depends on paying people well. So, Barry Bonds and Mark McGwire hit 70 plus home runs because they are paid so well, right? And where would we be if that did not happen? After all, imagine how much business is generated when a player hits 70 home runs. "It's good for baseball" and "it's good for business."

## THE MORAL CONSEQUENCES

You do not have to be a Nobel Prize–winning economist to ask the obvious question. If health care premiums are dramatically increasing, and doctors and hospitals are being paid the same or less, where is the money going? In standard business thinking, increased income and spending means your business is growing. And health care spending continues to grow. The annual amount spent in the United States is now above two trillion, or about twice as much as other countries spend—countries that have a health care system that is comprehensive and covers *all* its citizens.[34] But health care is different and does not fit the free market model or way of thinking that bigger is best, and we should grow, grow, and grow. Continued growth in the health care system means greater inefficiency. Economist Robert Kuttner coins it well when he says that health care involves "extra market values."[35] By this he means health care's impact in saving lives places it in a special category outside marketplace values. If you are injured or require immediate care, doctors are obligated to save your life and provide emergency care, even if you are homeless and without means to pay. In fact, it is the law—we mandate it. Hospitals and doctors must provide care even if they may not be paid for their services.

(To compensate, hospitals may file a lien on someone's house or a negative on a credit report. I recall an incident when my mother was furious when she discovered months after she had been hospitalized that a negative had been placed on her credit report. The hospital kept aggressively sending bills that her HMO contested but eventually paid. But it took too long, and the hospital expected my mother to pay the bill, so they filed a credit negative. Hospitals and doctors are amazingly aggressive, trying to survive the crazy game of trying to get paid for their services, and yes, trying to overcharge too. Sometimes doctors who are specialists will bill the patient even when the referral will be covered by the managed care insurer, such as a PPO or HMO plan, hoping the good and cooperative patient will send in a check.)

So herein is a sliver of good news. Emergency rooms are the manifestation of our society's recognition that there are exceptions, extra market values that are for the common good. Unfortunately, those values place an economic burden on some that threaten the safety net. The costs of emergency rooms are staggering. When patients do not have a doctor, they often seek care in an emergency room when it is not a real emergency. This is a significant factor in the increasing costs of health care.[36]

The health care crisis has a huge conflict in paying for emergency services. Insurance and managed care companies try hard to ratchet down what they will pay, as nothing will eliminate their profits faster, and the intense financial Armageddon has had a negative impact. Emergency rooms and trauma centers are closing—big time, especially in large cities. In Los Angeles so many have closed because they cannot make ends meet, it is frightening.[37] Today, if you have an auto accident in Los

Angeles, considerable time may elapse before getting you to the closest emergency room. Anyone well insured or not can die simply for lack of resources. One response, it seems, to Kuttner's extra market values is to simply get out of the business. Emergency services that cannot cover their costs cannot stay in business. More and more doctors dread the weekend or days they may be on ER duty and would rather opt out. But now there are fewer facilities anyway, and the general public is unaware of the consequences. After all, we often do not read the fine print in our health care policy until we get sick. Who has the time?

The ER system has a defined role in the importance of saving lives. Unfortunately, the misuse, overuse, and financial battles or fair price and pay in our market system are demolishing the system as a whole. But at least here we see concern or awareness of moral consequences. The rest of the health care financing mechanisms for ongoing care exclude many people. It should be unsurprising that some 46 million people who are uninsured are at risk for poorer health outcomes. The Institute of Medicine reports that 18,000 young adults die every year simply because they lack health insurance.[38] That is, persons who do not have coverage do not receive an adequate level of care for chronic illnesses. This comes out to 1,500 people each month. When terrorists killed 3,000 on September 11, there was a tremendous response. Yet that many die every two months without a word—a reality that is beyond moral consequences. Just as awful is the fact that the United States has a higher per capita mortality rate for infants than some Third World countries.[39] It is survival of the fittest out there, so do not lose your coverage. The extra market values of emergency care do not go any farther. If you have an accident or unexpected illness—good luck to you. Perhaps it will happen at a time and place that you will get adequate care.

By now, everyone is certainly burdened by increasing health care premiums, co-pays, and less coverage. A report on the increasing bankruptcies filed in the United States highlights the seriousness of the problem.[40] Half of all bankruptcies filed listed costs of health care as the reason. In other words, the financial costs of an accident or serious illness sank American workers into bankruptcy. Even more alarming, of those who cited this reason, 75 percent had health care insurance! That is, even with insurance coverage, you are susceptible to high costs for recovery and treatment that would overwhelm your finances. More recent reports indicate that the problem and vulnerability of Americans is getting worse.[41] All this if you just happen to be an unfortunate soul who has an accident or gets seriously ill. (Should this be your fate, I hope you will remember the bold advertisements for health care companies that you saw at the ball game or on TV.)

Even more appalling is the belief that you have a health policy only to have it pulled out from under you, or claims denied, because the insurance company probes your approved application to find evidence you lied or had a "preexisting condition." So many cases of this type of bait and switch have occurred in Southern California that former Los Angeles City Attorney Rocky Delgadillo decided to investigate. In an unprecedented move, Delgadillo set up a "prosecutor sponsored website" to collect information from patients and health care providers to assist him into fraud investigations of insurance companies.[42]

In the end analysis, the health care system is not really a system, but a nonsystem. There is nothing about it designed to protect you or assist you. If you get sick and need an intensive level of care, you must have the capacity to battle and argue with the managed care soldiers to get full coverage and the best-quality treatment. I guess we could say we have a great health care system—as long as you do not get sick.

If you are uninsured and need care, patients are now seeking services in Mexico, Singapore, New Zealand, and India. Even with travel costs, the savings for a surgery or treatment can amount to 60–90 percent. And the patient is treated like a guest, with much attention. Who could possibly imagine that? Last year approximately three-quarters of a million Americans paid for their own care abroad, or even received partial payment from their well-pleased insurance companies who were delighted to cover costs at low rates. U.S. patients can even be assisted by "medical travel companies" for their foreign trip.[43] As the quality of care improves in other countries, more of this will occur—unless, like the Medicare bill, Congress bans it.

## STRIKE ONE, TWO, THREE . . .

The economic holy wars of health care coverage and costs have a tremendous negative impact on our economy and interpersonal relationships. Recent workers' strikes are examples. In 2004, union grocery workers in California went on strike.[44] The primary reason? Health care costs. These grocery workers had what has now become a rare luxury in their benefits. They had health care benefits that were generous and had little or no co-payments. In addition, they did not have to pay out of their salary for the premiums, which were drastically rising. Saying ouch, and trembling in fear from competing Wal-Mart Superstores, the company dug in and forced a confrontation with the union. In a classic showdown, the strike seemed to frustrate and anger others not involved, and the grocery workers seemed to get little public support. Typically they were viewed as overpaid and "entitled" because workers at other companies did not receive the same rich health care benefits.

One of my patients, John, a forty-something engineer and ardent Republican, was delighted when the Republican Party repeatedly stood up at their national convention to berate their nemesis Michael Moore. Working for a small company of about a hundred employees, he had to pay about half of his own health care costs and wondered why on earth these grocery workers thought they did not have to. In an amazing statement, he reported: "They're driving up health care costs for all of us." Coming from an antiliberal and free market Republican, this statement stunned me. How could the negotiations of one group of workers for lower health care costs drive up costs for health care premiums? If health care truly is in the free market, then shouldn't "customers" and purchasers have a choice to shop and take the best price per value? Isn't a marketplace all about competition? Of course, this is not possible in health care unless you are in a large group, and the union in representing the workers took a stand. But the general public did not take much fancy in those nasty unions trying to get out of their responsibility of paying for health care—simply because *they* were having to pay more for it. Who do they think they are? The competition can get ugly among working people to get a better deal in health care costs when they themselves have no control over the financing mechanisms and prices. Survival of the economic fittest it is, and when total ruin, even bankruptcy can result, you would better fight hard to survive. If that means stamping out other workers and neighbors—well, then so be it. Not to be ignored in the process is the total amount of lost revenue and productivity for everyone when workers strike over health care benefits.

THE BEST LAID PLANS

In 2003, the State of California instituted the *California Health Care Options Project*,[45] an integrated study of nine different models of health care reform that policy experts proposed. Those participating included several organizations and professors from the University of California campuses in Los Angeles, San Diego, Berkeley, and San Francisco. Each of the nine models proposed were subjected to a microsimulation by the

Lewin Group and broke down as follows. Six models and proposals were expansions of the current health care system and could be described as incremental models—seeking reform in continued small steps. The other three models were comprehensive proposals of which two were single-payer models and the other was a health service model. The Lewin Group's final simulation analysis showed that these latter three models would provide comprehensive coverage for everyone and were projected to save California's citizens *billions of dollars* in health care costs. The other six incremental reform models fell short, leaving in place many of the policies that were not working well. All of these models were projected to *increase* health care costs to Californians. One of the six models proposed was a combination plan of an employer mandate and a single public program for everyone else. While this combination plan came close to meeting the goals of comprehensive coverage, it turned out to be the most expensive proposal put forth.[46] The systematic and data-based analysis was clear—a comprehensive model based on a single-payer system would save billions and provide care to all.

What prevents data-based and factual evidence from being implemented into policy in our democracy? Most would answer this question with the politics of it all, and the "special interests." But politics simply reflect our cultural viewpoint—even if the view is so factually incorrect. An examination of the facts seems nearly impossible because in discussion after discussion when people agree that our health care model is terrible, the solution is always thwarted by the automatic evil phrases of "government-run" and "socialism." These terms are like a person holding up a cross to a vampire which cowers and loses its evil and powerful influence. My favorite response to the knee-jerk socialism response is to ask the person if they read any paper that has a business section. I then ask them if they look at the page after page of small print with stocks from NYSE, ASE, NASDAQ, Small Cap, Options, Futures, and Bonds, and if, after looking at that every day, they see any evidence of socialism. But like a lot of fears, this one is unreasonable and without a logical basis. Fear of socialism is in the service of the prevailing roots of pure and unfettered entrepreneurial narcissism that dominates our culture and forms the basis for the rampant misconceptions of what would be best for all of us in health care today.

High health care costs in an employer-based system are killing our economy. In fact, employer-sponsored health care is a huge federal tax break. If employees had to claim their employee health care "benefits" as income, they would pay an estimated $126 billion in federal income tax.[47] In other words, private sector employer-sponsored health care is really part of a government-backed health care system. A National Health Care Plan, by spreading out the costs to everyone, would take the monkey off an employer's back. What will business do without this huge expense ($7,000 per employee)? Might they create jobs? Expand their business? Lower their prices? Of course, they will have to pay taxes on their increased profits, thus contributing to reducing our unacceptable budget deficit. Herein lies the seismic conclusion: A National Health Care Plan would stimulate and improve the economy. It would do this by creating jobs, promoting business expansion, lowering prices, reducing the budget deficit, and increasing our global competitiveness.

Even with the change in guard, President Obama favors compromise and is unwilling to change how health care is funded. These efforts will not lower prices. Proposed but resigned Health and Human Services Secretary Tom Daschle's recent book on health care does not cite the California Health Care Options Project but instead proposes a Federal Health Board modeled after other commissions and the Federal Reserve Board.[48] This board would have the power to set health care policy just as the Federal Reserve Board sets monetary policy. Daschle concludes: "A hybrid solution also has its flaws, but it has one distinct advantage over the others: It is politically and practically feasible."[49] This sounds good but avoids the battle necessary to let the facts be the determining factor in health care policy.

Nothing would be a stronger antidote to living in a culture of excess than the decision as a society to have a universal health care system. Whether this is done on a national basis or within each state, a universal approach would send a collective societal message that everyone's quality of life is important. It will certainly take bold, courageous, and visionary political leaders to implement this type of policy.

NOTES

1. Shakir, F. (2009, July 28). Jon Stewart gets Kristol to concede government can provide "first class healthcare." Retrieved July 31, 2009 from http://thinkprogress.org/2009/07/28/kristol-heath-care-soldiers/. Video of interview widely available on Internet sources.

2. Widely reported in all major newspapers and on television. See Rosen, I. (Producer). (2007, April 1). Under the influence. *60 Minutes* [Television broadcast]. New York: CBS Broadcasting. Retrieved January 12, 2009 from http://www.cbsnews.com/stories/2007/03/29/60minutes/main2625305.shtml; Boehlert, E. (2004, April 5). Lies, bribes

and hidden costs: Bush's Medicare quagmire and the striking parallels to Iraq. Salon.com. Retrieved February 1, 2009 from http://dir.salon.com/story/news/feature/2004/04/05/medicare/index.html.

3. Woolhandler, S., & Himmelstein, D. (2002). Paying for national health insurance—and not getting it. *Health Affairs*, 21:88–98. See also http://www.pnhp.org/news/2002/july/government_funds_60.php.

4. Girion, L., & Hiltzik, M. (2008, October 21). Patients pay more, get less—if they're lucky. *Los Angeles Times*, pp. A1, A16–A17. Article cites Lieutenant Governor John Garamendi for statistics on pregnancy/delivery in California.

5. The Henry J. Kaiser Family Foundation. (2005). *Annual Employee Health Benefits Survey*. Menlo Park, CA: The Henry J. Kaiser Family Foundation. Retrieved February 1, 2009 from http://www.kff.org/insurance/7315.cfm.

6. Catlin, A., et al. (2007). "National Health Spending in 2005: The Slowdown Continues." *Health Affairs*, January/February, pp. 142–153.

7. The Henry J. Kaiser Family Foundation. (2007). Health care costs: A primer. Menlo Park, CA: The Henry J. Kaiser Family Foundation. Retrieved February 1, 2009 from http://www.kff.org/insurance/upload/7670.pdf.

8. The National Coalition on Health Care. (2008). Facts on the cost of health insurance and health care. Retrieved January 12, 2009 from http://www.nchc.org/facts/cost.shtml.

9. Levey, N. (2009, January 6). Healthcare spending in U.S. slows. *Los Angeles Times*, p. A11.

10. Banks, J., Marmot, M., Oldfield, Z., & Smith, J. (2006). Diseases and disadvantage in U.S. and England. *JAMA*, 295 (16): 2037–2045.

11. Ibid. See also McCanne, D. (2003). Why incremental reforms will not solve the health care crisis. *JABFP*, 16 (3): 257–261.

12. Madigan, N. (2004, August 21). Los Angeles emergency care crisis deepens. *The New York Times*. Retrieved February 1, 2009 from http://query.nytimes.com/gst/fullpage.html?res=9C07E6D8163EF932A1575BC0A9629C8B63. Article reports that 70 hospital emergency rooms and trauma centers in California have closed since 1990.

13. For data on the nursing shortage, see American Association of Colleges of Nursing Web page: http://www.aacn.nche.edu/media/shortageresource.htm.

14. Institute of Medicine. (1989). *Controlling and changing patient care: The role of utilization management*, pp. 24–25. Washington, D.C.: National Academy of Sciences.

15. General Accounting Office. (1993). *Network based managed care plans*. (GAO/HRO 943). Washington, D.C.: U.S. General Accounting Office.

16. *Business Week*. (August 1994). A furor over mental health, p. 66–69. Kuttner, R. (December 1991). Sick joke. *New Republic*, p. 20–22.

17. Ellis, J. (June 1996). *Money Magazine*, p. 43.

18. National Institute of Mental Health. (2007, January 19). Soaring economic costs from depression a global issue. News release retrieved February 2, 2009 from http://www.nih.gov/news/pr/jan2007/nimh-19.htm.

19. Slosar, J. R., & Lettieri, R. (1997). Financing mechanisms in the delivery of mental health care services: Widgets or wisdom? In *Behavioral managed care sourcebook* (pp. 155–163). New York: Faulkner & Gray.

20. Forbes.com. (2005). Forbes lists of executive pay. Retrieved January 13, 2009 from http://www.forbes.com/static/pvp2005/LIRRI3M.html.

21. Dr. William McGuire joins settlement of UnitedHealth Group federal securities class action. (2008, September 10). *Reuters*. Retrieved February 2, 2009 from http://www.reuters.com/article/pressRelease/idUS161728+10-Sep-2008+PRN20080910?sp=true.

22. Anders, G. (2006, April 18). Health-care gold mines: Middlemen strike it rich. *The Wall Street Journal*, p. A1.

23. Dr. William McGuire joins settlement of UnitedHealth Group federal securities class action; CalPERS Office of Public Affairs. (2008, September 10). CalPERS recovers $30 million from UnitedHealth Group CEO. Retrieved February 2, 2009 from http://www.calpers.ca.gov/index.jsp?bc=/about/press/pr-2008/sep/recovers-30-million-unitedhealth.xml.

24. Graybow, M. (2009, January 13). UnitedHealth settles New York reimbursement probe. *Reuters*. Retrieved July 29, 2009 from http://www.reuters.com/article/businessNews/idUSTRE50C5V820090113. United Health settles lawsuit. (2009, January 16). *Los Angeles Times*, p. C3.

25. Gingrich has written extensively and conducted many interviews on the subject of improving health care. See Center for Health Transformation Web site at http://www.healthtransformation.net/.

26. Woolhandler, S., Campbell, T., & Himmelstein, D. U. (2003). Cost of healthcare administration in the U.S. and Canada. *New England Journal of Medicine*, 349:768–775. Woolhandler, S., & Himmelstein, D. U. (1991). The deteriorating administrative efficiency of the U.S. health care system. *New England Journal of Medicine*, 324:1253–1258.

27. Woolhandler, Campbell, & Himmelstein, Cost of healthcare administration in the U.S. and Canada, 768–775.

28. Ibid.

29. Ibid.

30. Aaron, H. (2003). Editorial. *New England Journal of Medicine*, 349.

31. Woolhandler, Campbell, & Himmelstein, Cost of healthcare administration in the U.S. and Canada, 768–775.

32. Daschle, T., Greenberger, S., & Lambrew, J. (2008). *Critical: What we can do about the health care crisis* (p. 103). New York: Thomas Dunne Books. Daschle sums up 2003 Medicare bill: "Taxpayers' costs have been higher than originally thought. And Medicare's solvency is now threatened by overpayments to private insurers built into the legislation."

33. Rosen, I. (Producer). (2007, April 1). Under the influence. *60 Minutes* [Television broadcast]. New York: CBS Broadcasting. Retrieved January 12, 2009 from http://www.cbsnews.com/stories/2007/03/29/60minutes/main2625305.shtml.

34. Musgrove, P. (Ed.). (2000). *The world health report 2000—Health systems: Improving performance*. Geneva: World Health Organization.

35. Kuttner, R. (1997). *Everything for sale: The virtues and limits of markets*. New York: Alfred A. Knopf.

36. Committee on the Consequences of Uninsurance, Institute of Medicine. (2002). *Care without coverage: Too little, too late*. Washington, D.C.: The National Academies Press.

37. Madigan, Los Angeles emergency care crisis deepens.

38. Committee on the Consequences of Uninsurance, *Care without coverage: Too little, too late*.

39. Reinhardt, U. E., Hussey, P. S., & Anderson, G. F. (2002). Cross national comparisons of health systems using OECD data. *Health Affairs*, 21:169–181.

40. Warren, F., Sullivan, T., & Jacoby, M. (2000). Medical problems and bankruptcy filings. Norton's Bankruptcy Advisor, May 2000. Available at SSRN: http://ssrn.com/abstract=224581.

41. Himmelstein, D. U., Thorne, D., Warren, E., & Woolhander, S. (2009). Medical bankruptcy in the U.S., 2007: A National Study. *American Journal of Medicine*. Retrieved July 31, 2009 from http://www.pnhp.org/new_bankruptcy_study/Bankruptcy-2009.pdf.

42. *California Chronicle*. (2008, April 19). LA City Attorney Rocky Delgadillo files civil law enforcement action against Blue Cross. Retrieved August 1, 2009 from http://www.californiachronicle.com/articles/view/59118. Rocky Delgadillo is no longer LA City Attorney and the Web page he set up is not accessible.

43. Dickerson, M. (2008, November 2). Ticket to treatment. *Los Angeles Times*, p. C1.

44. Broder, J. (2003, October 14). California supermarket strike deters shoppers. *The New York Times*. Retrieved February 2, 2009 from http://query.nytimes.com/gst/fullpage.html?res=9F0CE0DD113FF937A25753 C1A9659C8B63&sec=&spon=&pagewanted=1. Describes employers' battle to control health care costs versus workers' efforts to avoid out-of-pocket costs.

45. The Lewin Group. (2002). Cost and coverage analysis of nine proposals to expand health insurance coverage in California. Retrieved February 2, 2009 from http://www.lewin.com/content/publications/1626.pdf.

46. Ibid. See also McCanne, D. (2004). A national health insurance program for the United States. *PLoS Medicine*, 1 (2): 115–118.

47. Reich, R. (2008). *Supercapitalism*. New York: Alfred A. Knopf.

48. Daschle, Greenberger, & Lambrew, *Critical: What we can do about the health care crisis*.

49. Ibid.

# Chapter 6

# SOCIAL NARCISSISM: IMAGES, REALITY, AND HEROES

A hero cannot be a hero unless in a heroic world.
> —Nathaniel Hawthorne

We can't all be heroes because somebody has to sit on the curb and applaud when they go by.
> —Will Rogers

Image is everything. The line was used by pro tennis star Andre Agassi in 1990 for Canon cameras in an immensely successful ad campaign that captured the social zeitgeist. Agassi would later report the ad and statement was not representative of who he was. But the successful ad was alluring and linked nicely with the idea of a new image-capturing camera.[1] The message is: You are not you. You are your image. Success is based upon your image. Corporations know how important and defining image is, too. Companies spent about $3.5 billion in 2005 on public relations.[2] And as Americans, we also have an image.

Historian Daniel Boorstin has outlined the trends in how American culture has formed and defined our collective self-image. In his 1961 book, *The Image*, Boorstin described terms that are now part of our lexicon. For example, the "pseudo-event," described as an event designed only to be reported and to create an impression or image. This includes most media events, in particular "photo opportunities" and press conferences. Boorstin coined the phrase that defined a celebrity as "a person who is known for his well-knownness." In an introduction to a chapter in *The Image*, Boorstin recounts the anecdote of a friend who tells a mother she

has a beautiful baby. The mother responds: "Oh, that's nothing—
you should see his photograph!"[3] Today, some celebrities will even sell
pictures of their newborns to tabloid or entertainment news sources.

As we have progressed technologically beyond our wildest dreams,
images, celebrity, heroes, and reality have become a blur. At times, our
projections and fantasies seem real, and the boundaries between reality
and imagination are porous and undefined. The culture of excess allows
advertising to be more influential than any type of communication today.
Our constant world of fantasy, images, and heroes presented through
screen media and social media reflects the underlying cultural narcissism.
Boorstin called it "social narcissism," falling in love with the images we
have created—images that reflect ourselves and our culture.[4] Within this
image forming process, we idealize and fantasize about success. The
images we hold and pursue become our cultural definition of success.

In business or traditional career paths, the process or the "how" of success and wealth accumulation is through becoming a middleman or a
broker. This manipulative effort means getting into the middle position
of where the money is, so that you can control the flow toward you.
Hence, the dramatic surge into MBA programs and the activity of
entrepreneurial narcissism. But becoming "rich and famous" is a more
dramatic and immediate process. It is about getting discovered. One can
avoid the hard work and time-consuming traditional career process with
the instant discovery of success through media and technology.

Francisco, age 16, has been arrested for tagging. I am asked to do an
evaluation as there is concern about his mental health and eccentric
behavior. He struggles with reality. Immediately after I introduce myself
and explain the purpose of the evaluation, he tells me he hears voices.
Photographs of his tagging show his handiwork is unique, an art style with
flare and imagination. They are his style and become the evidence by
which authorities know it is him. He explains that others have become
successful by public tagging. He believes it is possible someone would
see his work, and that could lead to being discovered and a successful
career. Since it certainly is possible, who is to say this thought process is
not logical? Is his thinking realistic?

Being discovered is a major part of pop culture and "reality" shows.
Today's obsession with pop culture is profound. A media company called
4INFO is sponsored by revenue from advertisers. 4INFO reports it will
send 500 million text messages in 2008 to subscribers providing them
with an "alert" for celebrity gossip (85%) and sports scores (15%).[5]
Today's youth would rather watch a reality show than anything more

substantive. Emory University English professor Mark Bauerlein was presenting to college students. When he told them they are six times more likely to know who won *American Idol* than who is Speaker of the House, a student snapped back that this is because *American Idol* IS more important.[6] Indeed it is. In 2005, President Bush's State of the Union speech was preceded on Fox News by *American Idol*. At 8 p.m., *American Idol* averaged 26 million viewers. When President Bush came on at 9 p.m., the number dropped to 7.6 million viewers, a retention rate of 29 percent.[7]

Serious media professionals are in despair if their network leads with a story about Brittany Spears or who won *American Idol*. This trend, by reporting on pop culture as important news, also changes the definition of success, which now means becoming famous through a media source and being "discovered." This kind of success is instantaneous, a fantasy come true, and akin to the American Dream. Today, these fantasies are now more possible in an extremely immediate way. Even very young children pick up on this, and their worldview (reality) of success is different. Their images and heroes are different.


## THE *REAL HOUSEWIVES*

Traditional soap operas have taken a backseat to the ongoing lives of actual or "real" people. *American Idol* consists of a real competition with a winner, who then gets a music contract and usually hits it big. Rich and famous—mission accomplished. But the other types of reality shows follow people and make them images of a star or a model of success. The *Real Housewives of Orange County (RHOC)* is a reality-based show that follows the daily lives of several women and their families who live in upscale Orange County, California. Orange County, located between San Diego and Los Angeles, is an affluent, conservative, and Republican-dominated area. It has one of the highest median home prices in the nation.[8] In its fourth season, *RHOC* is a depiction of success based on wealth, fashion, and consumption.[9]

*RHOC* characters are portrayed as dynamic and active, enjoying huge homes, upscale restaurants, and flamboyant lifestyles. Episodes are worse than trivia, depicting dialogues and conflicts among the adults that can only be described as histrionic melodrama of social immaturity. Dialogues of the housewives' petty arguments are often filmed with their young children observing it all. Many scenes are of parties where someone yells "woo-hoo" and then characters get drunk. There is often joking about "getting wasted." Scenes follow in which the characters discuss someone's getting drunk the night before. A young son of one of the housewives hits on one of the other housewives. Gossip follows. Episodes that include the children portray how unashamedly spoiled the teens or young adults are—often acknowledged by youth and parents. A common theme is parents buying an 18- or 20-year-old an expensive new car.

In another episode, a teenage son of one of the housewives sits down for a session with his doting mom and a therapist. He cries and emotes about his substance abuse problem. The therapeutic message to the boy is: "You know what you have to do," and the audience supposedly sees the ensuing catharsis as something that is real. Somehow this type of self-disclosure is considered genuine. But nothing filmed in this manner can be a genuine experience. When cameras are filming every move and word, an individual assumes a completely different persona. This type of experience for a young male with a substance abuse problem is the last thing he needs. The heightened publicity, lack of boundaries for privacy and confidential issues, and video catharsis only feed emerging narcissistic characteristics. In contrast, the young person needs work with a professional who will help him establish boundaries of separation and individuation to adulthood, and develop internal self-regulation. A successful result can only be accomplished in a setting that has boundaries and structure and includes privacy. Highlighting the problem of narcissistic personality issues and development through this type of media exposure only exaggerates them.

This is true of the *Real Housewives* series overall. Characters have narcissistic tendencies that the video documentation exacerbates. Yet, the popularity of the show represents the admiration of these qualities as desirable and related to success and happiness. In this way, the show's interest represents the core basis of the culture of excess—documenting declining self-control and the growth of cultural narcissism.

The *Real Housewives* series now has spin-offs in New York City and Atlanta, the latter focusing on African American women.[10] Even accomplished newscaster Anderson Cooper of CNN publicly described his following and interest in the *Real Housewives of Atlanta*.[11] We have to be fair—today's cultural narcissism must employ our cultural diversity.

When I bring up *RHOC* to others, my social group laughs and shakes their head at what a superficial show it is. A family relative calls and after viewing the show in the Midwest asks: "Are people out there really like that?" He goes on to say he cannot imagine his daughters turning out as self-centered as those he sees on the program. Others report they know people exactly like the characters followed in the show. Although extreme, the series does depict an element of our culture and is a clear example of the psychological impact of the culture of excess. Moreover, the characters portrayed are idealized and viewed as someone you might like to be. On the *RHOC* Web page, a 10-item survey asks you to pick answers from choices about your personality and relationships. The results inform you which housewife you are most like. The characters on *RHOC* are portrayed as today's image of success. But if these "housewives" are "real," then reality and fantasy have merged.

## COMPETITIVE REALITY: THEN AND NOW

The possibility of instantaneous media success changes our perceptions of the world, workplace, and our relationships. It is the form of the new sense of reality I referred to earlier. Of course, this process dramatically heightens the importance of entertainment. But there are many types of "entertainment," offering more choices than ever before. Extreme sports, water and snow sports, online gaming, and even attempting to get on a reality show have expanded play and leisure activities. Some of these are pure leisure pursuits rather than the hard reality of true competitive sports. The traditional professional-level sports are an area of entertainment in which intense competition is real, and not what Boorstin calls a "pseudo-event." He explains the fascination with sports:

> But people—even twentieth-century Americans—will not so supinely allow themselves to be deprived of the last vestiges of spontaneous reality. By a new residual effect, then, we become doubly interested in any happenings which somehow seem to offer us an oasis of the uncontrived. One example is the American passion for news about crime and sports. This is not simply an effect of the degradation of public tastes to the trivial and the unserious. More significantly, it is one expression of our desperate hunger for the spontaneous, for the non-pseudo-event.[12]

A professional sports event is then spontaneous and uncontrived, in other words—real. It does not matter who you are, or that your family is wealthy, runs a big business, or your parent was president of something or went to Yale, but rather your performance between the lines. You compete on raw talent and skill. Attending a sports event can be considered an escape into reality, the fulfillment of a basic need to find a competition or an activity that is real. The worker leaves the office of business hype and exaggerations to enter the seemingly raw reality of a competitive event. This is despite the fact that some sports are not real (wrestling), and that commercialism increasingly pollutes the reality of the event. In addition, sports have a history and links to community and loyalty to where one grew up and lives. The historical significance of sports and city rivalries provides a depth that allows it to be used as a model to view changes in images and heroes. The image of a hero becomes a template of success. To admire an athlete who has the most exceptional skills seems normal. How these hero images change reflect cultural trends.

In 1959, Major League Baseball had eight teams in two leagues. The winner of the American League played the winner of the National League in the World Series. During the regular season, teams in each league never played a team from the other league. But in 1959, something different happened. The Chicago White Sox won the American League pennant, interrupting a long New York Yankee hegemony. And the new owner of the White Sox was a colorful entrepreneur named Bill Veeck. He walked with a peg leg from the Korean War and owned the White Sox from 1959 to 1963, and then later reemerged with the help of Mayor Daley to own the team in the 1970s. During his long career with several teams, Veeck initiated marketing in baseball and used many successful promotional events. He was responsible for bringing in the exploding scoreboard and fireworks. He once hired a midget to pinch hit to draw a walk. His marketing included having players from both teams engage in a contest of milking cows between games of a doubleheader, S & H green stamp day to attract women to the ballpark (it worked), and even Bartenders Day, when 3,500 bartenders got in for free.

When his outfielder Al Smith was struggling and being constantly booed by fans in the bleachers, Veeck set up "Smith Night." On August 26, 1959, in a stretch drive for the pennant, Veeck set the rules for Smith Night. Anyone who showed an ID that his or her name was Smith or anything close (Smthye, Smit, etc.) got in for free and had to wear a blue and white badge that read: "I'm a Smith and I'm for Al." That night, 5,253 Smiths showed up and sat in left field behind Smith, a number that was not counted among the 22,497 paying customers. Unfortunately, on his own special night, Smith did not do so well. He struck out twice and hit into a double play. Worse yet, he dropped a fly ball in a rally that led to a 7-6 loss.

Smith reported decades later to writer Bob Vanderberg that on that night he saw his milkman, "a Polish fellow" (Smith was African American), in

the stands. Asking him how he got in, the milkman said he used someone's tax bill that had "Smith" on it.

Al Smith was also well known for a photo showing him getting a beer in
the face during the World Series when he backed up against the outfield
wall, looked up, and a fan reaching for the Dodger home run knocked
his beer directly onto Smith's face. The historic photo symbolized the fate
of the Sox in the 4-2 game loss to the Dodgers in the Series.[13]

But another small promotional event tells the entire story of Veeck and
the image of a community-based owner. On Monday, July 20, 1959, an
impending strike at the steel mills was announced. The Gary, Indiana
and East Chicago shores of Lake Michigan provided thousands of jobs
for the working-class area I grew up in. President Eisenhower said no
immediate settlement to the strike seemed possible, and Veeck
responded. He announced that at the Saturday game against the Baltimore Orioles all striking steelworkers and steel management personnel
would be his guests. Veeck stated: "They might as well come to the ball-
game; they're not working."[14] On that Saturday, 7,445 steelworkers came
to the game for free. Consider the magnitude of this gesture and the
underlying philosophy. Can anyone imagine Disney, Fox, or the other
corporate entities and owners extending such an offer to striking union
workers? As noted earlier in the example of health care strikes, union
workers are by and large hated. And Veeck extended the gesture to
management as well, during a year in which the team was engaged in a
very close pennant race.

That year it did pay off. The team won the pennant and 10,000 people
rushed to Midway Airport to celebrate the night the team clinched the
pennant in a single, dramatic play-off game. The city even set off the
air-raid sirens. In the historic 1959 World Series, the White Sox lost to
the Dodgers who had just moved west and played in the Los Angeles
Coliseum. But a still record crowd of 92,706 fans attended game five of
the series.[15]

Veeck responded to the community and represented the working area
more effectively than a politician. White Sox ballpark was on the south
side, near the stockyards and steel mills. Anyone who has been near a
stockyard knows the effect. The smell of the stockyards in the heat of
summer is not pleasant. Veeck was immensely popular in Chicago, and
the team had not returned to the World Series since 1959, until their recent
World Series championship in 2005. At the games, Veeck mingled and sat
with the fans and listened to their needs. He was their owner. It was their
team. He made the community a better place.

In contrast to the affable and generous Bill Veeck, today's overpriced sports world demands a twenty-first-century owner who mimics the current corporate style. He or she must have that narcissistic quality and be able to locate and move players quickly, more like commodities than human players. One new sports owner, though not the only one, represents this enigma. Mark Cuban, owner of the Dallas Mavericks of the NBA, is described as an "American billionaire entrepreneur."[16] In January 2000, he purchased the Dallas team from Ross Perot for $285 million.

Cuban was an entrepreneur since youth, selling garbage bags in bulk at age 12 for profit. Described as a "system integrator and software reseller," he eventually started his own company, MicroSolutions, which was sold to CompuServe in 1990 for $6 million.[17] He went on to form Audionet, a company that broadcast live sports events on the Internet. Audionet changed its name to Broadcast.com and was acquired by Yahoo! for $5.04 billion in Yahoo! stock.[18] (To his credit, Cuban did not purge his wealth in the dot.com bubble burst.) Cuban was credited with the largest ever financial e-commerce transaction when he purchased his private Gulfstream V jet in 1999 for $40 million. In 2007, his net worth was listed at $2.3 billion, and he ranked number 407 on the *Forbes* list of the "World's Richest People."[19]

So how does Cuban run the Mavericks? His team's performance and his behavior demonstrate the pros and cons of Michael Maccoby's "productive narcissism."[20] Prior to Cuban coming on board, the Mavericks had a history of a winning percentage of just 40 percent. In the six years, Cuban has owned the team; the winning percentage has increased to 69 percent. The team has been in the play-offs each year, and made the finals in 2006, losing to Miami.[21]

Now the downside. Cuban sits near courtside, wears team shirts, and cannot control himself. He has run out on the court to scream at referees. In 2006, the league fined Cuban more than $1.6 million for 13 different incidents.[22] (Cuban reports he matches the league fines with an equal amount in charitable donations.) In one dramatic incident, Cuban criticized the league's director of officials stating he "wouldn't be able to manage a Dairy Queen." Dairy Queen management was offended, so Cuban worked for a day at the Dairy Queen in Coppell, Texas, serving Blizzards while giving penance.[23] Interestingly, Ross Perot, from whom Cuban purchased the Mavericks, used this same line when Perot participated in a presidential debate in 1992. I do not think Ross Perot ever worked a day at Dairy Queen.

Of course, Cuban gets away with the fines because money is no object, but a normal fan who ran out on the court could end up in jail (especially in Texas) and probably would be banned from attending games by the league. But for powerful CEOs, justice is not equal, and the fans and society revere Cuban's "success" and tolerate the behavior. After all, he has realized the American Dream in today's society and that is all that really matters. He has made enough money to own a professional sports team, and now he can do pretty much whatever he wants. When news reports indicated Cuban might purchase the historic Chicago Cubs, fans seemed excited.[24] They knew he had enough money to buy a pennant. The deal did not work out and later came the announcement that the SEC was investigating Cuban for insider trading—the trademark of a modern day executive and hero. However, in July of 2009 a federal judge dismissed the SEC lawsuit.[25]

The cultural fantasy of being a Cuban or a Veeck and owning your own sports team should not be underestimated. In the past 20 years, "fantasy" leagues have emerged as a vital business enterprise. Today, the Fantasy Sports Trade Association estimates there are about 27 million fantasy players that generate annual revenues between $800 million and $1 billion.[26] In these leagues, participants put money in and form their own team by having a draft day just like the big wigs do. Fantasy franchises bid against each other for team members among the athletes currently playing for real teams; a computer calculates each team's stats based on what the players actually do in real life. The fantasy league now allows you to be a real owner of your own team—to trade or wheel and deal like the real owners do—and in the end if your team's stats are in first place, you win the prize money. Of course, this is another modern day form of gambling, but instead of betting how stocks will do, you bet on ballplayers. "Owners" of a fantasy team have been known to call real teams themselves to find out about inside information like injuries or possible trades.

Which owner or entrepreneur do you prefer—Cuban or Veeck? They both seem equally idolized in their own day. The major difference seems to be in their outward display of behavior and personality. But unlike Veeck, I am not sure Cuban makes the community a better place. But others may think differently—Cuban contributed a million dollars to start a Fallen Patriot Fund to help families of Iraqi war veterans.[27] This is the twenty-first-century means to public acceptance and mitigation of any negative perceptions. But how can anyone say this generous donation is not a very patriotic and compassionate thing to do?

## QUIET HEROES

"Nice guys finish last" is one of my favorite quotes. But it was not a philosopher or existentialist who coined the phrase. It was baseball manager Leo Durocher who successfully managed the New York Giants in the 1950s. He was nicknamed "Leo the Lip," and sportswriters loved him because he was always popping off, giving them great quotes.[28] This was back in the days when a reporter took notes with pencil and pad in hand and ran back to a typewriter.

In 1954, Durocher managed a great young player—Willie Mays. The color barrier had already been broken by Jackie Robinson, so it was a little easier for Mays, a talented young outfielder and black athlete who seemed to have it all. With power, speed, and great defensive ability, Mays roamed center field, moving in to use a basket-style manner to catch fly balls rather than keeping both hands up, a more cautious and conservative way to catch high flies. Young players like me would try the basket style, only to drop the ball and hear their manager's voice: "When you get to the big leagues, you can catch like Willie Mays; for now, you use both hands and keep them up."

So the young phenom began the New York Giants '54 season on a terror. After 99 games he had 36 home runs. At that pace, he could break Babe Ruth's then record of 60 homers in one year. Remember the unbelievable furor when McGwire, Sammy Sosa, and then Bonds hit that many home runs. It is a big deal. But there was one problem: The Giants were losing, often by only one run. Durocher was worried, Mays's homers were often hit with no one on base, and thus only one run would score. So he approached his talented superstar and told him he wanted him to stop hitting home runs. Pointing out the situation, he asked Mays to try to get on base, use his speed to steal bases and hit more doubles and triples to drive in runs. Durocher was asking Mays to sacrifice his personal stats for the team. The talented Mays had no problem. He changed his style and that year had 33 doubles, 13 triples and batted .345.[29] He ended up with 41 home runs at the end of the year. But Durocher was right—the Giants went on to win the pennant. Could a manager successfully do that today? Would a manager even consider doing that today, or be so enthralled about the big PR record and the pressure to pursue what would really draw more fans to the game than winning—the breaking of the big record? Today, when the record is broken, a fight breaks out over catching the ball, which can be sold for big bucks. Lawsuits follow—I had it, no he had it, no I had it and he stole it from me. But Mays was a quiet hero in contrast to the sports heroes most noticed today. For some, the intense media attention makes you a hero and it is hard to be quiet about it.

## THE BIG O

Everyone knows who Michael Jordan is. And Magic Johnson. The NBA has grown tremendously popular in the past 20 years, but basketball followers and insiders know about the Big O, Oscar Robertson. Robertson played from 1960 to 1976 and was a quiet hero. In his passionate autobiography, Robertson has documented the amazing racial tension and turmoil of growing up in the 1960s in Indiana, the heartland of basketball.[30] He played in a different era and seldom shot 30 times a game like Jordan (he averaged 18.9 shots per game). In his era, it was harder by definition to get an "assist," defined as helping another player score a basket. Robertson estimates that by today's looser standard for scoring an assist, he would have had several thousand more assists. Not that he needed to add to his numbers. In basketball, scorers count three important stats—points scored, and the number of rebounds and assists made in the game. If you get ten or more of each in one game (ten points, ten rebounds, and ten assists), you are considered to have done everything— an exceptional achievement called a "triple double." On a given day in the NBA schedule, few, if any, players get a triple double. But Oscar Robertson, small by NBA standards at six feet five inches, actually *averaged* a triple double through an entire season. In 1961–62, only his second season in the NBA, Robertson averaged 30.8 points, 12.5 rebounds, and 11.4 assists per game.[31] He is the ONLY basketball player to accomplish this feat. At the end of his career, Robertson led the way with a lawsuit, settled after six years, which guaranteed free agency for NBA players. Robertson's high school team in Indiana was also involved in the story portrayed in the popular movie, *Hoosiers*, which was based on a true story of a small, rural high school that beat a powerful large high school for the state championship. His team was also upset by the small school, which was named Hickory in the movie. Robertson reports the large school that lost in the championship game was depicted in the movie as an all black team, but in fact was an integrated team.[32]

What modern day athlete went through what Robertson did? Today's young athletes do not have to face the social mistreatment of black athletes such as Jackie Robinson, Muhammad Ali, and Henry Aaron. The quiet heroes like Mays and Robertson have already blazed the trail.

Today's young athlete primarily has to try to stay out of trouble. In the epilogue to his autobiography, Robertson graciously addresses who is the best basketball player of all time; his comments on today's players are telling:

> Of course, speculation is beside the point. You can't alter history or change time. We live in the here and now; a new generation of players is maturing and becoming the game's leaders. Iverson and Webber, McGrady, Kevin Garnett, and Vince Carter among them. They're all very good, even great players, but if there's anything missing from their games, it's this: Some of these great basketball players hardly do anything to help the team or the other players on the team. I always thought that my role was to get the team going, get other players involved. You don't see that a lot anymore.[33]

In 1996, newspapers described his "biggest assist," donating his kidney to his daughter who was ill.

Mays and Robertson were quiet heroes. As young black athletes in the 1950s and 1960s, who could have encountered more social barriers and vicissitudes? In contrast, one radio program describes today's sports news as the "athlete arrest of the day." Sammy Sosa broke the home run record, and then in one game a few years later broke his bat and out spilled Superballs. His excuse was that the loaded bat was for batting practice, and in the game he just grabbed the wrong bat. Players laughed. Major League Baseball seized all his bats for examination, even the one in the Hall of Fame that Sosa used to break the record. There was big sigh of relief when further exam found nothing illegal in his bats.[34] But the damage to his reputation was done, opening the door to speculation that his physique was the result of steroids.

Mark McGwire, the first to break the record of 60 home runs per season, also has lost standing. When testifying in Congress in 2005, he refused to answer questions about whether he took steroids in his playing days, in effect invoking the Fifth Amendment against self-incrimination. At the same hearing, Rafeal Palmeiro did a full Clinton scene, pointing his finger and insisting he never used steroids. A few weeks later, media reported lab results that were positive for steroid use.[35]

The ethical conflict is taking its toll. Major League Baseball has been unwilling to set and enforce rules and regulations about drug or powerful supplement usage. Each passing month, more and more players who set records are exposed for using performance-enhancing drugs. As a result,

McGwire's and Sosa's records pose an ethical dilemma that blurs reality and threatens to negate the world records that dramatically increased baseball's financial success and survival. The questions remain: Are these really new world records, and can a cheater be the greatest player? Whether it is the athlete or today's CEO, many of our individual and culturally observed attainments of success become tainted and unsatisfying. In 2007, three players were nominated for the Baseball Hall of Fame: Cal Ripken, Tony Gwynn, and Mark McGwire. Ripken and Gwynn swept in easily, but McGwire did not, receiving less than 25 percent of the vote.[36] A clear message was sent—you have the record, but your peers question how you got it.

The competitive reality of a sports event is further threatened by the pollution of commercialism and excess. Today's sports stars do not encounter more stress or adversity than athletes in previous eras. Rather, they are in a sports world society that is more wealthy and materialistic, immediate and intense, and has a different sense of community. All major sports have extended their play-offs and seasons. The Super Bowl now goes into February. Major League Baseball drags to the end of October, with fans wearing parkas and gloves at the World Series. NBA play-offs go into May and June. College football, not wanting to miss out on potential profit, drags out the bowl games way beyond New Year's Day, enhancing the fans' long weekend stay in a city that grabs all the revenue it can. Scalping tickets as a side business is huge, and the price for a big game ticket can be more than some people make in a week or a month. Players switch teams so frequently, true fans cannot keep up. Despite the fact that they are far bigger, faster, and better athletes, any possible way to get ahead is fair game, and for many their hero status is something they cannot accept, they cannot carry. When they try, there is nothing quiet about it. If they have a legal or emotional problem, everyone knows about it.

## SELF-INFLICTED HEROES

Today's struggle to be a hero in sports and celebrity is different. The historical era of a struggle for civil rights is replaced by another social struggle—the evermore common malady of overcoming an addiction.

Current baseball slugger and star Josh Hamilton plays for the Texas Rangers. After years of missing games due to substance abuse and multiple drug rehab attempts, Hamilton found the Lord and recovered. "It's a God thing," he reports, frequently relating the story of how Christianity saved him.[37] He is an example of today's comeback kid story. After finally getting his act together, a Yankee Stadium crowd repeatedly shouted his name as he whacked balls into the stands in a home run derby contest before the All Star Game. He did not even win the contest.[38] But the public now identifies him as a hero, more so than the other sluggers in the derby who had not "recovered." Sports writers and other celebrities pick up on this means to notoriety, too.

The *New York Times* reporter David Carr, admitting to a crack cocaine addiction and mistreating women, was featured on the cover of the *New York Times Magazine*.[39] The *Chicago Sun-Times* reporter Neil Steinberg was arrested for a domestic dispute, and admitting he is a "drunkard," he wrote a nonfiction book promoted by the *Sun-Times*.[40] Sports columnist Mike Downey of the *Chicago Tribune* notices this trend among colleagues, athletes, and celebrities. In his short piece, "The 12 Steps to Success," he laments: "I need an addiction, man, I need it bad, real bad. Got to get me one."[41] Of course, celebrities who struggle with drugs are always featured too. Amy Winehouse, Charlie Sheen, Robert Downey, Jr.— many end up receiving the highest awards for their talents. They are considered more heroic than those who win recognition and awards without struggling with drugs.

But there are sad stories, too, as some do not fully recover. Former star Daryl Strawberry continued to have lapses continuing into his post-baseball years. And some athletes come clean. Marion Jones, female track star, won five medals in the 2000 Olympics. After years of rumors and reports she used performance-enhancing substances, Jones admitted to doing so. In October 2007, she emotionally acknowledged cheating, forfeited her Olympic medals, and retired from running. Caught up in the BALCO scandal, a company that sold these substances to top athletes, she lied to federal investigators. Jones even spent six months in jail in 2008.[42]

So the story can be double-edged and end up in tragedy, like the tragic case of actor Heath Ledger. Ledger, who suffered from a chronic sleep problem, died from an accidental overdose. Ledger's case points up the huge problem of prescription drug abuse. An estimated 20 percent of the U.S. population has used prescription drugs for nonmedical problems.[43] Ease of getting medications and the availability and quantity of new drugs are another manifestation of the culture of excess, with many trying to find drugs that are performance enhancers. Misuse sometimes leads to addictions and tragedy. Still, you can become a cultural hero if you can make a recovery. Struggle with it—up and down—and you will always have the public relations thing going. An athlete or celebrity who has a stable and healthy background just is not that interesting.


## COMMERCIALISM AND COMMUNITY

Professional sports are a part of the explosive capitalism and narcissistic entrepreneurialism of today. The public does not challenge the huge player salaries as much as the inflated CEO salaries. This is true even though a player can be paid millions and have a terrible year and not perform well. The impact of the commercialism in destroying the experience of the reality of sports seems also to just be something we accept. Yet the deep roots and history of a team in a community have a powerful and positive psychological impact in helping people feel connected and having a sense of identity. If we have experiences that are satisfying, have real competition and develop positive attachments and connections to others—shouldn't we try to preserve them?

When I moved to Southern California, I would go to the games when the White Sox would come to town against the hometown Angels. But after Disney acquired the Angels, I became quite reluctant to go. I also balked at price increases as I did not want to use my VISA card to go to a ball game. If I am visiting Chicago, I will go see a game at Sox Park (sorry, U.S. Cellular Field) or wonderful and nostalgic Wrigley Field. But my experience going to a Sox/Angels game after Disney took over was depressing.

A friend said let's go and we did. The Disney regime had already been in power for a few years now, after having brokered the hockey team, the Mighty Ducks. The new and rebuilt stadium was impressive. Large and scenic, it was also majestic. One visiting player noted that a structure in the outfield looked like the Matterhorn at Disneyland. Of course, advertising signs and messages were everywhere.

So now, sitting in the box seats behind the first base dugout, I want something to eat. I go down the exit in search of a hot dog or two, and find that Wienerschnitzel is the only option. Now, I have nothing against Wienerschnitzel; they seem like a solid franchise with clean and efficient fast food service. But I am at a ball game, a special event, with the sights and smells and experiences that have the potential for something enjoyable.

Then, I notice the price of the Wienerschnitzel hot dogs and extras is more than twice what it would be if I went to the one in my neighborhood. I cannot believe it. I am curious why everyone is lining up for fast food and not demanding something more real. In line just to talk to someone, I complain to a young adult woman that this is only Wienerschnitzel and these prices are not right. She looks at me in a strange and critical way that says so what, what's your problem?

Wandering to the end of the ramp in a depressed daze, I encounter a security guard who seems concerned about me. "What's wrong," he asks, "I'm trying to find some good food—not just Wienerschnitzel," I tell him. He tells me there is a deli where you can "order what you want," up on the next floor and down by the outfield. He points up and to the other side of the stadium. I wished I had sat up there instead of the box seats.

Hot dogs are out, but there must be good pizza. Wrong again. The choice is Domino's, another fast food option. Isn't Dominos known for its home delivery? Well, the vendors would bring it to you in your seat, but one slice of Domino's pizza is $5.25 (this was six years ago). And lest you think a baseball fan could bring in food to avoid these high prices, keep in mind that Disney was military-like in checking bags upon admission, making sure you did not even smuggle candy. After that, I did not go to a ball game for several years, even when the Angels won the World Series.

Disney got tired and dumped the Angels. Not enough profit, I think. The new owner, Artie Moreno, is a successful and popular millionaire businessman who quickly became involved in a huge legal dispute with the City of Anaheim. After signing a contract with the city and receiving all kinds of perks, he then later changed the name of the team to the Los Angeles Angels of Anaheim.[44] (For you sports fans, that is abbreviated LAA.) Turns out, the name Los Angeles is more lucrative for marketing income and dollars than Anaheim. It is a "market" thing, like using the name Beverly Hills. Of course, the City of Anaheim called foul and embracing their new owner's definition of "community" filed a lawsuit. Meanwhile, Moreno was allowed to keep the name LAA. At first, I wondered if the players are confused—asking who do I really play for? But not in the least, by their own admission; they know who writes their paychecks.

All this is seen as amusing and just a normal part of entertainment and living in the twenty-first-century sports world. The lawsuit posed an interesting and exciting dilemma, but in today's worldview these kinds of legal battles and lawsuits are OK; we do not seem to get mad at the trial lawyers. A good old fight about money—it is part of truth, justice, and the American Way, and I would guess that most people are pulling for the owner—his inherent and God-given right to make as much money as possible. After all, if God had intended baseball to benefit the community and fans of a city,

God would have named the teams right there in the Bible. Moreno won the lengthy lawsuit, as the contract was poorly worded and did not disallow LAA.[45] Of course, the conflict between city and team was not resolved, but life (business) goes on. We have to add the standard defense for owner Moreno—he is generous in supporting programs in the community.

Yet conflicts such as the Moreno-Anaheim dispute interfere with one of the most important contributions the institution of sports can make; that is, the sense of community, group identity, and bonding to where one grows up and lives, which contributes to a healthy view of reality. These core values are squashed by the hype of profit seeking and stardom, the pursuit of narcissistic individualism at the expense of community development.

Contrast the LA/Orange County world with the colorful history of the beloved Chicago Cubs, a team that since 1909 has repeatedly come close but has failed to win a pennant and play in the World Series. In moments before losing a final play-off game, fans who have attended games for 20 and 30 years at Wrigley Field break down in tears. Their players are heroes with whom fans have a strong emotional attachment and caring. Consider the case of third baseman Ron Santo, who played 15 years in Major League Baseball, 14 of those with the Chicago Cubs. Santo was an All Star in nine seasons and won five consecutive Gold Glove awards for excellence in fielding. A popular player, he continues as the broadcaster for the team today.

Through most of his career, *Santo kept a secret*. At age 18, he had been diagnosed with diabetes and given a life expectancy of 25 years. But in 1971, three years before his last game, he revealed his condition on "Ron Santo Day" at Wrigley Field. Santo, born in 1940, had both legs amputated in 2001 and 2002. Since 1974, he has raised more than $50 million for the Juvenile Diabetes Research Foundation through an annual Ron Santo walk. One special fan inspired by Santo, Bill Holden, made a walk of 2,100 miles from Arizona to Chicago and raised $250,000 for diabetes research. When Santo's uniform number was retired on a special day in 2003 at Wrigley Field, Bill Holden came through the outfield door, walked onto the field, and embraced Santo. There was applause, but mostly not a dry eye in the house. This story is depicted in an emotional documentary, *This Old Cub*,[46] written and produced by Santo's son. Anyone would be emotionally affected by this story, but if your roots or family are from the Chicago area, the story reinforces your sense of community beyond belief. In 2005, Santo was considered for the Baseball Hall of Fame but missed the mark by eight votes. When his number was retired in Chicago at Wrigley Field, Santo told the home crowd: "This is *my* Hall of Fame."[47]

The fixation on pop culture, celebrity, and star athletes represents cultural trends toward fantasies of immediate success and social narcissism. We fall in love with the images we have created. The increased possibilities for fantasy activity further distort our view of reality. Sports, with its historical significance and attachment to community, helps provide an experience that offers competitive reality—if only it can be protected from the excesses of commercialism. Images and heroes have changed from causes of social justice to recovery of self-inflicted maladies in the culture of excess.

Fast-moving and changing images of attainment, an ideal, success, and heroes contribute to the growth of the culture of excess. The overidealization of media figures and obsession with their struggles and "recovery" are a part of the growth of cultural narcissism. In this case, there is more of a social narcissism to the process—falling in love with the images of success. We crave and desire to be successful like the stars. We want to act, look, and dress like they do. The intensity and obsessiveness creates a huge entertainment financial empire that invites commercialism and the profit from entrepreneurial narcissism. In traditional sports, this increased commercialism can be excessive and harm the historical significance and attachment to the community and its identity.

The development of identity for individuals growing up in their community is an important indicator for a healthy society. As individuals, teens and young adults must answer the question "Who am I?" The answer to this question of identity development is much harder today than ever before.

## NOTES

1. Agassi made comments and was quoted about the label and image in several places, including *Men's Journal* of August 1995. See also Brown, N. (2009, January 19). Andre Agassi: Image isn't everything. *Signs of the Times.* Retrieved January 19, 2009 from http://www.signsofthetimes.org.au /archives/2004/january_february/article5.shtm.

2. Reich, R. (2008). *Supercapitalism* (p. 178). New York: Alfred A. Knopf.

3. Boorstin, D. (1992). *The Image: A guide to pseudo-events in America* (Vintage Books ed.). New York: Vintage Books.

4. Ibid. Social Narcissism, pp. 257–258.

5. Klayman, B. (2008, September 25). Technology spurs growth of fantasy sports in U.S. *Reuters*. Retrieved February 7, 2009 from http://www.reuters.com/article/sportsNews/idUSTRE48O02L20080925.

6. Bauerlein, M. (2008). *The dumbest generation: How the digital age stupefies young Americans and jeopardizes our future* (p. 42). New York: Jeremy P. Tarcher/Penguin.

7. Moraes, L. (2005, February 4). State of the Union: A smaller audience. *The Washington Post*, p. C07.

8. Orange County Demographics, see http://egov.ocgov.com/portal/site/ocgov/; see also http://www.muninetguide.com/states/california/Orange.php.

9. Dunlop, S. (Executive Producer). (2007). *The real housewives of Orange County*. Season 3. [Television series]. New York: Bravo. Episodes can be viewed at http://www.bravotv.com/the-real-housewives-of-orange-county.

10. Brings, K., Call, M., Fraenkel, J., & Pupa, D. (Producers). (2008). *The real housewives of New York City*. Season 2. [Television series]. New York: Bravo. Episodes can be viewed at http://www.bravotv.com/the-real-housewives-of-new-york-city; Taub, N., Jones, T., & Platt, J. (2008). *The Real Housewives of Atlanta*. Season 1. [Television series]. New York: Bravo. This series features five housewives, four of whom are African American, described as "five glamorous Southern belles." Episodes can be viewed at http://www.bravotv.com/the-real-housewives-of-atlanta.

11. *The Huffington Post*. (2008, November 4). Anderson Cooper: Loves factual reporting, dance and "Real Housewives of Atlanta." Retrieved February 7, 2009 from http://www.huffingtonpost.com/2008/11/04/anderson-cooper-loves-fac_n_141078.html.

12. Boorstin, D. (1992). *The image: A guide to pseudo-events in America* (p. 254). New York: Vintage Books.

13. Vanderberg, B. (1999). *'59 Summer of the Sox*. Champaign, IL: Sports Publishing Inc. Smith story on p. 118.

14. Ibid. Quote by Veeck, p. 100.

15. All three games at the converted Los Angeles Coliseum in the 1959 World Series drew more than 92,000 fans. Converting the field for the newly arrived Dodgers baseball team meant putting a very short fence in

left field at only 250 feet but with a 42-foot high wall. The Dodgers had a player named Wally Moon, who even though he was left handed perfected an inside-out swing to hit the ball off of and over the short left field wall. His efforts were called "Moon shots."

16. Frommer, D. (2009, February 14). Dot-com billionaire: Mark Cuban. Forbes.com. Retrieved February 7, 2009 from http://www.forbes.com/2006/02/11/mark-cuban-money_cx_de_money06_0214cuban.html.

17. Swartz, J. (2004, April 25). Losing's not an option for Cuban. *USA Today.* Retrieved February 7, 2009 from http://www.usatoday.com/money/2004-04-25-cuban_x.htm.

18. Junnarkar, S. (1999, July 20). Yahoo completes Broadcast.com acquisition. CNET News. Retrieved February 7, 2009 from http://news.cnet.com/Yahoo-completes-Broadcast.com-acquisition/2100-1023_3-228762.htm.

19. Forbes.com. (2007, March 8). Special report: The world's billionaires. Retrieved February 7, 2009 from http://www.forbes.com/lists/2007/10/07billionaires_The-Worlds-Billionaires_Rank_17.html.

20. Maccoby, M. (2003). *The Productive Narcissist.* New York: Broadway Books.

21. databaseBasketball.com. (2009). Dallas Mavericks (1980–). Retrieved February 7, 2009 from http://www.databasebasketball.com/teams/teampage.htm?tm=dal&lg=n. See also http://www.nba.com/finals2006/.

22. ABC News. (2006, June 20). Cuban slammed with $250,000 fine. Retrieved February 7, 2009 from http://abcnews.go.com/Sports/story?id=2098577&page=1.

23. The Associated Press. (January 17, 2002). Mavs owner serves smiles and ice cream. *The Daily Texan online.* Retrieved February 7, 2009 from http://www.dailytexanonline.com/sports/1.1266192.

24. Mariotti, J. (2006, May 30). Pitiful Cubs could use a maverick owner. *Chicago Sun-Times*; The Associated Press. (2007, July 13). Mark Cuban applies to buy Chicago Cubs. Retrieved February 7, 2009 from http://www.redorbit.com/news/sports/999310/mark_cuban_applies_to_buy_chicago_cubs/index.html.

25. Robbins, L., & Sanati, C. (2009, July 17). Judge dismisses suit against Cuban. *New York Times.* Retrieved July 31, 2009 from http://www.nytimes.com/2009/07/18/business/18Insider.html.

26. Klayman, B. (2008, September 25). Technology spurs growth of fantasy sports in U.S. *Reuters*. Retrieved February 7, 2009 from http://www.reuters.com/article/sportsNews/idUSTRE48O02L20080925.

27. Cuban gave a million dollars to start Fallen Patriot Fund through Bank of America. See http://www.fallenpatriotfund.org/4_16_03.html.

28. Robinson, R. (1993, April 4). Baseball; A bad guy who finished first. *The New York Times*. Retrieved February 7, 2009 from http://query.nytimes.com/gst/fullpage.html?res=9F0CE5D71639F937A35757C0A965958260&sec=&spon=. This is a review of Gerald Eskenazi's book, *The Lip: A Biography of Leo Durocher*. The book notes that Durocher never really said those exact four words, "nice guys finish last," but that reporters rephrased his statement for impact.

29. Mink, M. (2000, August 23). Baseball player Willie Mays: He gave every game his all. *Investors Business Daily*, p. A4.

30. Robertson, O. (2003). *The Big O: My life, my times, my game*. New York: Rodale Inc.

31. NBA Media Ventures. (2009). *NBA Encyclopedia, Playoff Edition*. Retrieved February 7, 2009 from http://www.nba.com/history/players/robertson_summary.html.

32. Robertson, *The Big O: My life, my times, my game*, pp. 40–41.

33. Ibid.

34. O'Conner, Ian. (2003, June 5). Sammy's fall from grace hurts image. *USA Today*. Retrieved February 7, 2009 from http://www.usatoday.com/sports/columnist/oconnor/2003-06-04-oconnor_x.htm.

35. Roberts, J. (2005, March 18). McGwire's testimony leaves doubts. CBS New. Retrieved February 7, 2009 from http://www.cbsnews.com/stories/2005/03/18/entertainment/main681498.shtml.

36. Blum, R. (2007, January 10). McGwire strikes out; Gwynn, Ripken in. The Associated Press. Retrieved February 7, 2009 from http://www.redorbit.com/news/sports/795818/mcgwire_strikes_out_gwynn_ripken_in/index.html.

37. Jones, R. (2008, November 6). Hamilton on his success: "It's a God thing." *Daily Reflector*. Retrieved February 7, 2009 from http://www.reflector.com/sports/hamilton-on-his-success-its-a-god-thing-227786.html.

38. Verducci, T. (2008, December 29). Moment of the year: Baseball. *Sports Illustrated*. Retrieved February 7, 2009 from http://sportsillustrated.cnn.com/2008/writers/tom_verducci/12/29/moment.of.the.year/.

Verducci describes the Hamilton home run derby event at Yankee Stadium as a "public redemption of a crack addict."

39. Carr, D. (2008, July 20). Me and my girls. *The New York Times Magazine*. Retrieved February 7, 2009 from http://www.nytimes.com/2008/07/20/magazine/20Carr-t.html.

40. Miner, M. (2008, May 29). Steinberg on Steinberg. *Chicago Reader*. Retrieved February 7, 2009 from http://www.chicagoreader.com/features/stories/hottype/080529/. The article is a review of Steinberg, N. (2008). *Drunkard: A hard drinking life*. New York: Penguin.

41. Downey, M. (2008, July 23). The 12 steps to success. *Los Angeles Times*, p. A17.

42. Norris, M. (2007, October 7). Marion Jones pleads guilty in drug case, retires. *NPR, All things considered*. Retrieved March 1, 2009 from http://www.npr.org/templates/story/story.php?storyId=15060426; Associated Press. (March 7, 2008). Marion Jones starts 6 month prison term. Retrieved March 1, 2009 from http://www.cbc.ca/sports/amateur/story/2008/03/07/marion-jones-prison.html.

43. MedlinePlus. (2009). Prescription drug abuse. Retrieved February 7, 2009 from http://www.nlm.nih.gov/medlineplus/prescriptiondrug abuse.html.

44. Digiovanna, M. (2005, January 4). Name change is hot Angel topic. *Los Angeles Times*, p. D-11.

45. The Associated Press. (2006, February 9). Jurors reject Anaheim claim in Angel's name change dispute. *USA Today*. Retrieved February 7, 2009 from http://www.usatoday.com/sports/baseball/al/angels/2006-02-09-name-change_x.htm.

46. Comstock, T., & Santo, J. (Producers), Santo, J. (Director). (2004). *This old cub*. [Motion picture]. United States: Emerging Pictures.

47. Jauss, B. (2003, September 29). Santo: Flag "my hall of fame." *Chicago Tribune*. Retrieved February 7, 2009 from http://www.chicago tribune.com/sports/cs-030929santoretired,0,3733336.story.

# Chapter 7

# MULTIPLE IDENTITY: ISN'T THAT SPECIAL

I am what I am and that's all that I am
I'm Popeye the Sailor Man

—Elzie Segar, "Popeye Song"

Leonard Nimoy, an accomplished actor who has played many diverse and successful roles, is certainly best known for his character Spock in the *Star Trek* television series. Spock, described as "half-human and half-Vulcan," is a character that still fascinates the public. Nimoy played the character from 1966 to 1969 and received three Emmy nominations for his role.[1]

Nimoy wrote an autobiography in 1977 titled *I Am Not Spock*, suggesting to many that he was rejecting the role and the character he had successfully played. Nimoy reported he was only trying to draw a distinction between himself and Spock. Meanwhile, the series ended and the motion picture *Star Trek* was released with great success. Nimoy made amends for the first autobiography; in 1995, he published another, titled *I Am Spock*. In this book he explained away the first autobiography to the fans. He reported the first title was misperceived and that the Spock character has not changed and is a part of him.[2] Writers for *The Simpsons* could not resist. In one episode the character Comic Book Guy purchases three books—*I Am Not Spock*, *I Am Spock*, and *I Am Not Scotty*.[3] In 2002, Dan Castellaneta, the voice of Homer Simpson, released a comedy album titled *I Am Not Homer*.[4]

Today's screen and social media can certainly provide much complexity to self-definition, identity, and the identity development process.

Cultural pressures are everywhere to try to describe who we are, what our roles are, our commitments, and finally our own personality. The end goal of our formative years in our teens and early adulthood is to establish an answer to the question: Who am I? The end goal is described as "identity achievement," the attainment of a clear self-definition and direction in one's life. Along the way, we often encounter an "identity crisis." Today the complex process of identity development represents the conflict between developing a healthy sense of self and cultural excess.

## MAMA: I LOVE ME

Erik Erikson (1902–94) was one of the most influential psychologists of all time. His immensely popular books included *Gandhi's Truth*, which describes the origins of militant nonviolence and which was awarded a Pulitzer Prize. Trained in psychoanalysis and analyzed by Anna Freud, Erikson was a psychoanalyst who extended Freudian theory. He placed greater emphasis on the importance of the ego over the id. But it was Erikson's developmental theory (referred to as a psychosocial theory of development) and emphasis on ego identity that remains so profoundly important today. Unlike Piaget and Freud, Erikson's developmental theory covers the entire life span—from cradle to grave or womb to tomb—and emphasizes the teen years, a time when the focus is on resolving and struggling for an identity.

Erikson's personal story of identity was revealing. He was born out of wedlock to Danish parents. His father left his mother before he was born, and his mother never told him about his father. When his mother moved to Germany, she married Erik's pediatrician, Dr. Homburger. As a child, Erikson grew up unaware that Homburger was not his natural father, and he kept the last name Homburger until age 37.

When Erikson went to school in Germany, he did not fit in. German students would not accept him because his stepfather was Jewish. Jewish students rejected him because he had Nordic features. As an adult, the identity conflict continued. Erikson fell in love with Joan Serson, who became pregnant. But Erikson refused to marry her. Friends pointed out he would be repeating the pattern of his father, allowing his child to have the societal mark of illegitimacy. Finally, he did marry her—three times—in civil, Jewish, and Protestant ceremonies.[5]

Other researchers have greatly expanded Erikson's emphasis on the identity process and how the process unfolds for teens and young adults.

Notably, James Marcia utilized a semi-structured interview process to present a model of four exploratory stages. He emphasized that identity achievement involved the degree of exploration and commitment to an identity in more specific areas such as vocational identity, religious identity, and gender identity. Marcia concluded that in adolescence a crisis evolves as the youth reevaluates old or existing values and makes a commitment to certain values or roles. The four stages he delineated are noteworthy for the terms used: diffusion, foreclosure, moratorium, and achievement.[6]

John, age 21, is a premed major. His father is a successful doctor with a specialty area. By age 10, John knew he would grow up to be a doctor. He also knew his father could get him into medical school at his prestigious alma mater. In identity theory, John is in foreclosure. He has not explored any alternatives or other career options. There is no crisis for John as he has made a commitment without going through a crisis stage. Many friends tell John he is lucky—he knows what he wants even as they are struggling to find something they want to pursue in school.

John is concerned about his 18-year-old brother, Ron, who has graduated from high school and is working as a waiter. Ron surfs most of the time and parties. He has no crisis and has not committed to anything—at least not yet. To some, he is described as lost or floundering, with no direction in his life. Ron's stage is described as identity diffusion.

Their sister, Carol, age 19, is in her first year in college. She has already changed her major twice. She has tried some different volunteer jobs to see if she liked the work. But right now, she is not trying anything, just taking the usual required classes. She seems to be stuck in her exploration. Carol has been having a crisis and is unsure what she wants to pursue. Soon, however, she will set out to explore another area. Carol is described as in the stage of identity moratorium.

So which process is healthy? Researchers have found that a back and forth process of exploration seems normal. A young person tries something, then steps back (moratorium), tries something again with some success (achievement), steps back, and continues with this pattern. Researchers call this a MAMA cycle, a process of exploration and commitment (moratorium to achievement repeated) that leads to more successful outcomes.[7]

The process of this back and forth exploration to try to find one's identity is a healthy one. Of course, so many familial factors determine the identity road that an individual more or less travels. Cases where things are not going well are referred to as negative identity, when a teen may completely reject parental values. For example, a preacher's son resorts to drinking and lawbreaking behavior. A voice tells some of us: No way am I going to be like my parents!

Today's cultural forces have a significant impact on the normal MAMA cycles of teens and young adults. Everything is faster today, and the lure of what has been called sudden wealth syndrome must influence self-definition and identity formation. Within a background of cultural narcissism, today's young person highlights "me" with fast and multiple cycles of MAMA. Of course, there are now possibilities for media levels of success/achievement in these cycles. Twenty-eight-year-old Marcus Lehman was a graduate of Emory University Medical School. He became a celebrity on the *Survivor* reality show in 2008, with the usual bare chest pictures splashed everywhere. An episode made big news when his penis was exposed while running.[8] Such celebrity would not exactly fit the identity or role one would expect for his or her family doctor.

But a doctor or a celebrity—it is all the same—why limit oneself? Today's fast-paced possibilities and opportunities open the door to unlimited identities. Why just choose one when multiple identities are possible and more exciting? A doctor and an actor or TV star. Why not? Yet today, the process of identity exploration that Marcia describes is faster, can change quickly, and is more expansive than ever before. Constantly evolving and changing, it has more threads, more choices, and more paths. And we love choices and unlimited possibilities. A research study of 30 young adults analyzed their "personal narratives," written stories, and explanations of how their religious views and sexuality developed. Researchers aimed to ascertain what factors the young adults considered to be constraints and facilitators to their identity attainment. The conclusion was that at least for these young adults, identity was attained not through crisis and commitment but rather through a self-actualizing process; that is, a process of continuous growth and development toward attaining a level of complete fulfillment.[9]

The term self-actualization is historically related to Abraham Maslow's well-known hierarchy of needs. Maslow's humanistic theory stated that we cannot attain self-actualization unless our basic needs of hunger and safety are satisfied. (Poor people are then quite limited.) Believing that we are always trying for complete self-fulfillment, Maslow grouped needs hierarchically into a pyramid model, with physiological needs as the base and self-actualization at the top. He intensively studied successful and famous people to identify the components of a self-actualized person, but his process was critiqued as not being very scientific. He could not find too many self-actualized people to match his definition. In the end he concluded less than 1 percent of people were self-actualized.[10] The model, however, is reflected today in those people who attempt to climb the highest mountain because it is there or engage in risky extreme sports.

The phenomenon of today's youth engaging in a sort of self-actualization process of identity development is another symptom of our culture of excess. We explore more, develop more options, become over-committed, and even blur fantasy with reality. Consistency and a single-minded commitment are out. Why get boxed in with one identity? (Besides, traditional identities are boring.) Look at me—see how many things I can do. This self-actualizing paradigm also fits nicely with the highly valued "multitasking." If you can do many things at the same time, you are many people. More are better than few. Few are better than one.

But the self-actualizing tendency of identity development eventually has to be resolved. We cannot continue with open possibilities all our lives and for multiple identities. Despite the constant mantra of "inventing and reinventing" ourselves, we make choices and declare ourselves as com-mitted to an identity. William James, one of the founders of psychology, described this process more than a century ago:

> With most objects of desire, physical nature restricts our choice to but one of many represented goods, and even so, it is here. I am often confronted by the necessity of standing by one of my empirical selves and relinquishing the rest. Not that I would not, if I could, be both handsome and fat and well-dressed, and a great athlete, make a million in a year, be a wit, a bon vivant and a lady-killer, as well as philosopher, a philanthropist, statesman, warrior and African explorer, as well as a "tone poet" and saint. But the thing is simply impossible ... such different characters may conceivably at the outset of life be alike, possible to a man. But to make any one of them actual, the rest must more or less be suppressed. So the secret of this truest, strongest, deepest self must review the list carefully and pick out the one in which to stake his salvation.[11]

Within the self-actualizing process of identity development, rapid MAMA cycles, and the immediate "me" of social media, another related psychological need emerges—the tremendous desire to emerge as "suc-cessful" by being remarkably different, even unique. The powerful urge to stand out from the crowd and be recognized can result in multiple identities and some interesting alternatives in how we represent ourselves and how we look. The trend is always to be unique and cool, in response to the pressure to be different, and today's media culture provides many avenues for doing so.


## MAVERICKS AND METROSEXUALS

A maverick is defined as someone who is an independent thinker, a nonconformist, or perhaps even a rebel and someone who can be a lone dissenter. The term fits the uniqueness factor and has the capacity also to tap into people's frustration and anger with the status quo, or in fact, with life in general. Countless famous and successful people in the arts and sciences have been called "mavericks." The term is often applied to them post-success; that is, their success is often attributed to their being different and unique—a maverick. And as for being a rebel, that has always been a popular icon in today's society, ranging from James Dean to the "bad boys" of rock and roll and sports.

In one research study, people communicated pro or con messages on an issue to a group of subjects. Some communicators were defined as mavericks, or specifically, individuals who had quit an organization over the issue that was being presented to the group of subjects. The other communicators were defined as members of the organization and people who supported the organization's position on the issue. The group of subjects perceived those presenters defined as mavericks as being fair and more trustworthy than the non-maverick presenters. In addition, maverick presenters were able to elicit more changes of opinion among the group members. Subjects perceived the mavericks' conclusions as "better justified by the facts."[12]

The mavericks, as defined in this study, would seem quite admirable—those who had left an organization on principle, an action that probably rarely occurs. Today's definition of a maverick seems much broader, including the rebels, eccentrics, and the lone dissenters who may be partially crazy. Still, it seems that to proclaim oneself a maverick is a good thing and an identity that many people aspire to attain. To be a maverick makes one unique, draws attention, and may give oneself more credibility. This may be true even if the title is self-proclaimed.

But there are complicating factors to the image of being a maverick. Senator John McCain was always defined as a maverick throughout his career. Recently, the maverick status did not work, at least in winning the Presidency. In politics, being a maverick may not be as powerful a force as former Speaker of the House Sam Rayburn's famous dictum: "To get along, go along."

When McCain ran in 2000, he was very popular and appeared to be the front-runner to win the Republican nomination for the Presidency. The maverick thing seemed to be working. But apparently McCain's being a maverick and his independent status did not sit well with his party's establishment. McCain's own party turned against him with an active campaign which included ugly rumors. The party quickly sought out another candidate and pushed George Bush to the forefront, who eventually won the nomination.[13] The whole process left McCain and many others bitter.

Although McCain achieved the Republican nomination in 2008, some remnants of this conflict may have still persisted. While trying to maintain his maverick status, this time he also courted others and their views, something that compromised and detracted from his maverick identity. He then tried to enhance that identity, selecting Alaska Governor Sarah Palin, considered another maverick, as his running mate. But it did not work. Palin was even lampooned on *Saturday Night Live* by Tina Fey who described how she was going to do "mavericky" things if elected.

The selection of Palin as VP highlighted the complexity of gender identity development. The traditional female role/image has of course dramatically changed. But there seems to be a similarity in the vitriol and intensity of response to females who emerge for a powerful position and the media spotlight. Hillary Clinton and Sarah Palin are completely different in ideology and experience. However, they did share the polarizing aspect of either being strongly admired or strongly disliked. This polarizing aspect is obvious and glaring. Palin's emergence fits the models being discussed. She had a fast emergence into the path of success. Many assessed her as not qualified or having enough experience to be the VP. While she represented today's fast-track model of identity development to success, reality set in about how and why she got there. Realizing Senator McCain was 72 years old and it could be more possible she would be president did not help. Being a maverick was not enough.

The complexity of female gender identity has also been illuminated by author Susan Faludi who carefully documented what happened after 9/11. In Faludi's book *The Terror Dream*,[14] she documents the reemergence after the 9/11 attacks of traditional identities, from "security moms" to "hawks." John Wayne resurfaced as the male image and the frail helpless woman as the female image. From a cultural perspective, underneath the superficial attempts to be different and expand identity development, gender identity looms as an unresolved area subject to intense emotional reactions.

Gender identity provides another arena in which to seek an avant-garde identity. A metrosexual is defined as a heterosexual male who is very concerned about his appearance and who demonstrates characteristics of a stereotypic gay lifestyle.[15] In other words, the metrosexual is a male who willingly displays feminine traits and a strong aesthetic sense. He might use several hair products, have his nails manicured, and spend a lot of time and money on his appearance. Mark Simpson originated the term in articles in 1994, but mostly developed the concept in his 2002 Salon.com article titled, "Meet the Metrosexual."[16] In this article, Simpson utilized David Beckham, international star and a soccer player, as an example of metrosexual. Acknowledgment and popularity of the term followed, and it is frequently referenced in media portrayals. For example, the television show *Queer Eye for the Straight Guy* involves homosexual males who offer consulting services to clueless heterosexual men seeking to shape up their appearance and lifestyle to impress women.

What is most remarkable about the metrosexual identity is how it clearly seems to advance consumerism. After all, if men begin to use female products, a dramatic expansion of business and sales will occur. Simpson notes that the metrosexual follows the dramatic trend toward increased consumerism, imitating images seen in the media. As such, the metrosexual becomes a narcissist, falling in love with himself or idealistic images of himself that he wants to portray to others.[17] In this sense, the metrosexual, through continuing to perfect appearance and lifestyle, is in effect saying, "Hey, look at me." Marketing specialists have tried to capitalize further on the popularity of the metrosexual term and its support of consumerism. Additional terms for spin-off types of identity did not seem to stick. The term "ubersexual" was advanced for a while, along with the term "heteropolitan." Neither caught on.[18]

But the metrosexual identity is another part of a self-actualizing identity process. Continuing to grow and change into this particular path involves expansion of one's gender identity. Simpson hit it right by noting its relationship to narcissism and falling in love with oneself. In addition, it relates to the materialism of cultural excess. The metrosexual is described as an "urban male" and someone who thus has a considerable amount of money to spend on consumer products. In particular, as the rich and famous expand their lifestyles and enhance their appearances, we can watch them do so.

## TATTOO ME TATTOO YOU

I decided to have dinner at a local restaurant. I am by myself, so I sit at the bar and order from the menu. The bartender/waiter seems to be about 25 years old, and I notice he has tattoos on both arms. A short while later, three attractive young women come in and sit at the opposite end of the bar. When the waiter goes to take their order, they ask about his tattoos. An animated discussion follows, as he shows them both arms, explaining the meaning and significance of his tattoos and that he got them while in the military service. They are impressed, admiring his tattoos on both arms. The process is an eye opener for me, as meeting and flirting with the opposite sex certainly has changed.

Tattoos are fashionable. A Pew Research report in 2006 indicates that about 36 percent of 18- to 25-year-olds have one or more tattoos. Interestingly, 40 percent of individuals in the age range between 26 and 40 have at least one or more tattoos. In Pew's overall sample, 54 percent had gotten a tattoo, had dyed their hair a nontraditional color, or had some sort of body piercing in a place other than the ear lobe. However, tattoos remained the most popular form of expression.[19] A 2003 Harris Poll found similar results, reporting 36 percent of persons between the ages of 25 and 29 having tattoos.[20] In addition, the tattoo artistry is a developing business venture. More than 20,000 tattoo parlors are estimated to be operating in the United States. One article reported that tattoos are the sixth fastest growing retail business in the United States.[21]

The normative aspect of getting a tattoo represents a cultural change. It used to be that tattoos were associated with criminals and gangsters. They still are. Tattoos are used to identify them, or even provide evidence of gang membership. Traditional research reports also indicate that tattoos are correlated with risky behavior, such as substance abuse.[22] In addition, the Food and Drug Administration points out that tattoos can expose people to infections, and then people who are dissatisfied with their tattoos may later want them removed.[23] Nevertheless, tattoos are now a popular item for the general public. Individuals may have many complex reasons for getting tattoos, and one is the obvious aspect of sexuality. Thirty-four percent of those who get tattoos report that they feel sexier, though this tendency is higher for females than males.[24]

Roger, age 20, has been coming to therapy for about six weeks. He flunked out of college and is now working and trying to find himself. His parents are quite concerned, viewing him as in the identity diffusion stage—lost and without focus. They make the referral to my office.

He reluctantly keeps the appointment, and acknowledges that quite often he sinks into depression. Finally, in one session he shows up sporting a new tattoo. He continues to look at it as he sits in front of me. I have to state the obvious: "I see you've gotten a tattoo." He then shows me the tattoo, which is a phrase lettered on his arm. He explains the meaning of the statement—a self-affirming, motivational statement that has meaning to him. At a loss initially, I refrain from asking why he would do that, and we explore the significance of the tattoo and the statement.

Michael Atkinson, a sociologist at McMaster University in Ontario, Canada, is an expert on tattoos. He refers to tattoos as "the socio-genesis of a body art." Atkinson, utilizing a participant observer process, collected data from direct observation and involvement in the community of body art documenting the complexities of why people get tattoos. Atkinson describes tattoos as "a personal identity construction." He analyzes the sociological aspect, describing the body as a "text of culture." Body modification, such as a tattoo, serves multiple purposes in identity development. Atkinson believes that the motivation is much broader than simply the desire to be unique and cool or an attempt at individualism. He even reports that body modifications are ways of communicating and demonstrating self-control; in other words, a way to "release anger in a restricted manner." He certainly seems correct. I have had people tell me several stories of significance regarding their tattoos. They use their body to express a wide range of emotions. Tattoos may even be words or symbols in a foreign language or culture. They may be a means of dealing with grief and loss or remembering a deceased loved one. Tattoos are a very complex form of identity development and involve a significant aspect of expression and externalization of feelings.[25]

And they are ubiquitous. One can hardly avoid noticing tattoos. Watch any NBA basketball game on TV, and you cannot help but notice all the tattoos the players have. They seem to become more noticeable every year. When a player is shooting a free throw, it is hard not to be distracted by the multiple tattoos covering the player's arms. Tattoos also seem to be a way for young people to connect with each other, as in the scene I reported at the restaurant. Today's young modern couple enjoy the process of "tattoo me and tattoo you," as both partners obtain their own significant tattoo and maintain their own separate sense of identity. Bonded—but yet separate and unique.

Just as I check my personal reaction to tattoos, the generation gap is apparent. Walking down the hall at my office, a young adult female is talking openly on her cell phone. She tells her friend that she visited her father and reports: "I had to have the tattoo talk with him." Some parents just do not understand. In addition, you still hear the term "tramp stamp," referring to women who have a tattoo on their lower back. As the story goes, women who have a tattoo here are considered sexually promiscuous and not the sort of girl you take home to meet your parents.

A further step in body modification may not be so complex. Cosmetic surgery is simply about looking and feeling better. Improvement in one's appearance can often be presented as a makeover and "a new me." It, too, is big business. The American Society for Aesthetic Plastic Surgery (ASAPS) reported that from 1997 through 2007 the total number of cosmetic medical procedures performed in the United States increased 450 percent. From 1997 through 2005, surgical procedures have increased by 119 percent, while nonsurgical procedures increased by 726 percent. The most commonly performed procedure was Botox injections, described as a nonsurgical procedure. The most popular surgical procedures were liposuction and breast augmentation.

Ninety percent of all cosmetic surgeries are undertaken by women. More than half of these cosmetic procedures are performed in an office with about 28 percent performed at surgical centers, and only 17 percent at hospitals. The cost figure is noteworthy. The American public spent more than $13 billion on cosmetic procedures in 2007, or $8.3 billion for surgical procedures and $4.7 billion for nonsurgical procedures.[26]

Cosmetic surgery has more serious risks than getting an infection from the tattoo process or ending up simply with a bad tattoo. Horror stories emerge of disfigurement or even death from procedures performed by unqualified or irresponsible practitioners. As for the costs reported above, cosmetic surgery is easily the most expensive form of body modification. Thus, cosmetic surgery is a more elite direct form of body modification— and improved identity—related to socioeconomic status. Not surprising, most cosmetic surgeries are obtained by Caucasians, at 80 percent.[27]

VIRTUAL IDENTITIES

In today's era of technology, it is possible to have multiple identity sources, not just involving your body. Anyone can adopt a digital identity. Combine the digital identity with a fantasy world and the possibilities for identity attainment increase. In the virtual world of online games, a computer avatar is a representation designed and created by the user. Creating your own avatar allows you to live up to the slogan for joining the U.S. Army—"be all that you can be."

Avatars are often described as alter egos. An avatar can be anything—animal, hero/heroine, cartoon character—you name it. There are generic avatars one can adopt for use, but you do not want to be caught dead with one of those in the virtual online gaming world. That would be like being the new kid at school who dresses funny. The skill comes in creating your own personal avatar, an interactive character. The customization involves changing anything from body type, skin, clothing, hair, or any aspect of your appearance. In addition, your new identity can jump, fly, dance, hop, skip planets, or even create other objects. The avatar becomes an entity unto itself as your new identity collects and acquires things through performance in the virtual world game. These accumulations also can be anything, such as virtual money, tools, food, and material possessions.[28]

Jeremy Bailenson, an assistant professor at Stanford University, directs the "Virtual Human Interaction Lab" and has become a well-known researcher in the area involving the interaction of virtual reality and the field of psychology. Bailenson was trained as a cognitive psychologist, but his interests evolved into the virtual world. After receiving a grant from the National Science Foundation, Bailenson began conducting research on virtual-human interactions. He has concentrated considerably on the virtual classroom and using avatars for teaching. Bailenson reports, "My virtual representation of me, commonly known as an avatar, can outperform me as a teacher any day."[29]

Bailenson and colleagues have developed cutting-edge technology at their lab at Stanford that has enabled them to build avatars that look identical to the person represented. This includes using sophisticated devices to mimic gestures, touch, and hand movements. This precise technology can thus be transmitted through computers. Through this capacity, a digital avatar of a teacher has precision and demonstrated effectiveness. As Bailenson states, "A teacher's avatar has powers that just don't exist in physical space."[30]

Bailenson's technology has created a digital avatar representing a teacher who mimics the students in the class. In a number of laboratory studies, the researchers examined head movement, handshakes, and nonverbal behavior of students. Relying on previous research, Bailenson notes that when someone nonverbally mimics another person, displaying their similar movements, they maximize their social influence. People who mimic are seen as more likable and more persuasive than people who do not mimic. In a series of laboratory studies, Bailenson and colleagues demonstrated that if a teacher practices "virtual nonverbal mimicry," positive results are elicited. Virtual nonverbal mimicry is defined as perceiving the student's nonverbal actions and then transforming the teacher's nonverbal behavior to mimic or resemble the student's motions. All this is done through sophisticated computer equipment.

This mimicking has profound results. First of all, students are not conscious of or aware of the mimicking. In addition, they pay more attention to the virtual teacher, directing their gaze much more to these teachers who mimic than the teachers who behave in a normal manner. Finally, they are more influenced by the mimicking teachers than the teachers who behave naturally. Since they are more influenced by the mimicking teachers, they are more likely to follow their instructions and respond positively to a lesson.[31]

It does not stop there. Bailenson has created studies in which people watch their own avatars, in this case cartoon versions that represent themselves, and when their avatars become fat and gain weight by overeating, these persons in real life are more likely to adopt a weight loss plan. Likewise, people who observe their avatars slimming down by running on a treadmill become motivated to exercise more.[32] This may not be as innovative or creative as it sounds. Classic behavioral research from the 1970s and 1980s has shown that you can change your behavior or overcome fears by watching others or a film of others.[33] In this case, the observation is just of yourself. Unless the key factor is in actually controlling the avatar, then this also becomes a virtual version of "practice makes perfect." The principles of modeling and imitation remain the same, and have long been established as ways to change behavior. Today's version is just more high tech.

Other experiments carried out by Bailenson show that when "ordinary looking people" are assigned to very beautiful avatars and spend time with them in virtual reality, when they visit dating services later, they choose potential mates who are more attractive. This is in contrast to people who assume less attractive avatars.[34] Bailenson is aware of the power of his research and has refused to participate in studies that might sway the influence of voters on political candidates. He also realizes that this technology would certainly be used in marketing to promote products and services. But the bottom line is that by participating in a virtual world with an identity of an avatar totally created by one's own doing, this process can involve changes in real-world life. Bailenson states: "Our virtual identity is not separate from our physical identity."[35] I certainly hope he is wrong.

## IDENTITY HERE AND GONE

With all the travails and struggles to be unique and develop one's identity, it is disconcerting to realize your identity can be stolen. If your computer hardware is damaged, it does not matter what software you develop. The hardware of your identity is your name, driver's and Social Security numbers, and the financial history you have developed. One of the fastest growing crimes in the Unites States has been identity theft. While all sorts of electronic stealing and scams occur daily in financial transactions, someone can steal your entire identity and cause tremendous damage to your name and history. Trying to sort it out can be a nightmare. The crime is certainly psychologically violent. In 2004, the Department of Justice (DOJ) did a six-month survey to determine the extent of identity theft in the United States. They reported that in this six-month period, 3.6 million households experienced some form of identity theft, about 3 percent of all households in the country. The dollar value estimate of the loss total was reported at $3.2 *billion*.[36] The amount in 2004 pales in comparison to reports in the following years. While much of these costs are reimbursable by the financial institutions, two-thirds of those victims in the DOJ study reported a financial loss that averaged $1,290. Worse, 25 percent reported the problem was continuing. The problem can sometimes be resolved quickly in one day but can also last for about thirty days until it is taken care of and life returns to normal. Thirty-four percent of victims reported they had been contacted by a debt collector.[37] What a way to find out your credit has been ruined. The good news is that with increased awareness and regulations and enforcement, recent data shows improvement in a decline of the number of incidents and resolving the theft. A survey of 5,000 telephone interviews by Javelin Strategy & Research in 2006 provides estimates that incidents have declined by 12 percent from 2005. Cost/loss estimates in 2006 are only estimated at $49.3 billion, down from 55.7 billion in 2005. Once again, take a double look at the magnitude of these estimated dollar amounts. The report states that the number of incidents has declined for the past four years as we now all expect to have our information, identity, and money stolen, and our awareness reduces our odds of victimization. Time to resolve the matter has been lowered to about five hours from twenty-five in 2005.[38] We are getting much better at dealing with anticipated fraud.

By now, the fear of identity fraud is worse than the possibility of its actual occurrence. Identity theft and fraud protection is now a growth industry with banks and financial institutions offering services of "protection" for anywhere from $10 to $18 per month. But most of these only offer protection for the fraud of someone creating a new account in your name. This is only one of seven types of identity fraud and accounts for a very small proportion of occurrences. These plans only offer a way to tell you when an existing account has been violated, notifying you after you are already a victim.[39] As usual, the fear takes over, and many consumers are then conned further by the financial industry.

Still, we now carry with us the hypervigilance that someone will steal our personal information and history—a part of our self—and this is now just expected. We now struggle to develop our identity in a complex and overwhelming environment, and we struggle to protect it too. That takes a whole lot of energy. It makes us defensive.

Identity attainment and achievement is complex in today's technological society. Commitment and consistency prove difficult. The prevailing attitude about developing identity is that of going through a buffet line and picking what you want in whatever amount you want. The excess in our culture is not just with materialism but with our psychological self, our self-image, and our identity. What constitutes success needs to be redefined, by either a new generation or by cultural changes *we* must make collectively.

## NOTES

1. *Wikipedia: The Free Encyclopedia*. Retrieved February 14, 2009 from http://en.wikipedia.org/wiki/Leonard_Nimoy.

2. Nimoy, L. (1975). *I am not Spock*. Cutchogue, NY: Buccaneer Books. Nimoy, L. (1997). *I am Spock*. Cutchogue, NY: Buccaneer Books.

3. The South African TV Authority, Actor Profiles. Retrieved February 14, 2009 from http://www.tvsa.co.za/actorprofile.asp?actorid=2698.

4. Castellaneta, D. (2002). [Recorded by D. Castellaneta]. *I am not Homer*. [CD]. Los Angeles: Oglio Records.

5. Schultz, D., & Schultz, S. E. (2005). Erik Erikson. In D. Schultz & S. E. Shultz, *Theories of Personality* (8th ed.). Chapter 8: Erik Erikson. Belmont, CA: Thomson Wadsworth.

6. Stephen, J., Fraser, E., & Marcia J. E. (1992). Moratorium-Achievement (MAMA). Cycles in lifespan identity development: Value orientations and reasoning system correlates. *Journal of Adolescence*, 3:283–300.

7. Luyckx, K., Goossens, L., Soenens, B., & Beters, W. (2006). Unpacking commitment and exploration: Preliminary validation of an integrative model of late adolescent identity formation. *Journal of Adolescence*, 29:361–378.

8. Dehnart, A. (2008, September 28). Marcus Lehman's penis exposed on Survivor. Reality Blurred.com. Retrieved February 2, 2009 from http://www.realityblurred.com/realitytv/archives/survivor_gabon/2008_Sep_28 _marcus_penis.

9. Schachter, E. (2002). Identity constraints: The perceived structural requirements of a "good" identity. *Human Development*, 45:416–433.

10. Schultz, D., & Schultz, S. E. (2005). In D. Schultz & S. E. Schultz, *Theories of Personality* (8th ed.). Chapter 11: Abraham Maslow. Belmont, CA: Thomson Wadsworth.

11. Schachter, Identity constraints, 45:416–433.

12. Dutton, D. (1973). The maverick effect: Increased communicator credibility as a result of abandoning a career. *Canadian Journal of Behavioural Science*, 5 (2): 145–151.

13. Banks, A. (2008, January 14). Dirty tricks, South Carolina, and John McCain. *The Nation*. Http://www.thenation.com/doc/20080128/ banks.

14. Faludi, S. (2007). *The terror dream: Fear and fantasy in post 9/11 America*. New York: Metropolitan Books.

15. McFedries, P. *Wordspy*. Retrieved February 14, 2009 from http://www.wordspy.com/words/metrosexual.asp.

16. Simpson, M. (2002, July 22). Meet the metrosexual. He's well dressed, narcissistic and obsessed with butts. But don't call him gay. Salon.com. Retrieved February 14, 2009 from http://dir.salon.com/story/ent/feature/2002/07/22/metrosexual/.

17. Ibid.

18. Simpson, M. (2007, May 18). When the issue comes out. Guardian.co.uk. Retrieved February 14, 2009 from http://www.guardian .co.uk/commentisfree/2007/may/18/whentheissuecomesout.

19. Pew Research Center. (January 2007). *How young people view their lives, futures and politics: A portrait of Generation Next* (p. 21). Washington, D.C.: Pew Research Center.

20. Sever, J. M. (2003, October 8). A third of Americans with tattoos say they make them feel more sexy. *The Harris Poll #58*. Retrieved

February 14, 2009 from http://www.harrisinteractive.com/harris_poll/index.asp?PID=407.

21. Lord, M., & Lehmann-Haupt, R. (1997, October 26). A hole in the head? A parent's guide to tattoos, piercings, and worse. *U.S. News & World Report*. Retrieved February 14, 2009 from http://www.usnews.com/usnews/culture/articles/971103/archive_008193.htm.

22. Carroll, S., Riffenburgh, R., Roberts, T., & Myhre, E. (2002). Tattoos and body piercings as indicators of adolescent risk-taking behaviors. *Pediatrics*, 109 (6): 1021–1027. Roberts, T., & Ryan, S. (2002). Tattooing and high-risk behavior in adolescents. *Pediatrics*, 110 (6): 1058–1083.

23. U.S. Food and Drug Administration. (2008). *Tattoos and permanent makeup*. Retrieved February 14, 2009 from http://vm.cfsan.fda.gov/~dms/cos-204.html.

24. Sever, A third of Americans with tattoos say they make them feel more sexy.

25. Atkinson, M. (2003). *Tattooed: The Sociogenesis of a body art*. Toronto: University of Toronto Press. Atkinson, M. (2002). Pretty in ink: Conformity, resistance, and negotiation in women's tattooing. *Sex Roles*, 47 (5/6): 219–236. Atkinson, M. (2004). Tattooing and civilizing processes: Body modification as self-control. *The Canadian Review of Sociology and Anthropology*, 41 (2): 125–140. Anderson, M., & Sansone, R. (2003). Tattooing as a means of acute affect regulation. *Clinical Psychology and Psychotherapy*, 10:316–318.

26. American Society for Aesthetic Plastic Surgery. (2008, February 25). Cosmetic procedures in 2007. Retrieved February 1, 2009 from http://www.surgery.org/press/news-release.php?iid=491.

27. Ibid.

28. Kayne, R. (2007–2009). What is a computer avatar? WiseGEEK.com. Retrieved February 1, 2009 from http://www.wisegeek.com/what-is-a-computer-avatar.htm. Egen, S. (2005, June 20). The history of avatars. Imediaconnection.com. Retrieved February 14, 2009 from http://www.imediaconnection.com/content/6165.asp.

29. Bailenson, J. (2008). Why digital avatars make the best teachers. *The Chronicle of Higher Education*, 54 (30): B27.

30. Ibid.

31. Ibid.

32. Foster, A. (2008). What happens in a virtual world has a real-world impact, a scholar finds. *The Chronicle of Higher Education*, 54 (30): A14.

33. Albert Bandura has published countless books and research on imitation and modeling and its impact on learning and behavior. This research started with the well-known bobo doll experiment in which children who had watched an adult hit a bobo doll were more aggressive than children who had not seen the adult model.

34. Foster, What happens in a virtual world has a real-world impact, a scholar finds, A14.

35. Ibid.

36. U.S. Department of Justice, Office of Justice Programs. (2006, April 2). 3.6 million U.S. households learned they were identity theft victims during a six-month period in 2004. Retrieved February 14, 2009 from http://www.ojp.usdoj.gov/newsroom/pressreleases/2006/BJS06039.htm.

37. Ibid.

38. Mincer, J. (2007, February 7). Identity fraud declined 12% in prior year. *The Wall Street Journal*, p. B5A.

39. Kristof, K. (2008, September 14). Personal finance: Identity theft monitoring devices: Worth it? Most firms charge for basic fraud alerts that consumers could set up for themselves for free. *Los Angeles Times*, p. C3.

# Chapter 8

# GENERATION WE

Personality change follows change in behavior. Since we are what we do, if we want to change what we are we must begin by changing what we do, must undertake a new mode of action. Since the impact of such action is change it will run afoul of existing entrenched forces which will protest and resist. The new mode will be experienced as difficult, unpleasant, forced, unnatural, anxiety-provoking. It may be undertaken lightly but can be sustained only by considerable effort of will. Change will occur only if such action is maintained over a long period of time.

—Allen Wheelis, *How People Change*

A farmer had a donkey that would do anything he was asked. When told to stop, the donkey stopped. When told to eat, he ate. One day the farmer sold the donkey. That same day, the new owner complained to the farmer. "That donkey won't obey me. When you ask, he will sit, stop, eat—anything. For me, he does nothing." The farmer picked up a two-by-four and walloped the donkey. "He obeys," the farmer explained. "But first you have to get his attention."[1]

The American public has been whacked. They are shocked and attentive. By now the financial impact of a culture of excess has hit full force. The financial failures and downturn have been coming for a long time as Americans have lost self-control and lived way beyond their means. Assessment, solutions, and changing the trend of excess are complex. Economic spending plans are critiqued as counterproductive, allowing the culture of excess to continue without facing full responsibility for creating the failure. To take a more psychological perspective, it would be important to understand what has happened. Without some awareness and insight into how we got here, the same patterns would just continue. This is the same reason one goes to therapy to try to understand and change the way we are, the way we relate, the way we integrate our feelings. We explore how we experience and bind our anxiety, which increases our coping, changes how we respond, and improves our relationships. Then, slowly, change can occur. From a sociological perspective, understanding the interactive cultural trends allows for breaking the links in the cycle. We can then begin to go in a new direction and develop more comprehensive solutions.

The culture of excess involves a cycle of interactive components. Increased normative levels of narcissism foster entitlement and higher or even grandiose expectations. This, coupled with the immediacy and power of technology, increases impulsivity leading to the most important factor—the loss of self-control. From declining self-control follows increased risk-taking and deception. These processes involve tremendous manipulative behavior that also becomes normative. The outcomes of risk-taking and deception demand a response to correct failures, and our resources become drained. Declining self-control is the result of the underlying development of cultural narcissism, our shared sense of entitlement and unrealistic expectations.

The workplace has become a culture in and of itself, from which must emerge a new generation of business leaders who will demand checks on entitlement and narcissism. As the federal government sought to respond to the economic crisis at the end of 2008, a $350 billion "bailout" was given to banks supposedly to keep the economy from complete collapse. But when Merrill Lynch was sold to Bank of America in December 2008, Merrill Lynch executives took an early bonus before the sale was completed. Even though the firm lost $27 billion that year, Merrill distributed $3.6 billion to 700 employees. The top four persons received $121 million. One hundred and forty-nine employees received $3 million or more. Had the $3.6 billion been distributed to all 39,000 Merrill employees, each person could have received $91,000.[2] Too bad this isn't just one egregious example—as the pattern continues. In 2008, nine of the biggest banks paid out $32 billion in bonuses after taking in $175 billion in bailout funds. This included almost 5,000 financial executives who received a bonus larger than $1 million.[3] This continuous sense of entitlement in business leaders—that in this case is nothing but pure greed—will be halted by a new generation that demands self-control in business leaders through enforced regulation. It is unfortunate, but at this point only a strong response from government can stop the pigs at the trough. The Merrill Lynch story is typical. Other companies tried to hide their bonuses, calling them "retention awards," arguing that these are acceptable and necessary for business.

Many business owners do believe in equitable sharing. Taiwanese immigrants John Tu and David Sun formed Kingston Technology in the early 1990s in Fountain Valley, California. Kingston makes memory devices for computers. After attaining sales of more than a billion dollars, in 1996 they sold 80 percent of the company for $1.5 billion. They shared the profits with all 550 employees. The average payout for each employee was $130,000. Following the bonuses, Kingston's sales tripled to $3.8 billion. Their workforce increased by a factor of 6 to 3,300.[4]

In the home environment, awareness of entitlement falls upon parents. Ron, age 38, comes to therapy because he is getting a divorce. He travels a lot, the divorce is not yet finalized, and he still lives with his wife and sons. He is worried and not sure what to do about the boys, ages seven and nine. "They'll play video games all weekend," he laments, "unless I stop them." He tries to communicate with his wife about setting boundaries for the boys, but the relationship is strained. Ron relates that he told his son to feed the dog, but the food was left on a counter instead of being placed on the floor where the dog could eat. Ron checked himself before he lost his temper. He complains that his sons expect him to buy them everything they want. Ron is looking ahead and can envision his boys may not develop with enough self-control as they get older. He comes to realize, now is the time to respond with more limits as a parent. Ron recognizes that initially he may overregulate to create the intensity needed to get his sons' full attention—just like the farmer that whacked the donkey.

At school, the sense of entitlement also involves parents. Psychologist and parent training expert Madeline Levine titled her presentation: "Parenting the average child." Few signed up. "Nobody believed they had an average child," she reports.[5] The parental attitudes seem converted to student entitlement. About one-third of college students surveyed at the University of California, Irvine reported they expected to get a B grade just for attending lectures. Forty percent reported they deserved a B grade for completing required course reading.[6] The regulators at schools face the same tough battle to have stricter standards for parents and children, and especially to resist the pressure they feel to inflate grades.

In the interaction of culture (in all settings) and personality development, culture has come to dominate. Culture and personality development interact in a loop that feeds on itself. The challenge in redirecting both ourselves and our culture is to recognize the circular development that compounds the problem. Maria was only 22 when she came for therapy. She had been to the emergency room on three occasions in the past two months. She could not breathe and had heart palpitations each time. Her heart was fine, but now she feared going out, worried she would have another panic attack. She switched desks with a coworker at work to sit by the door in case she needed a fast exit. When she went grocery shopping, she went only to a small store where she knew where all the exits were. Eventually, Maria decided to return to where she grew up, a small rural town where she knew she would have family connections and feel less stress. Her fear of having another panic attack altered her behavior and lifestyle. Her symptoms built on symptoms and occurred on top of an underlying problem. So it is in our culture. The cycle of excess and narcissistic entitlement continues in a loop and alters the way we live. We have problem on top of problem, and sorting it out becomes a process in and of itself.

In the cycle of excess and cultural narcissism, repetition and a combination of intertwining factors elicit deeper psychological issues. Narcissistic entitlement combined with cyber-capitalism has produced a generation that is "me" focused. Our self-definition and identity have been altered. Boundaries between images and reality merge. The combination of entitlement and expectations of reward with altered images of relationships and attachments contribute to a concept of success that is both superficial and inflated. In the end, "success" motivated by grandiosity and unrealistic expectations does not yield satisfaction or happiness when it is supposedly attained. Who we are as individuals and as a society, how we connect, and our attachments to others have changed.


SUCCESS AND WE

To address current trends, our culture must develop a new generation that will move toward a different concept and process of attaining success or "making it." This new concept is based on connectedness with culture and has a broader perspective of inclusiveness. It also involves having less sense of entitlement, more realistic expectations, and more willingness to regulate one's own behavior and the marketplace we live in. These are the components needed to develop a Generation of We. To effect these changes will mean challenging basic economic assumptions and the elevated status of established economic theories and principles. In turn, we must challenge our current definition of success. The transition from a "me" society to a "we" society can be framed as the classic dichotomy of individualism versus collectivism. But it is a larger and more complex issue than that.

Generation We would then have to embrace a concept of success that is interactive between culture and personality and able to break the cycle. The last election focused on political change and the election clearly indicated a desire to do so. We argue about change, looking for a direction to go in. Much of the time, we feel like we are pursuing a direction that will be the same old thing. Sometimes the process seems like we are lost, a pattern that also goes in a circle and is self-defeating. Frustrated, we feel we have become a society unable to help itself. Frequently, we hear the expression that our collective or organized efforts of government only make matters worse.

The literature in social psychology is extensive in arguing about the issue of what comes first in order to change. Is it necessary to change behavior first, for change to occur—or is it necessary to change attitude before behavior change can occur? The dichotomy of behavior versus attitude for individuals to change is also applicable to our culture. Changes in individual behavior will principally follow changes dictated by policy. Our mass consumption society will only redirect when forced too. Narcissistic entitlement is too high—self-control is pummeled and expectations of voluntary change are naïve. The cycle and patterns of the culture of excess are too ingrained. As a result, regulation in policy will be an important factor in the change process, and replace the conscious efforts of deregulation and no regulation. As discussed earlier, the cultural deregulation and no regulation movement has deregulated our inner mechanisms of individual self-control. Changes in attitude and thinking will also be related to policy; however, confrontation must occur between current attitudes and thinking that is "me based." Challenging some existing and entrenched beliefs about economics and economic growth will be necessary for change to occur.

Positive psychology with all its fine intent cannot deal with the outcomes of a culture of excess. Promoting resilience, optimism, and undoing "learned helplessness" while desirable at the individual level will help one survive the culture of excess but will not create a new generation. Positive psychology cannot respond to the increased risk-taking and the quagmire that we are now in. This is partly due to the strength of existing economic philosophy of open-ended capitalism.

Formation of a new generation will be able to break the cycle of excess and begin positive change by redefining success. There are several areas involved in this transition and describing how to do it. These areas include: Identity and Materialism; Quantitative Thinking and Mood Regulation; Coping with Devaluation; Media Reform; New Measurements of Success; and Economic Redefinition.

## IDENTITY AND MATERIALISM

The redefinition of success for a healthier generation will need people with a different form of self-definition and identity. Somehow, development of who one is needs to be separated from materialism and wealth accumulation. Currently, a successful person is a wealthy person and monetary success drives self-definition. The path to this success and wealth (career or business) is of some interest because others will want to emulate the process, but for too many, the end point of wealth is what really matters. No wonder today's young people seek a fast and expedient way to success and wealth. But the way of the rich and famous or the self-actualizing identity development process is ultimately unable to provide a satisfying form of success. It is too quick and ephemeral or too expansive and fragmented. In addition, the process of exploring everything, or multiple identities, does not allow for self-reflection and a more careful establishment of identity development and who one is. The rich and famous approach is different than the recommended moratorium achievement or the MAMA cycle described in Chapter 7.

The shortcut to success through fame and fortune may simply be an escape from the longer and fiercely competitive identity/success/wealth model of the marketplace. Basing one's self identity on material wealth impacts our connectedness and the quality of our lives and health. This is obvious to those in the mental health field. Several research studies by psychologist Suniya Luthar show that children from more affluent suburban homes are more likely to be depressed and anxious and to abuse drugs and alcohol than children from less advantaged homes. Luthar reports children from affluent homes react to pressure to achieve at school, believing such achievement is what their parents value most.[7] Success supersedes who they are or their emotional needs and the culture constantly reinforces this message.

Changing this model of materialism will take a while as this generation has been stamped for it. Surveys of incoming college students document the belief that wealth is more important than developing a sense of oneself in the world. Ongoing surveys of college freshmen ask them to rate the importance of factors in their life goals. In 2003, 74 percent of freshmen cited as "very important" to be "well off financially." In 1971, 50 percent of college freshmen chose this answer. In contrast, the option "to develop a meaningful philosophy of life" was cited by 40 percent of college freshmen in 2003, its lowest level to date. The idea that college helps one prepare for life through the development of a solid self-identity has gradually declined from 80 percent of freshmen in 1968 who cited this as very important to only 40 percent today.[8] On a graph, the two choices dramatically cross paths in the mid-1970s, then separate to present day, where they seem to be leveling off at the rates cited above. Today's student goes to college not to help them learn and cope effectively in life but primarily to be sure they make more money. This perspective has a significant impact on their attitude toward learning in their formative years, and a profound impact on their identity development.

Yet current events are not without true stories of heroism and competence and examples of those with a healthy sense of identity. On January 15, 2009, pilot Sully Sullenberg safely landed a US Airways jet airplane in the Hudson River after the plane struck a flock of geese and lost its engines. All 150 passengers survived. The much-needed story of Sullenberg and crew provided a dramatic relief to the ongoing economic failures at the time. Sullenberg was a quiet and conscientious pilot—a consistent person who performed when needed most. Reports surfaced later how Sullenberg wrote a letter to his local library informing them he was late in returning a book—a book about safety and accountability. Sullenberg testified to Congress that his profession has been decimated. He told Congress that many pilots, including him, had lost their retirement funds. The economic malaise in the airline industry dramatically changed the profession. He reported that when pilots were let go and then later offered jobs and asked to return as pilots, 60 percent of them refused. He reported that he could not find one case where pilots would be able to recommend that their children become pilots. He insisted to Congress that he was not exaggerating.[9] Despite all the adversity, he persisted, maintaining his professional standards and continued development. He sustained his self-identity as a pilot—a professional—even though his prototype had become devalued by economic dysfunction. His career identity persisted, and until he suddenly went from quiet hero to public hero, most people would never have fully appreciated him.

Many other professionals are people you hear least about. For example, Daniel Patrick Moynihan was an ambassador to the United Nations and to India who worked in the Kennedy, Johnson, Nixon, and Ford administrations. As early as 1969 he recommended to NATO that acid rain and the greenhouse effect be dealt with. As a sociologist, he became an expert on poverty and the welfare state, documenting the pervasive problem of children raised by only their mothers. When he clearly pointed out the problem of absent fathers in African American families as far back as in the 1960s, he was called a racist. Continuing all his accomplishments brought him to the U.S. Senate from 1976 to 2000. Moynihan was described as a person who wrote more books than most people have read. Following his retirement from elected office, Moynihan lectured at colleges on the culture of politics today. He stated: "We have lessened our capacity for large national initiatives. Something's lacking. Can it be that our energies have run out?"

Moynihan died in 2003, his last residence an apartment on Pennsylvania Avenue in Washington, D.C.[10] Do we hear much about his successful career and contributions? Is there anyone in politics today who comes close to his devotion to public office, expertise, and accomplishments? Is there any young politician who can develop and be as accomplished? Perhaps *Forbes* magazine can develop a ranking of the most accomplished professionals in their fields, without any mention of their earnings or wealth. Or perhaps we can publish a list of the most accomplished and *underpaid* professionals in their field.

To reinstate a healthy process of identity development in our culture means altering the established model of success from one based on wealth to one based on the basic aspects of good work—consistency and competency. The definition of a "profession" has been fragmented and competes with the self-actualizing process of identity development and the drive to get rich quick. Economic conditions and lack of stability also impede pursuing a profession, affecting identity development in the important area of work and career. As a result, today's generation lacks self-identity based on a career path that reflects consistent training, experience, and competence. Young emerging workers learn quickly you make money by becoming a broker, not spending too much time at a profession. The increase in MBA degrees and the decline in professions like engineering highlight the problem. Other professions that require longer preparation and training must be elevated in economic status to avoid shortages. Acting to increase degrees in the professions, in contrast to more degrees in finance or MBA, can have a significant impact on the development of a more stable and healthier identity development model. But this cannot be done when parents who have chosen professions dissuade their children from pursuing similar careers. Significant change will involve policy leaders who make sure we allow the professions to develop and thrive.

## QUANTITATIVE THINKING AND MOOD REGULATION

Dan and Marie, in their mid-thirties, consult with me about their 14-year-old son Bryan. He has had trouble at school because he has challenged the types of assignments he receives. Dan and Marie have trouble confronting Bryan about the problem. "We want him to think out of the box," they report, and then express a belief that schools can be too regimented and hinder creative thinking. It seems very important today that we think "out of the box" or in a different or creative way. That is how you are successful or get ahead. Traditional thinking or completing an assignment from school may not achieve this end. Then, by the time you get older and graduate, you will not be prepared for the business marketplace. You will be ordinary. You will not be successful.

Most people believe in the mind/body relationship—the way we think is related to our body, our mood, and our health. The entire basis of cognitive behavior therapy (CBT) is to help someone change the way he or she thinks. CBT is the highly recommended course of treatment for depression and has become the primary method of therapy taught in most graduate psychology programs. Although CBT can be overrated and cases of depression are varied and complex, most everyone agrees that ways of thinking impact mood.

Today's prevalence of screen media promotes a certain kind of thinking. This thinking is more immediate, impulsive, and faster. Time online with gaming even leads to addiction. Children and adults have trouble sitting and listening to a speaker for too long without getting on their laptop or cell phone. But screen activities whether for business or leisure require a dramatically different kind of thinking than does comprehension and problem-solving. We might label screen time as technological thinking, a distinct product of the culture of excess. Survey data shows that third to twelfth graders spend an average of more than six hours a day in "screen time," which includes television, Internet/computer, video gaming, and DVDs. The time jumps to eight hours if we include "multitasking" as when someone watches television and plays on the computer at the same time. In contrast, children spend an average of 23 minutes a day reading a book, either for school or leisure.[11]

The increase in technological thinking is at the expense of more traditional quantitative thinking. Quantitative thinking involves a more sustained, intentional, and focused process necessary for comprehension and problem-solving. Time and again when evaluating children and teens, I obtain adequate scores on reading words and mastering vocabulary but lower scores on comprehension, the area that is the key determinant for how well a student is functioning. Many have bemoaned the decline in reading time and recommended more efforts in this area. But reading without comprehension may not address the issue. Efforts to improve students' miserable scores in math and quantitative analysis could help to offset the impact of technological thinking.

We can also offset technological thinking in another way. It may come as a surprise that developing quantitative thinking and avoiding the short-focused technological thinking can be responded to by learning a second language. Like math, our school system does not emphasize or require learning a second language. Other countries do far better, with many adults able to understand and speak at least some English. Young children (before age 10) easily learn a second language. Research studies of young students who become bilingual show significant improvement in cognitive skills. Researchers have found that bilingual students (when compared to monolingual students) have increased abilities in selective attention, analytical reasoning, and both cognitive flexibility and complexity. Overall, they are "easier to resist distraction," and the increased skills extend further into solving nonverbal problems that involve conflicting material and sustained attention. This powerful research may even suggest improved maturation in social development and judgment.[12]

Unfortunately, technological thinking dominates our lives. It seems that today we have thought so far "out of the box" that we no longer know where the box is. Efforts for immediate answers and creative solutions take precedence over thorough analysis. In this regard, traditional quantitative thinking is even considered old-fashioned and unnecessary. What is fashionable is to think quickly and to be different.

Although computers and technology enable us to analyze data more thoroughly than ever before, technological thinkers dismiss quantitative thinking. For example, the technological capabilities and rapidity of Internet searches have even led some to question the core aspects of science and data analysis. In a recent issue of *Wired* magazine, an analysis of Google searches renders the following observation:

> Google's founding philosophy is that we don't know why this page is better than that one: If the statistics of incoming links say it is, that's good enough. No semantic or causal analysis is required. That's why Google can translate languages without actually "knowing" them (given equal corpus data, Google can translate Klingon into Farsi as easily as it can translate French into German).

Speaking at a conference, Google's research director offered: "All models are wrong, and increasingly you can succeed without them." The *Wired* article goes on to explain mega-data and mathematics are replacing human behavior theories from linguistics to psychology.

> Who knows why people do what they do? The point is they do it, and we can track and measure it with unprecedented fidelity. With enough data, the numbers speak for themselves.[13]

According to technological thinkers, models, systematic analysis, data analysis, and the scientific method can be brushed aside by a way of thinking that breeds immediacy without history or depth. But such an analysis is sophomoric and similar to that of a teenager, or maybe today's techno teen. Numbers do not speak for themselves. And putting together more numbers requires *more* comprehensive and quantitative analysis. The importance of controlled trials (consider the placebo effect) and conceptualization of findings is the heart of unbiased conclusions and important decisions that affect our lives. In contrast, technological thinking leads to uncontrolled and limited analysis and false conclusions.

Certainly, the point here is not to argue against the use of computers or technology but to emphasize that the type of thinking that predominates today is related to impulsivity and mood regulation. If more time is spent on quantitative thinking, mood regulation will improve because mood is related to thinking. Increased quantitative thinking will decrease impulsive thinking and behavior. Mood regulation and impulse control are the foundation for self-control. A person who has self-regulation of his or her mood is more focused, has better comprehension skills, and has more consistent thinking and behavior. In other words, a better employee and someone you would want to hire.

In this area, psychology is putting forth an honorable effort. By insisting on critical thinking, college assignments demand a student explore, research, and present all sides of an issue. While this may not be pure quantitative thinking, it does require depth and focus that lead to comprehension and integration. When I have taught classes for adult students in a Master's program, I have noticed a difference in improved writing and quantitative thinking in students who have had a psychology major.

Of course, time spent on screen media and technological thinking is often for social reasons and escape. But the social aspect is starting to be challenged by the possibility that all the time spent on sites like Facebook, MySpace, or Twitter is shortening attention spans. In an unfolding scientific debate, neuroscientists are expressing concern that the fast pace and stimulation are rewiring our brains.[14] As a result, parents have a huge dilemma—should they limit their children's access to online games, celebrity alerts, and even cell phones? Text messaging cannot replace face-to-face communication, though indeed it may do so. There can be no doubt that parents should regulate these activities more. But then they would have to regulate their own use also. How many parents know the recommendations of the Academy of Pediatrics that advises against any screen exposure before the child is age 2? Or, their recommendation limiting screen time to two hours a day as children grow up?[15] Sorting out the positives of technology for children must be pitted against controlling exposure. Our mood depends on it. And if our mood depends on it, so does our self-control and our behavior.

Parents can be an important part of the solution by monitoring access to technological thinking and encouraging quantitative thinking. Schools must spend more time on quantitative problem-solving and math instruction in the early years. Acquiring a second language at an early age also has profound advantages. Teaching and testing must focus on the student developing comprehension of what they read and study. This does not require thinking out of the box.

## COPING WITH DEVALUATION

Entitlement and grand expectations are the manifestations of cultural narcissism and must have some roots in order to continue to grow. These roots develop in reaction to the cultural/economic conditions that lead to a sense of being devalued. Devaluation is a process that is gradual and erodes one's sense of self. A person may feel that others get ahead at school or in the workplace by unfair processes. Or, by social comparison, someone may feel they have spent much more time or effort than others in developing skills that are not economically valued.

Devaluation is prevalent in the process of *how* we get ahead or attain success. The "isms"—favoritism, cronyism, and nepotism—are familiar pathways in a culture of excess. The sense of entitlement leads to these pathways but these factors are so out of control, they contribute greatly to a process where many feel devalued. Redefining healthy success means purifying the process so that these shortcuts are minimized. This is a huge challenge since someone has to enforce rules that limit what we used to call a "conflict of interest."

Although students can certainly experience this feeling, devaluation can peak in middle age. People obtain a job or career and then feel dissatisfied —that they cannot apply their skills in ways they would like to and that their knowledge is not recognized or rewarded by the marketplace. They see others with less knowledge or education who are overpaid and viewed as successful. Recent data on suicide rates provide some interesting data about the middle-aged. In a five-year analysis of the nation's death rates recently reported by the Centers for Disease Control, the suicide rate among 45- to 54-year-olds increased nearly 20 percent from 1999 to 2004, the latest year studied. This by far outpaced changes in nearly every other age group. This spike in middle-age suicide has never occurred before. Experts are stumped.[16] More analysis and breakdown might answer why this spike occurred, but hopelessness and cultural devaluation must be considered.

Devaluation occurs for the skilled and highly educated professional worker and the middle-class worker who makes less and cannot make ends meet. A doctor with years of education and skill performs a surgery that takes several hours. She bills the insurance carrier for the services. The insurance company sends an all-inclusive payment of less than half the amount billed. It is entirely possible for a hospital or a skilled doctor to barely break even on a procedure when all is said and done.

The devaluation is also apparent in the bashing of American workers who are constantly devalued and under attack as they attempt to organize through unions. Nothing demonstrates more clearly this attitude toward workers than the Supreme Court decision in *Ledbetter v. Goodyear Tire*. Lilly Ledbetter had worked at Goodyear for 20 years. When she was hired her salary was equal to male coworkers. But over the years her pay raises did not match those of her male peers. By the time she retired in 1998, her monthly salary was $3,727 versus $4,286 for the men. Ledbetter was unaware of the disparity until near the end of her career when she sued under federal law for discrimination. She won her case and was awarded $3 million in back pay and $360,000 in punitive damages. But on appeal the court reversed the award, stating that claims must be filed within 180 days after the unlawful practice occurred. But Ledbetter had not known the discrimination occurred until years later. The U.S. Supreme Court, in a five-to-four decision, also ruled against Ledbetter.[17] Ledbetter did not file in time.

In this case the court ruled the timeline applies even if the discrimination is not apparent to the worker and even if it continues from there. Imagine if someone you knew cheated and stole from you for 10 years. The theft is still ongoing. But you did not know it. You then went to the authorities after you discovered you have been a victim. But the police said they could not help you because you should have come to them within 180 days of when the crime started. So if you plan to steal or cheat, make sure you do not get caught in the first six months—then you are home free. Better yet, you now have a victim for life because you can continue with no consequences.

This verdict is like a sledge hammer against all workers. In addition to this gross unfairness, employers often prevent or inform employees they are not to talk about their salaries with coworkers. An employee who is caught can be in jeopardy of losing his or her job. The Ledbetter case has at least drawn a response. In order to correct the loophole and guarantee workers' rights, the first bill President Obama signed into law in January 2009 was the Lilly Ledbetter Fair Pay Act.[18]

We can frame these cases of unfair treatment as discrimination, a word that then attracts all the political groups who rage about lawsuits and "rights." It seems to be more helpful to focus upon the effect—a devaluation of all workers. For older workers, devaluation may take another form in a culture of excess that demands profit over skill. Our society is full of successful losers. Every day people who work hard and do actually attain success are often not rewarded but may even lose their jobs. In a well-known and growing trend, many companies cut workers and high performers to reduce costs, then hire younger, less experienced, and less expensive workers to do the same job. In an article in the *Wall Street Journal* in 2003, employees of Circuit City documented their stories concerning a push to sell like entrepreneurs, and even after years of increased sales and success, were abruptly let go simply to reduce costs. All in all 3,900 employees were let go. Younger and less experienced employees were hired at lower salaries. Workers learned to keep track of their own sales performance to convince the next employer to hire them.[19] In 2008, Circuit City laid off more workers, making the newswire again. Even Jay Leno made a quip in his monologue on the *Tonight Show* that Circuit City could solve its problem and not lay off anyone if they just cut the salary of their CEO—a social statement that is laughed at and applauded because it is logically true. In January 2009, Circuit City announced bankruptcy and liquidation.[20] Shoppers came out quickly looking for bargains, but that is not how it works. The announcement is to get shoppers in, but lower prices do not happen until maybe the last few hours of desperation time.

Workers in their forties and fifties, who cannot get jobs because they are too experienced or overqualified (in other words, they cost too much), recognize the trend. To maintain a high level of profit, companies must hire less skilled or less experienced workers. Disillusionment is bound to result when these corporate practices intersect with the powerful societal message in our democracy to do your best, work hard, and play by the rules. Isn't this what parents teach their children? But the rules have fundamentally changed. Today, we must be able to cope psychologically with the loss inherent in the possibility that working hard does not lead to success. As you get older, depending where you work, you must be careful about getting too good at what you do.

Retribution for the unbelievable excesses of those in economically advantageous positions would help address the public outrage and at least assuage feelings of devaluation. Those who profited by manipulation and deceit, along with those who failed to enforce regulations, should be public enemy number one. Many were involved in the economic downturn that began in the fall of 2008. Yet, little is heard about those who rated mortgage loans AAA when they were not. As a result these bad loans were packaged and sold to naïve buyers all over the world. Why haven't these rating agencies been held responsible for the collapse? Many other areas are worth exploring. Who invented and promoted credit default swaps? Instead of being held accountable for their mistakes, these same entities that already cheated us are benefiting from federal "bailout" funding. These days, it appears that if you play by the rules and are honest, you get punished, and if you manipulate and cheat, you get even further ahead. This is the expressed statement of cultural devaluation that is on the tip of everyone's tongue.

Economic devaluation in the marketplace must be a factor that takes a toll in depression, shorter life spans, and the increase of middle-age suicide among Americans. A Generation We must return fair play to the workplace and hold accountable those who have dishonestly profited; they should return their ill-gotten gains. Although precautions should be made to avoid a witch hunt or just envious vindictiveness, repayment should include confiscating jewelry, designer shoes, and Lamborghinis passed on to spouse and family. Overall, only increased regulation and enforcement of the markets will address this underlying psychological condition that is part of the roots of cultural narcissism. For too many years, there have been no cops on the beat.

Until a Generation We takes hold, we have no choice but to find ways to cope with devaluation in the workplace. When young people complain about these issues, I frequently respond: "Who told you life was fair?" There will always be some inequities and the "isms" in the work world.

But a new generation will demand more effort to control them. Coping with devaluation and accepting the inequalities are easier if you have a healthy self-definition and clear identity of who you are.


## MEDIA REFORM

Media and rapid technology infuse the public with information that leads to impulsivity, anxieties, fears, misperceptions, and poor decisions. Broadcasting corporations should be obligated to operate in the public interest, but profit making, as in everything else, usually wins out. On the other side of the question, credible media persons complain that they are easily blamed when something goes wrong. A politician can garner public sympathy and support by blaming the media for attacking him. And his success in doing so reflects the public's anger and mistrust of media in general.

I turn on the late night news on a local channel of a major network hoping to hear some local news and also what newly elected President Obama had to say in his speech that day. What comes on is a "breaking news" story—once again, a man has led police on a slow speed pursuit. The broadcasters go on and on speculating who might be in the expensive car as they cover the "story" from the air and on land. They believe the chase followed a report of domestic violence. After continuous coverage and the car even stopping on the freeway, the news program time allotment is over. No news tonight. The next program comes on.

Paul Newman cited this anecdote demonstrating how media can manipulate the headlines. A reporter asks him if he beats his wife. He responds strongly: "No, I don't beat my wife." The headline the next day states: "Newman denies beating wife."[21] The impact and power of bad events is a well-researched fact. Negative events and information have more power than positive, whether they are experienced through trauma, relationship issues, interpersonal interactions, or learning situations. We naturally become more active in avoiding bad events than pursuing good ones. Negative impressions and negative stereotypes are much harder to prove wrong. Impression formation is one domain of psychological research that demonstrates this point. Studies have shown that negative information is processed more thoroughly and impacts a final impression more than positive information. Hearing something bad about somebody has more of an impact upon us than hearing something good. Researchers sum it up simply: "Bad is stronger than good."[22] This effect is magnified through the 24/7 presence of media and the mantra "if it bleeds it leads."

The National Conference of Media Reform has held four annual forums, doubling attendance since its first conference and now attracting approximately 4,000 people. The leader is Bill Moyers, one of the most esteemed journalists of our time. Moyers was the deputy director of the Peace Corps for President Kennedy and served as a special assistant to President Johnson. Honored many times by all sorts of media organizations, Moyers has received more than 30 Emmy Awards from the Academy of Television Arts and Sciences. In a keynote address at the 2007 conference, Moyers stated that media reform is a social movement that will be the next major movement in the country since the civil rights movement. He pointed out that the media no longer acts effectively as a corrective factor in our lives; investigative newspaper reporters, who are best at providing this balance, are continuing to be laid off as newspapers cut staff to maintain profit. Other major concerns at the conference included the larger issues of corporate and government control of the news and information delivery, including potential control of access to the Internet. Current policies and actions of the Federal Communications Commission were critiqued as "market-driven media policies," the end result of which is less validity to what is reported. Can broadcasters from big corporations really examine important issues capably and fairly? What happens when the public interest and profit making collide? Coverage of local politics and news is in decline.[23] Major newspapers long associated with their cities and communities are closing down. Many believe that print newspapers will die.

The Social Science Research Council and Free Press is a group that emphasizes a systematic analysis of issues through working group round-tables and documentation of the needs for quantitative research, access to data, and research on specific communities. The council has outlined desirable future decisions and policy actions through federal legislation and the FCC. An organization like the SSRC is certainly what the doctor ordered. In trying to make a "more public social science," SSRC President Craig Calhoun poses this question: "How can growth and equity be effectively combined in economic development, and how can attention to the political, social, and cultural concomitants of economic change be integrated into development agendas?"[24] In other words, can there be a balance between corporate-controlled media, government control, and the public good?

Obviously, news that serves to inform citizens in a democracy needs to be separated from entertainment. The blending of news and entertainment has been much railed about since the 1990s. The conclusion is evident. Entertainment *is* news. Although specialized media outlets capture an overdone and pathetic story like that of Anna Nicole Smith, many credible journalists complain about having to report on this type of entertainment news. Likewise, why should the top news of the day include who won *Survivor* or *American Idol*? The vanity of these stories and sagas detract from important news issues. Entertainment is different from news and should be separated. Perhaps we can tax entertainment news at the same rate we tax cigarettes and alcohol.

Similarly, we must also question why networks cover live car chases. Why is it important to see some loser abandon a car and run through people's backyards? A summary report would suffice rather than continuous live coverage that increases either adrenaline or unnecessary fear.

In the public interest, media reformers should borrow from the model of positive psychology and organize a Positive Media Movement, establishing guidelines on coverage of live police car chases and possible traumas and emergencies that can even amount to nothing. Standards for privacy should also be part of the discussion, as the invasion of privacy has greatly impacted our sense of security and the ability to enjoy our lives.

## NEW MEASUREMENTS OF SUCCESS

Today's simplistic model of success is essentially tied to business economics, and more money equates to more success. The most desirable person to hire is the one who provides more sales volume and thus more profit for the company. They get the biggest office.

But is there an upper limit to increased sales or to the concept of more? Must the GDP always be used as the sole indicator of how well a country is doing? Is it possible to have a decrease in the GDP while at the same time Americans report a sense of success? Of course. This requires that success is defined in a more comprehensive way, one that actually reflects the quality of our lives.

Researchers have focused on an approach called quality of life measurement (QOL). From 1982 to 2005, more than 50,000 academic citations using the term "quality of life" were found across a broad range of academic disciplines.[25] Unfortunately, discussions about "quality of life" in the popular media define the term as economic prosperity, reflecting the current definition that equates more income and more consumption with improved quality of life.[26] But, in fact, we have reached a point at which excess is not an indicator of success, but of failure.

The indicators of quality of life must be multidimensional, with economic factors only one measurement among many. And these economic factors must not be the simplistic dollar amounts, but rather should be weighted according to importance. Advanced statistical techniques can be used to calculate both objective and subjective factors of quality of life. The subjective factors include happiness and life satisfaction measures; objective measures include economic activity, productivity, and other variables such as literacy rate or life expectancy. The measures together will encompass broad social, economic, and health factors. Total indices in combinations of many of these factors can also be developed. The United Nations already uses an index called the Human Development Index (HDI) which is a composite of measures of educational attainment, life expectancy, and income. More specific quality of life scales include the Human Poverty Index (HPI) which measures the level of poverty; the Gender-Related Development Index (GDI) which measures gender inequality; and the Gender Empowerment Index (GEI) which measures gender equality in economic and political involvement and decision making. These index measures are far more comprehensive and specific in providing data about quality of life than anything reported in the United States today.[27]

Academic researchers are ready to pursue instrumentation and methodology for quality of life measures and quality of life indices. Would an improvement in quality of life automatically mean an increase in GDP? What will be the relationship between QOL and GDP? More may not always be better, and success need not be defined by economic growth alone. Even more important, quality of life indices can be used for policy decisions. Data can be extracted by region and state, allowing resources to be directed to areas of greatest need. Less waste and fewer special-interest earmarks will result.

As a result, quality of life indices can provide the new definition of success that can help develop a "we-based culture." Success for a generation of "we" will be more inclusive and reflect what people are experiencing and feeling and the needs that they have. Generation We will define and measure success in a more comprehensive and meaningful manner.

## ECONOMIC REDEFINITION

Redefining and measuring success with different outcome variables can help lead to changes in our view of economic theory, philosophy, and practices. After all, the pursuit of self-interest through the marketplace is not inherently immoral. Economic theory and practice, however, has been given too much credibility. As noted by economist Duncan Foley, economics is a "speculative philosophical discourse" and not a science.[28] It is value laden. Too much attention has been paid to economic factors and theory; too little attention to the psychological impact of the economic direction we have followed.

Current economic philosophy today is principally based on the idea that what is good for American business is good for the American people. Generation We proposes a reverse of this philosophy. In a we-based society, the operating philosophy would be that what is good for the American people is good for American business.

One prime example in the direction of this new philosophy would be the challenge of health care policy. As noted in Chapter 5, the evidence for a universal health care plan is overwhelming. The psychological importance of changing health care is underestimated. Providing a health care system that provides security for all Americans and is affordable will be a huge step forward toward a new philosophy that benefits the American public and not purely business interests. Overall, a significant segment of our society badly wants policies that are we-based. The green environmental movement historically has been we-based, though often cajoled and laughed at by those with a me-based economic philosophy. The desire for a universal health care plan and the continued growth of the green movement signify Americans' desire for a new generation based on the concept of "we."

The opposing forces to any change in economic practice remain entrenched. In particular, opposition is intense among those of the libertarian movement, which avows that government should be as small as possible and not be involved in people's lives. The philosophy is that as long as my individual actions do not bother anyone, then everyone, especially government, should leave me alone. The position is similar to isolationism, a philosophy unwilling to realize that almost all of our behavior has an impact on someone else. The libertarian position supports the development of the Me Generation, and it has contributed to deregulation, no regulation, and the development of a culture of excess. Now more than ever before this position needs to be challenged.

One way to do this is through fostering change in our attitude toward our own government. Political reactions to a "tax and spend" model of government has led to a "no tax and spend" government. The antitax policy is part of a self-defeating negative attitude toward our own government. Thomas Paine, British intellectual who influenced both the

American and French revolutions, is known for his quote that government, even in its best state, is but a *necessary evil*. He added that "in its worst state, an intolerable one."[29] Ronald Reagan, with his powerful communication skills, made the philosophy more pragmatic when he said that government is not the solution, but rather the problem. He stated that the public's worst fear is when someone says: "I'm from the government and I'm here to help."[30]

But consider what the depiction of government as a necessary evil and harmful means to a democracy in which government is people. If government is a necessary evil, the implication is that the people in government are also a necessary evil, in which case our entire democracy is evil. The impact of this attitude is that younger Americans carry not only increased levels of narcissism but at some level have an underlying assumption that the government is not good and therefore that taxes should not be paid. Government as evil influences the young minds to develop extreme individualism to counteract a government that is against them.

Generation We must redefine democratic government as positive, a government "by the people" who are not a necessary evil, but in fact are necessarily good. Government reform must embrace those who want a "good" but, more important, an efficient and fair government. President Obama seems to understand this. His election and efforts are in the direction of developing a healthy view of government and its role.

More involvement in government activities is needed rather than the antigovernment attitude of libertarianism. And leaders must stop bashing government. As an example, when Michael Steele became chair of the Republican Party, he expressed in an interview that government jobs are not really jobs. He implied only private jobs really matter.[31] To foster a Generation We, antigovernment attitudes must be replaced with those that reflect a cultural identity of we the people, and a willingness to value, protect, and participate in our system of government.

Some changes are already evident and offer some hope. Of course, a new and young President, a historic election of an African American, brings excitement and yearning for fair play and equality. Out of necessity, Americans have consumed less and have begun to save more than ever before. The savings rate has increased as Americans are forced to live within their means. There is more discussion of the need for regulation and willingness to reestablish previous regulations or develop and expand existing rules. On the other hand, the narcissistic entitlement of financial leaders abounds. Stories of major financial deceit and fraud continue to emerge. Other leaders and groups want to stall health care reform and dilute any proposed changes. Their political opposition is intense. Many Americans have no choice but to cut back, save, and conserve financial resources. Others who have money continue to indulge, often at the expense of others. The intense conflict between Generation Me and Generation We has just begun. Will there be a lower standard of consumption and sustained conservation by the American public? Can we have economic growth without creating a bubble that bursts and destroys lives? In order for Generation We to prevail, positive changes in self-control and risk-taking must be sustained.

Finally, Generation We will need to (1) adopt a healthier model of identity development; (2) increase quantitative thinking to improve mood regulation and self-control; (3) make efforts to change the emphasis of what media reports; (4) develop quality of life measurements of success; and (5) challenge the existing economic philosophy and antigovernment viewpoints. That's a lot—but only through such an ambitious challenge can we evolve from a culture of excess into one with a definition of success that maximizes the full depth of human potential.

## NOTES

1. Minuchin, S., & Fishman, H. C. (1981). Chapter 9: Intensity. In *Family Therapy Techniques* (p. 116). Cambridge, MA: Harvard University Press.

2. De la Merced, M., & Story, L. (2009, February 11). Nearly 700 at Merrill in million dollar club. *The New York Times*, p. B1.

3. Hamilton, W. (2009, July 31). Payouts lavish despite bailouts. *LA Times*, p. A1.

4. Moskowitz, M. (2007, September 23). We love our jobs, just ask us. *The New York Times*, p. BU1.

5. Novotny, A. (2009). The price of affluence. *APA Monitor*, 40 (1): 50.

6. Greenberger, E., Lassard, J., Chen, C., & Farruggia, S. (2008). Self-entitled college students: Contributions of personality, parenting, and motivational factors. *Journal of Youth and Adolescence*, 37 (10): 1193–1204.

7. Luthar, S. S., & Becker, B. E. (2002). Privileged but pressured? A study of affluent youth. *Child Development*, 73:1593–1610. Luthar, S. S. (2003). The culture of affluence: Psychological costs of material wealth. *Child Development*, 74:1581–1593.

8. Santrock, J. (2005). Social psychology. In *Psychology 7* (p. 685). New York: McGraw-Hill.

9. Office of the Mayor. (2009, February 9). Mayor Bloomberg presents captain and crew of US Airways Flight 1549 with keys to the city. Retrieved March 7, 2009 from http://www.nyc.gov. Associated Press. (2009, February 24). Sully Sullenberger tells Congress he worries for the future of the airlines industry. Retrieved March 7, 2009 from http://www.kron.com/News/ArticleView/tabid/298/smid/1126/ArticleID/531/reftab/36/t/Sully-Sullenberg-Tells-Congress-He-Worries-for-the-Future-of-the-Airline-Industry/Default.aspx.

10. Will, G. (2003, March 27). Pat Moynihan, RIP. Retrieved March 7, 2009 from http://townhall.com/columnists/GeorgeWill/2003/03/27/pat_moynihan,_rip. CBS News. (2003, March 26). Former Senator Moynihan dead at 76.

11. Bauerlein, M. (2008). *The dumbest generation: How the digital age stupefies young Americans and jeopardizes our future* (p. 77). New York: Jeremy P. Tarcher/Penguin.

12. Santrock, J. (2008). *Life span development*. Chapter 10: Physical and cognitive development in middle and late childhood (p. 344). New York, NY: McGraw Hill. See also Bialystok, E. (1999). Cognitive complexity and attentional control in the bilingual mind. *Child Development*, 70 (3): 636–644. Bialystok, E. (2007). Cognitive effects of bilingualism: How linguistic experience leads to cognitive change. *The International Journal of Bilingual Education and Bilingualism*, 10 (3): 210–223.

13. Anderson, C. (2008). The end of theory: The data deluge makes the scientific method obsolete. *Wired Magazine*, 16.07.

14. Derbyshire, D. (2009, February 24). Social websites harm children's brains: Chilling warning to parents from top neuroscientist. *Daily Mail*. Retrieved March 7, 2009 from http://www.dailymail.co.uk/news/article-1153583.

15. American Academy of Pediatrics. (2001). Policy statement: Children, adolescents and television. *Pediatrics*, 107 (2): 423–426. See also American Academy of Pediatrics, www.aap.org.

16. Cohen, P. (2008, February 19). Midlife suicide rises, puzzling researchers. *The New York Times*. Retrieved March 7, 2009 from http://www.nytimes.com/2008/02/19/us/19suicide.html?_r=1&emc=eta1.

17. Greenhouse, G. (2007, May 30). Justices' ruling limits suits on pay disparity. *The New York Times*. Retrieved March 7, 2009 from http://www.nytimes.com/2007/05/30/washington/30scotus.html. Ford, R. T. (2007, May 30). Bad think: The Supreme Court mixes up intending to screw over your employee and actually doing it. *Slate*. Retrieved March 7, 2009 from http://www.slate.com/id/2167286/.

18. Stolberg, S. G. (2009, January 29). Obama signs equal pay legislation. *The New York Times*. Retrieved March 7, 2009 from http://www.nytimes.com/2009/01/30/us/politics/30ledbetter-web.html.

19. Tejada, C., & McWilliams, G. (2003, June 11). Left behind—Casualties of a changing job market. *The Wall Street Journal*, p. A1. Wilcox, R. (2003, October 13). For seven tales of lost jobs, the next chapters. *The Wall Street Journal*, p. A14.

20. Bustillo, M. (2009, January 17). Retailer Circuit City to liquidate—4,000 workers will lose jobs. *The Wall Street Journal*, p. B1.

21. CNN Transcripts. (2008, September 27). Paul Newman tribute. *Larry King Live*. Retrieved March 7, 2009 from http://transcripts.cnn.com/TRANSCRIPTS/0809/27/lkl.01.html.

22. Baumeister, R., Bratslavsky, E., Finkenauer, C., & Vohs, K. (2001). Bad is stronger than good. *Review of General Psychology*, 5 (4): 323–370.

23. VanDalsen, R. (2007, March 7). Looking back at the 2007 National Conference for Media Reform. *IndyBay*. Retrieved March 7, 2009 from http://www.indybay.org/newsitems/2007/03/07/18373910.php. Smith, C. F. (2007, February 11). Something's out there—or should be. *Baltimore Sun*, p. 27A.

24. Calhoun, C. (May 20, 2008). Toward a more public social science, Social Science Research Coalition presidential address. Retrieved March 7, 2009 from http://www.ssrc.org/program_areas/ps/public_ss.pdf.

25. Constanza, R., et al. (2008). An integrative approach to quality of life measurement, research, and policy. Institut Veolia Environment. *Surveys and Perspectives Integrating Environment and Society*, 1:11–15.

26. Ibid.

27. UN Human Development indices retrieved March 1, 2009 from http://hdr.undp.org/en/humandev/hdi/. Kasser, T., & Kanner, A. (2004). *Psychology and consumer culture: The struggle for a good life in a materialistic world*. Washington, D.C.: American Psychological Association.

28. Foley, D. (2006). *Adam's fallacy: A guide to economic theology.* Cambridge, MA: Harvard University Press.

29. Paine, Thomas. (1776). Quote from *Common sense.* Retrieved March 1, 2009 from http://www.bartleby.com/133/1.html.

30. Ronald Reagan quotes retrieved March 7, 2009 from http:// thinkexist.com/quotes/with/keyword/ronald_reagan/.

31. ABC News. (2009, February 8). Larry Summers and Michael Steele. *This week with George Stephanopoulos.* Transcript retrieved March 7, 2009 from http://abcnews.go.com/print?id=6830708.

# SELECTED BIBLIOGRAPHY

American Psychiatric Association. (2004). *Diagnostic and statistical manual of mental disorders* (4th ed.). Washington, D.C.: American Psychiatric Association.

Anders, G. (2006, April 18). Health-Care gold mines: Middlemen strike it rich; Rewarding career: As patients, doctors, feel pinch, Insurer's CEO makes a billion; Unitedhealth directors strive to please "brilliant" chief; New questions on options; Selling trout for 40 cents a pound. *Wall Street Journal*, p. A1.

Anderson, C. (2008, July 23). The end of theory: The data deluge makes the scientific method obsolete. *Wired*, 16.07.

Anderson, G. F., Hussey, P. S., Frogner, B. K., & Waters, H. R. (2005). Health spending in the United States and the rest of the world. *Health Affairs*, Vol. 24 (4), pp. 903–914.

Anderson, M., & Sansone, R. (2003). Tattooing as a means of acute affect regulation. *Clinical Psychology and Psychotherapy*, Vol. 10, pp. 316–318.

Atkinson, M. (2002). Pretty in ink: Conformity, resistance, and negotiation in women's tattooing. *Sex Roles*, Vol. 47 (5/6), pp. 219–236.

———. (2003). *Tattooed: The sociogenesis of a body art*. Toronto: University of Toronto Press.

———. (2004). Tattooing and civilizing processes: Body modification as self-control. *The Canadian Review of Sociology and Anthropology*, Vol. 41 (2), pp. 125–140.

Ayres, Ian, & Donohue, John J., III. (April 2003). Shooting down the "More Guns, Less Crime" hypothesis. *Stanford Law Review*, Vol. 55 (4), p. 1193.

Babiak, P., & Hare, R. (2006). *Snakes in suits: When psychopaths go to work*. New York: Harper Collins.

Bailenson, J. (2008, April 4). Why digital avatars make the best teachers. *The Chronicle of Higher Education*. Section: Information Technology. Opinion piece. Vol. 54 (30), p. B27.

Bauerlein, M. (2008). *The dumbest generation: How the digital age stupefies young Americans and jeopardizes our future*. New York: Jeremy P. Tarkin/Penguin.

Baumeister, R. (March 2002). Yielding to temptation: Self-control failure, impulsive purchasing, and consumer behavior. *Journal of Consumer Research*, Gainesville, Vol. 28 (4), pp. 670–676.

Baumeister, R., Bratslavsky, E., Finkenauer, C., & Vohs, K. (2001). Bad is stronger than good. *Review of General Psychology*, Vol. 5 (4), pp. 323–370.

Baumeister, R., Sparks, E., Stillman, T., & Vohs, K. (2007). Free will in consumer behavior: Self-control, ego depletion, and choice. *Journal of Consumer Psychology*, Vol. 18, pp. 4–13.

Berger, K. S. (2006). *The developing person: Through childhood and adolescence* (7th ed.). Chapter 12. New York: Worth Publishers.

Bernard, Claude. *An introduction to the study of experimental medicine*. First published in 1865, translated to English and published in 1927. Republished in 1957 by Dover Publications, New York.

Blatt, S. J. (1995). The destructiveness of perfectionism: Implications for the treatment of depression. *American Psychologist*, Vol. 50, pp. 1003–1020.

Blatt, S. J., Quinlan, D. M., Pilkonis, P. A., & Shea, M. T. (1995). Impact of perfectionism and need for approval on the brief treatment of depression: The National Institute of Mental Health Treatment of Depression Collaborative Research Program revisited. *Journal of Consulting and Clinical Psychology*, Vol. 63, pp. 125–132.

Blatt, S. J., Zuroff, D. C., Sanislow, C. A., & Pilkonis, P. A. (1998). When and how perfectionism impedes the brief treatment of depression. Further analyses of the National Institute of Mental Health Treatment of Depression Collaborative Research Program. *Journal of Consulting and Clinical Psychology*, Vol. 66, pp. 423–428.

Bogle, J. (2005). *The battle for the soul of capitalism*. New Haven, CT: Yale University Press.

Boorstin, D. (1992). *The image: A guide to pseudo-events in America*. New York: Vintage Books.

Bushman, B., Bonacci, A., van Dijk, M., & Baumeister, R. (2003). Narcissism, sexual refusal, and aggression: Testing a narcissistic reactance model of sexual coercion. *Journal of Personality and Social Psychology*, Vol. 84, pp. 1027–1040.

Callahan, D. (2004). *The cheating culture: Why more Americans are doing wrong to get ahead*. Orlando, FL: Harcourt Books.

Campbell, W. K., Goodie, A., & Foster, J. (2004). Narcissism, confidence, and risk attitude. *Journal of Behavioral Decision Making*, Vol. 17 (4), pp. 297–311.

Carroll, S., Riffenburgh, R., Roberts, T., & Myhre, E. (2002). Tattoos and body piercings as indicators of adolescent risk-taking behaviors. *Pediatrics*, Vol. 109 (6), pp. 1021–1027.

Collom, E. (May 2005). The ins and outs of homeschooling: The determinants of parental motivations and student achievement. *Education and Urban Society*, Vol. 37 (3), pp. 307–335.

Constanza, R., et al. (2008). 20 other authors listed from academic departments at University of Vermont. An integrative approach to quality of life measurement, research, and policy. *Institut Veolia Environment. Surveys and Perspectives Integrating Environment and Society*, Vol. 1, pp. 11–15.

Csikszentmihalyi, M. (1999). If we are so rich, why aren't we happy? *American Psychologist*, Vol. 54 (10), 821–827.

Dasche, Tom, Greenberger, S., & Lambrew, J. (2008). *Critical: What we can do about the health-care crisis*. New York: Thomas Dunne Books.

Department of Justice. (2006). 3.6 Million U.S. households learned they were identity theft victims during a six-month period in 2004. Report dated April 2, 2006.

Dutton, D. (1973). The maverick effect: Increased communicator credibility as a result of abandoning a career. *Canadian Journal of Behavioural Science*, Vol. 5 (2), pp. 145–151.

Easterbrook, G. (2004). *The progress paradox. How life gets better while people feel worse*. New York, NY: Random House.

Economic Research Service. (May 2004). The economics of obesity: Report on the workshop held at USDA's Economic Research Service. Report E-FAN No. 04004.

Exline, J., Baumeister, R., Bushman, B., Campbell, W. K., & Finkel, E. (2004). Too proud to let go: Narcissistic entitlement as a barrier to forgiveness. *Journal of Personality and Social Psychology*, Vol. 87, pp. 894–912.

Faludi, S. (2007). *The terror dream: Fear and fantasy in post 9/11 America*. New York: Metropolitan Books.

Fernando, J. (1998). The etiology of narcissistic personality disorder. *Psychoanalytic St. Child*, Vol. 53, pp. 141–158.

———. (2000). Superego analysis in narcissistic patients with superego pathology. *Canadian Journal of Psychoanalysis*, Vol. 8, pp. 99–117.

Foley, D. (2006). *Adam's fallacy: A guide to economic theology*. Cambridge, MA: Harvard University Press.

Foster, A. (2008, April 4). What happens in a virtual world has a real-world impact, a scholar finds. *The Chronicle of Higher Education*. Section: Information Technology. Vol. 54 (30), p. A14.

Frankfurt, H. (2005). *On bullshit*. Princeton, NJ: Princeton University Press.

Franko, D. L., et al. (2004). What predicts suicide attempts in women with eating disorders? *Psychological Medicine*, Vol. 34, pp. 843–853.

Fuchs, V. (1993). *The future of health policy*. Cambridge, MA: Harvard University Press.

Gates, J. (2001). *Democracy at risk: Rescuing main street from Wall Street*. New York: Perseus Publishing.

General Accounting Office. (1996, July 2). Resolution Trust Corporation's 1995 and 1994 financial statements, General Accounting Office.

Gilbert, D. (2007). *Stumbling on happiness*. New York: First Vintage Books.

Glaberson, William. (1999, June 6). The $2.9 million cup of coffee; When the verdict is just a fantasy. *New York Times*.

Glenn, David. (2003, May 9). "More Guns, Less Crime" thesis rests on a flawed statistical design, scholars argue. *The Chronicle of Higher Education*, Vol. 49 (35), p. A18.

Greenberger, E., Lassard, J., Chen, C., & Farruggia, S. (2008). Self-entitled college students: Contributions of personality, parenting, and motivational factors. *Journal of Youth & Adolescence*, Vol. 37 (10), pp. 1193–1204.

Hansen, J. (2007). *24/7: How cell phones and the internet change the way we live, work, and play*. Westport, CT: Praeger Publishers.

Hare, R. (1999). *Without conscience: The disturbing world of the psychopaths among us*. New York: Guilford Publications.

Hemenway, David. (1998). More guns, less crime: Understanding crime and gun-control laws/Making a killing: The business of guns in America. *The New England Journal of Medicine* Vol. 339 (27), pp. 2029–2030.

Hewitt, P. L., & Flett, G. L. (1990). Perfectionism and depression: A multidimensional analysis. *Journal of Social Behavior and Personality*, Vol. 5, pp. 423–438.

————. (1991). Perfectionism in the self and social contexts. Conceptualization, assessment, and association with psychopathology. *Journal of Personality and Social Psychology*, Vol. 60, pp. 456–470.

Hewitt, P. L., Flett G. L., & Donovan, W. T. (1992). Perfectionism and suicidal potential. *British Journal of Clinical Psychology*, Vol. 31, pp. 181–190.

Hewitt, P. L., Flett, G. L., Donovan, W. T., & Mikail, S. F. (1991). The multidimensional perfectionism scale. Reliability, validity, and psychometric properties in psychiatric samples. *Psychological Assessment: A Journal of Consulting and Clinical Psychology*, Vol. 3, pp. 464–468.

Hewitt, P. L., Flett, G. L., & Weber, C. (1994). Dimensions of perfectionism and suicidal potential. *Cognitive Therapy & Research*, Vol. 18, pp. 439–460.

Institute of Medicine. (1989). *Controlling costs and changing patient care: The role of utilization management*. Washington, D.C.: National Academy of Sciences.

Jacoby, Susan. (2008). *The age of American unreason*. New York: Pantheon Books.

John, O., & Robins, R. (1994). Accuracy and bias in self-perception: Individual differences and self-enhancement and the role of narcissism. *Journal of Personality and Social Psychology*, Vol. 66, pp. 206–219.

Josephson Institute Center for Youth Ethics. (2008). *The ethics of American youth: 2002, 2004, 2006 & 2008*.

Jost, J. (October 2006). The end of the end of ideology. *American Psychologist*, Vol. 61 (7), pp. 651–670.

Kaplan, A. (2007, January 1). Intermittent explosive disorder: Common but underappreciated. *Psychiatric Times*, Vol. 24 (1).

Kasser, T., & Kanner, A. (eds.). (2004). *Psychology and consumer culture*. American Psychological Association.

Kessler, R. C., Coccaro, E. F., Fava, M., Jaeger, S., Jin, R., & Walters, E. (2006). The prevalence and correlates of DSM-IV intermittent explosive disorder in the National Comorbidity Survey Replication. *Archives of General Psychiatry*, Vol. 63 (6), pp. 669–678.

Khantzian, E. (2005). Pathological gambling: A clinical guide to treatment. *The American Journal of Psychiatry*, Vol. 162, p. 1992. Review of text on gambling: *Pathological gambling: A clinical guide to treatment*. Edited by Jon E. Grant and Marc N. Potenza, Washington, D.C.: American Psychiatric Publishing, 2004.

Klosterman, C. (2004). *Sex, drugs, and cocoa puffs*. New York: Scribner.

Kohut, H. (1966). Forms and transformations of narcissism. *Journal of the American Psychoanalytic Association*, Vol. 14, pp. 243–272.

Kurtz, H. (2003, June 23). A little snag in those frivolous suits; U.S. News's examples were "myths." *Washington Post*.

Kuttner, R. (1997). *Everything for sale: The virtues and limits of markets*. New York: Alfred A. Knopf.

Lasch, C. (1979). *The culture of narcissism*. New York: W. W. Norton.

Levin, M. (2005, August 15). Coverage of big awards for plaintiffs helps distort view of legal system; In most such cases, the verdicts are either later rejected or the amounts are severely lowered. *Los Angeles Times*, p. C1.

Linn, S. (2004). *Consuming kids: The hostile takeover of childhood*. New York: The New Press.

Lott, J. (1998). *More guns less crime*. Chicago: University of Chicago press.

Luthar, S. S. (2003). The culture of affluence: Psychological costs of material wealth. *Child Development*, Vol. 74, pp. 1581–1593.

Luthar, S. S., & Becker, B. E. (2002). Privileged but pressured?: A study of affluent youth. *Child Development*, Vol. 73, pp. 1593–1610.

Luyckx, K., Goossens, L., Soenens, B., & Beters, W. (2006). Unpacking commitment and exploration: Preliminary validation of an integrative model of late adolescent identity formation. *Journal of Adolescence*, Vol. 29, pp. 361–378.

Lyman, Donald R., & Miller, Joshua D. (December 2004). Personality pathways to impulsive behavior and their relations to deviance: Results from three samples. *Journal of Quantitative Criminology*, Vol. 20 (4), pp. 319–341.

Maccoby, M. (2003). *The productive narcissist*. New York: Broadway Books.

Marano, Hara Estroff. (November/December 2004). A nation of wimps. *Psychology Today*, New York, Vol. 37 (6), pp. 58–68.

McEwen, W. (2005). *Married to the brand: Why consumers bond with some brands for life*. New York: Gallup Press.

McLean Hospital. (2007, February 4). Binge eating more common than other eating disorders, survey finds. *ScienceDaily*.

McNally, R., Bryant, R., & Ehlers, A. (November 2003). Psychological science in the public interest. *American Psychological Society*, Vol. 4 (2), pp. 55–68.

Mencimer, S. (October 2004). False alarm; How the media helps the insurance industry and the GOP promote the myth of America's "lawsuit crisis." *The Washington Monthly*.

Mihoces, G. (2008, May 30). Brain trumps hand: Mental acuity under pressure is needed to be successful on poker's big stage. *USA Today: World Series of Poker, Special section*.

Millar, H. R., Wardell, F., Vyvyan, J. P., Naji, S. A., Prescott, G. J., & Eagles, J. M. (2005). Anorexia nervosa mortality in Notheast Scotland, 1965–1999. *American Journal of Psychiatry*, Vol. 162, pp. 753–757.

Millon, T., Davis, R., Millon, C., Escovar, L., & Meagher, S. (2000). *Personality disorders in modern life*. New York: Wiley.

Minuchin, S., & Fishman, H. C. (1981). *Family therapy techniques*. Cambridge, MA: Harvard University Press.

Morrison, A. (1989). *Shame: The underside of narcissism*. Hillsdale, NJ: The Analytic Press.

Myers, David. (2005). *Social psychology* (8th ed.). New York: McGraw-Hill.

National Institute of Mental Health. (2006). *Facts about panic disorder*. Publication No. OM-99 4155, updated February 17, 2006.

Paul, G. (2005). Cross national correlations of quantifiable societal health with popular religiosity and secularism in the prosperous democracies. *Journal of Religion & Society*, Vol. 7, pp. 1–14.

Pew Center on the States. (2008, February 28). Pew report finds more than one in 100 adults are behind bars. Pew Center on the States Public Performance Project.

Pew Research Center. (2007). *How young people view their lives, futures and politics. A portrait of generation next*. Report released January 9, 2007.

Pipher, Mary. (1994). *Reviving Ophelia: Saving the selves of adolescent girls*. New York: Ballantine Books.

Potter, N. N. (2004). Perplexing issues in personality disorders. *Current Opinion in Psychiatry*, Vol. 17, pp. 487–492.

Raskin, R., & Hall, C. (1979). A narcissistic personality inventory. *Psychological Reports*, Vol. 45, p. 590.

Reich, R. (2008). *Supercapitalism*. New York: Alfred A. Knopf.

Reid, W., Dorr, D., Walker, J., & Bonner, J. (Eds.). (1986). *Unmasking the psychopath*. New York: W. W. Norton.

Reinhardt, U. E., Hussey, P. S., & Anderson, G. F. (2002). Cross national comparisons of health systems using OECD data, 1999. *Health Affairs*, Vol. 21, pp. 169–181.

Roberts, T., & Ryan, S. (2002). Tattooing and high-risk behavior in adolescents. *Pediatrics*, Vol. 110 (6), pp. 1058–1083.

Robertson, Oscar. (2003). *Oscar Robertson: The Big O: My life, my times, my game*. New York: Rodale Inc.

Santrock, J. (2005). *Psychology 7*. New York: McGraw-Hill.

———. (2007). *Adolescence*. New York: McGraw-Hill.

Schachter, E. (2002). Identity constraints: The perceived structural requirements of a "good" identity. *Human Development*, Vol. 45, pp. 416–433.

Schaie, K. Warner, Willis, S., & Caskie, G. L. L. (June 2004). The Seattle Longitudinal Study: Relationship between personality and cognition. *NeuroPsychology Cognition*, Vol. 11, pp. 304–324.

Schor, J. (1999). The new politics of consumption: Why Americans want so much more than they need. *Boston Review*, Summer Issue.

———. (2004). *Born to buy: The commercialized child and the new consumer culture. How consumer culture undermines children's well-being*. New York: Scribner.

Schultz, D., & Schultz, S. E. (2005). *Theories of Personality* (8th ed.). Belmont, CA: Thomson Wadsworth.

———. (2006). *Psychology & Work Today* (9th ed.). New Jersey: Prentice Hall.

Simpson, Mark. (2002, July 22). Meet the metrosexual. *Salon.com*.

Slosar, J. R. (2002). The role of perfectionism in law enforcement suicide. Paper presented at FBI Quantico Symposium on Law Enforcement Suicide on September 23, 1999. In *Law Enforcement & Suicide*, Edited by Sheehan & Warren, FBI Academy, Behavioral Sciences Unit, Quantico, VA, 2001, pp. 539–549.

Steele, M. (2008, May 23). Fantasy 5 fantasy fix; Enticing the poor to gamble more is a crazy solution to California's budget mess. *Los Angeles Times*, p. A.29.

Stephen, J., Fraser, E., & Marcia J. E. (1992). Moratorium-achievement (MAMA) cycles in lifespan identity development: Value orientations and reasoning system correlates. *Journal of Adolescence*, Vol. 3, pp. 283–300.

Symington, N. (1993). *Narcissism: A new theory*. London: Karnac Books.

Tavris, C., & Aronson, E. (2007). *Mistakes were made (but not by me): Why we justify foolish beliefs, bad decisions, and hurtful acts.* Orlando, FL: Harcourt Books.

The Lewin Group. (2002). Cost and coverage analysis of nine proposals to expand health insurance coverage in California. Falls Church, VA: Prepared for the California Health and Human Services Agency.

Tice, Dianne T., Bratslavsky, E., & Baumeister, R. (2001). Emotional distress regulation takes precedence over impulse control: If you feel bad, do it! *Journal of Personality and Social Psychology*, Vol. 80 (1), pp. 53–67.

Trull, T., & Durrett, C. (2005). Categorical and dimensional models of personality disorder. *Annual Review of Clinical Psychology*, Vol. 1, pp. 335–380.

Trzesniewski, K., Donnellan, M. B., & Robins, R. (2008). Is "generation me" really more narcissistic than previous generations? *Journal of Personality*, Vol. 76 (4): 903–918.

Twenge, J. (2006). *Generation me: Why today's young Americans are more confident, assertive, entitled—and more miserable than ever before.* New York: The Free Press.

Twenge, J., Konrath, S., Foster, J., Campbell, W. K., & Bushman, B. (2008). Egos inflating over time: A cross temporal analysis of the narcissistic personality inventory. *Journal of Personality*, Vol. 76 (4), pp. 875–901.

Twenge, J. M., & Campbell, W. K. (2003). "Isn't it fun to get the respect that we're going to deserve?" Narcissism, social rejection, and aggression. *Personality and Social Psychology Bulletin*, Vol. 29, pp. 261–272.

VanDalsen, R. (2007, March 7). Looking back at the 2007 National Conference for Media Reform. *IndyBay*. Retrieved March 7, 2009 from http://www.indybay.org/newsitems/2007/03/07/18373910.php.

Vanderberg, Bob. (1999). *'59 Summer of the Sox*. Champaign, IL: Sports Publishing Inc.

Viorst, J. (1986). *Necessary losses: The loves, illusions, dependencies and impossible expectations that all of us have to give up in order to grow.* New York: Simon and Schuster.

Wallace, H., & Baumeister, R. (2002). The performance of narcissists rises and falls with perceived opportunity for glory. *Journal of Personality and Social Psychology*, Vol. 82, pp. 819–834.

Westen, D., & Arkowitz-Westen, L. (1998). Limitations of Axis II in diagnosing personality pathology in clinical practice. *American Journal of Psychiatry*, Vol. 155, pp. 1767–1771.

Willman, D. (2004, December 22). The National Institutes of Health: Public servant or private marketer?; Doctors have long relied on the NIH to set medical standards. But with its researchers accepting fees and stock from drug companies, will that change? A continuing examination by *The Times* shows an unabashed mingling of science and commerce. *Los Angeles Times*, p. A1.

Wise, C. (2002, March 25). Profit folly: How firms convert red ink to black via pro forma. *Investors Business Daily*.

Wood, S., & Bettman, J. (2007). Predicting happiness: How normative feeling rules influence (and even reverse) durability bias. *Journal of Consumer Psychology*, Vol. 17 (3), 188–201.

Woolhandler, S., Campbell, T., & Himmelstein, D. U. (2003). Cost of healthcare administration in the U.S. and Canada. *New England Journal of Medicine*, Vol. 349, pp. 768–775.

Woolhandler, S., & Himmelstein, D. U. (1991). The deteriorating administrative efficiency of the U.S. Health care system. *New England Journal of Medicine*, Vol. 324, pp. 1253–1258.

———. (2002). Paying for national health insurance—and not getting it. *Health Affairs*, Vol. 21, pp. 88–98.

# INDEX

# ABOUT THE AUTHOR

J. R. SLOSAR is a clinical psychologist in private practice in Irvine, CA. In the past 25 years, he has provided direct clinical and consulting services in a variety of diverse settings. He has taught classes at several colleges and universities, and is an adjunct assistant professor at Chapman University.